AN *AMERICAN GIRL* ANTHOLOGY

Susan Honeyman, Series Editor

AN *AMERICAN GIRL* ANTHOLOGY

Finding Ourselves in the
Pleasant Company Universe

Edited by
Justine Orlovsky-Schnitzler and KC Hysmith

University Press of Mississippi / Jackson

The University Press of Mississippi is the scholarly publishing agency of the Mississippi Institutions of Higher Learning: Alcorn State University, Delta State University, Jackson State University, Mississippi State University, Mississippi University for Women, Mississippi Valley State University, University of Mississippi, and University of Southern Mississippi.

www.upress.state.ms.us

The University Press of Mississippi is a member
of the Association of University Presses.

Any discriminatory or derogatory language or hate speech regarding race, ethnicity, religion, sex, gender, class, national origin, age, or disability that has been retained or appears in elided form is in no way an endorsement of the use of such language outside a scholarly context.

Copyright 2025 by University Press of Mississippi
All rights reserved
Manufactured in the United States of America

∞

Publisher: University Press of Mississippi, Jackson, USA
Authorised GPSR Safety Representative: Easy Access System Europe -
Mustamäe tee 50, 10621 Tallinn, Estonia, *gpsr.requests@easproject.com*

Library of Congress Cataloging-in-Publication Data

Names: Orlovsky-Schnitzler, Justine, editor. | Hysmith, KC
(Katherine C.), editor.
Title: An American Girl anthology : finding ourselves in the Pleasant
Company universe / Justine Orlovsky-Schnitzler, KC Hysmith.
Other titles: Cultures of childhood.
Description: Jackson : University Press of Mississippi, 2025. | Series:
Cultures of childhood | Includes bibliographical references and index.
Identifiers: LCCN 2025004392 (print) | LCCN 2025004393 (ebook) | ISBN
9781496849700 (hardback) | ISBN 9781496858061 (trade paperback) | ISBN
9781496858078 (epub) | ISBN 9781496858085 (epub) | ISBN 9781496858092
(pdf) | ISBN 9781496858108 (pdf)
Subjects: LCSH: Pleasant Company. | American Girl (Firm) | American Girl
dolls—History. | American Girl dolls—Social aspects. | Character
dolls—United States. | Dollmakers—United States. | Girls—United
States—Social conditions.
Classification: LCC NK4894.3.A64 A64 2025 (print) | LCC NK4894.3.A64
(ebook) | DDC 688.7/221—dc23/eng/20250220
LC record available at https://lccn.loc.gov/2025004392
LC ebook record available at https://lccn.loc.gov/2025004393

British Library Cataloging-in-Publication Data available

AN
AMERICAN
GIRL
ANTHOLOGY

Finding Ourselves in the
Pleasant Company Universe

Edited by
Justine Orlovsky-Schnitzler and KC Hysmith

University Press of Mississippi / Jackson

The University Press of Mississippi is the scholarly publishing agency of the Mississippi Institutions of Higher Learning: Alcorn State University, Delta State University, Jackson State University, Mississippi State University, Mississippi University for Women, Mississippi Valley State University, University of Mississippi, and University of Southern Mississippi.

www.upress.state.ms.us

The University Press of Mississippi is a member
of the Association of University Presses.

Any discriminatory or derogatory language or hate speech regarding race, ethnicity, religion, sex, gender, class, national origin, age, or disability that has been retained or appears in elided form is in no way an endorsement of the use of such language outside a scholarly context.

Copyright 2025 by University Press of Mississippi
All rights reserved
Manufactured in the United States of America

∞

Publisher: University Press of Mississippi, Jackson, USA
Authorised GPSR Safety Representative: Easy Access System Europe - Mustamäe tee 50, 10621 Tallinn, Estonia, *gpsr.requests@easproject.com*

Library of Congress Cataloging-in-Publication Data

Names: Orlovsky-Schnitzler, Justine, editor. | Hysmith, KC
(Katherine C.), editor.
Title: An American Girl anthology : finding ourselves in the Pleasant
Company universe / Justine Orlovsky-Schnitzler, KC Hysmith.
Other titles: Cultures of childhood.
Description: Jackson : University Press of Mississippi, 2025. | Series:
Cultures of childhood | Includes bibliographical references and index.
Identifiers: LCCN 2025004392 (print) | LCCN 2025004393 (ebook) | ISBN
9781496849700 (hardback) | ISBN 9781496858061 (trade paperback) | ISBN
9781496858078 (epub) | ISBN 9781496858085 (epub) | ISBN 9781496858092
(pdf) | ISBN 9781496858108 (pdf)
Subjects: LCSH: Pleasant Company. | American Girl (Firm) | American Girl
dolls—History. | American Girl dolls—Social aspects. | Character
dolls—United States. | Dollmakers—United States. | Girls—United
States—Social conditions.
Classification: LCC NK4894.3.A64 A64 2025 (print) | LCC NK4894.3.A64
(ebook) | DDC 688.7/221—dc23/eng/20250220
LC record available at https://lccn.loc.gov/2025004392
LC ebook record available at https://lccn.loc.gov/2025004393

British Library Cataloging-in-Publication Data available

Contents

List of Abbreviations and American Girl Timeline. ix

Introduction: The Making of an American Girl Universe xiii
    Justine Orlovsky-Schnitzler and KC Hysmith

Part 1: Consuming American Girl

Breeches, Silks, and Flowered Hats: Aspirational Clothing,
Sartorial Labor, and Mattel's American Girl Brand 3
    Abigail C. Fine

"Eating Breakfast Like It's 1774": American Girl Cookbooks,
Gender, and Identity-Making through Food History 18
    KC Hysmith and Esther Martin

Places, Parties, and Purchases: Creativity and/against
Consumerism in the American Girl Experience 29
    Juliette Holder

Part 2: Who Gets to Be an American Girl?

Where Is My Disability Community?
A Comparative Close Reading of Children's Historical Fiction 41
    Marissa J. Spear

How the Irish (Doll) Became White: The Nellie O'Malley
AG Story Arc 59
    Mary M. Burke

Belonging and Indigeneity in the American Girl Universe 72
    Sheena Roetman-Wynn

Ivy Ling, Corinne Tan, and Chinese American Misrepresentation
in American Girl 83
    Mackenzie Kwok

Caught Between "Jewish" and "American": Rebecca Rubin
and the Americanization of the Jewish Immigrant Experience 95
    Samantha Pickette

Part 3: American Girl Teaches a Lesson

"Nothing but Each Other and Hope": Addy and the
Black Feminist Tradition 115
    Cary Tide

Teaching Girl(')s History: American Girls,
Curricular Standards, and Historians .128
    Tara Strauch

As American (Girl) as Girl Scout Cookies. 142
    Janine B. Napierkowski

The Care and Keeping of Me: A Moment, a Year, a Book,
and Returning Home to Our Changing Bodies, Again and Again 154
    Hannah Matthews

"Selfish or Annoying": Etiquette, Gender, and Race
in *Oops! The Manners Guide for Girls* 165
    Mary Berman

Part 4: Making American Girl Our Own

"Maybe I Could Be Part of the Story Too": Making Meaning and
Understanding American Jewish Identity through American Girl 179
   Rebekkah Rubin

Interpreting, Imagining, and Inventing Queer Pasts and Futures
through American Girl 195
   Laura Traister

An Interview with the Creators of the
"Hellicity Merriman" Meme Account 213
   Justine Orlovsky-Schnitzler

Conclusion: American Girls Forever. 225
   Justine Orlovsky-Schnitzler and KC Hysmith

Acknowledgments 233

About the Contributors 237

Index 241

List of Abbreviations and American Girl Timeline

Abbreviations

AG—American Girl

AGIG—American Girl Instagram

MG—middle grade (reading level)

TCAKOY—The Care and Keeping of You: The Body Book for Girls

YA—young adult (reading level)

Timeline

1941	Pleasant Rowland is born.
Early 1980s	Rowland collaborates with Colonial Williamsburg and gets the idea for a children-oriented historical doll.
1986	The first American Girl catalog is launched; the first three historical dolls—Kirsten Larson, Samantha Parkington, and Molly McIntire—are released.
1989	Pleasant Company does $30 million in sales.
1991	Felicity Merriman (fourth historical character) is released.
1993	Addy Walker (fifth historical character) is released.
1997	Josefina Montoya (sixth historical character) is released.

1998	Pleasant Rowland abruptly sells Pleasant Company to Mattel, her former competitor.
2000	Kit Kittredge (seventh historical character) is released.
2002	Kaya'aton'my (eighth historical character) is released.
2004	The first best friend doll—Nellie O'Malley—is released.
2007	Julie Albright (ninth historical character) and Ivy Ling are released.
2009	Rebecca Rubin (tenth historical character) is released.
2011	Cécile Rey and Marcie-Grace Gardner (eleventh and twelfth historical characters) are released.
2012	Caroline Abbott (thirteenth historical character) is released.
2014	American Girl overhauls the original historical doll lineup into the "BeForever" line.
2015	Maryellen Larkin (fourteenth historical character) is released.
2016	Melody Ellison (fifteenth historical character) is released.
2017	Nanea Mitchell (sixteenth historical character) is released.
2020	American Girl relaunches the original six historical dolls; Courtney Moore (seventeenth historical character) is released.
2022	Claudie Wells (eighteenth historical character) is released.
2023	Twin sisters Nicki and Isabel Hoffman (nineteenth and twentieth historical characters) are released.

List of Abbreviations and American Girl Timeline

Abbreviations

AG—American Girl
AGIG—American Girl Instagram
MG—middle grade (reading level)
TCAKOY—The Care and Keeping of You: The Body Book for Girls
YA—young adult (reading level)

Timeline

1941	Pleasant Rowland is born.
Early 1980s	Rowland collaborates with Colonial Williamsburg and gets the idea for a children-oriented historical doll.
1986	The first American Girl catalog is launched; the first three historical dolls—Kirsten Larson, Samantha Parkington, and Molly McIntire—are released.
1989	Pleasant Company does $30 million in sales.
1991	Felicity Merriman (fourth historical character) is released.
1993	Addy Walker (fifth historical character) is released.
1997	Josefina Montoya (sixth historical character) is released.

1998	Pleasant Rowland abruptly sells Pleasant Company to Mattel, her former competitor.
2000	Kit Kittredge (seventh historical character) is released.
2002	Kaya'aton'my (eighth historical character) is released.
2004	The first best friend doll—Nellie O'Malley—is released.
2007	Julie Albright (ninth historical character) and Ivy Ling are released.
2009	Rebecca Rubin (tenth historical character) is released.
2011	Cécile Rey and Marcie-Grace Gardner (eleventh and twelfth historical characters) are released.
2012	Caroline Abbott (thirteenth historical character) is released.
2014	American Girl overhauls the original historical doll lineup into the "BeForever" line.
2015	Maryellen Larkin (fourteenth historical character) is released.
2016	Melody Ellison (fifteenth historical character) is released.
2017	Nanea Mitchell (sixteenth historical character) is released.
2020	American Girl relaunches the original six historical dolls; Courtney Moore (seventeenth historical character) is released.
2022	Claudie Wells (eighteenth historical character) is released.
2023	Twin sisters Nicki and Isabel Hoffman (nineteenth and twentieth historical characters) are released.

AN
AMERICAN
GIRL
ANTHOLOGY

INTRODUCTION

The Making of an American Girl Universe

Justine Orlovsky-Schnitzler and KC Hysmith

Samantha. Molly. Kirsten. Addy. Kaya. On their own, these names aren't particularly alerting. Together? You likely know *exactly* what we're talking about. American Girl dolls, books, and accessories have been a part of millions of people's lives since 1986. What set American Girl (and its corporate creator, Pleasant Company) apart from its competitors (at least originally) was a willingness to go against the contemporary grain of toy manufacturing. Different, too, were the elaborate and immersive backstories given to each doll character. Interviewing the creators behind unofficial American Girl social media accounts for the *Huffington Post* in 2022, Ruth Etiesit Samuel posits: "The allure of the American Girl Doll brand lies in its hyper specificity and character-building in comparison to other doll brands. While Barbie played on imagination, American Girl dolls were defined characters with stories outlining their flaws and struggles, from Kit Kittredge's nosiness to Julie Albright grappling with adjusting to her parents' divorce."[1] That specificity in personality extended to the tactile: American Girl offers hyper-detailed accessories that speak to the time and place each doll (and by extension, each child playing with them) is living in. Inside Molly McIntire's School Bag (retailing in 1986 for $20; reissued in 2022 for $42), you'll find a vintage-looking report card with impeccable cursive handwriting detailing a C+ in mathematics. Consider Barbie's two hundred plus jobs; to our knowledge, she's been an ace at every single one of them. "American Girl is intensely focused on making a product that is fun to play with," one of the social media account creators told Samuel, "but also seemingly building allure around it that is not focused on perfection, idealism and romanticism but rather, to some extent, history, education, imperfection and pure girlhood."

We're rounding the corner on a new chapter for the company and the American Girl extended universe, so to speak; many of those who played with the dolls first in the late eighties and nineties have children of their own, while many of the youngest millennials and oldest members of Gen Z are reliving (and rewriting) their childhoods with a new ecosystem of memes and adult collecting. A cross section of these two groups includes the original AG generation (who may or may not have children), now in possession of the disposable incomes needed to buy themselves or their children the dolls (and all the accessories) they never had. Writers, including those found in this anthology, are revisiting the effect certain dolls and books in the American Girl catalog have had on their sense of identity. And pundits continue to fan the flames of imagined culture wars as they lament everything from the company's steps toward trans inclusion to the gender presentation of the dolls themselves. Consider, for example, the introduction of Logan in 2017: American Girl's first *boy* doll. In short: American Girl—as a product line, as a brand, and as shorthand for American girlhood, broadly construed—is more relevant than ever, thirty-eight years after its debut.

This anthology has several objectives. It is an examination of the democratizing power of the internet and the intoxicating power of nostalgia. It is an academic consideration of the ways in which American Girl and Pleasant Company have shaped senses of self-worth and hopes for the future (and created many lifelong consumers in the process). Finally, and perhaps most importantly, it is a reflective ode to the children—and *Girls*—many of us used to be. Along the way, we hope readers will take seriously American Girl's influence and place within larger cultural conversations. As the American Girl brand evolved, so has its consumer base. The company endeavored at its founding to give attention to girlhood and illustrate a cultural narrative of progress for girls and women across the nation. While the brand has evolved to capture new lived experiences of American girlhood (with varying degrees of success), those who once belonged to its original target audience grew up and began to question whether the prescriptive storytelling of their youths led to realistic versions of American adulthood. Despite the often-disappointing discrepancies between Pleasant Company's universe and real life, fans keep returning to the American Girl community to help them navigate real world issues.

American Girl was created by Pleasant Rowland, a former elementary school teacher and reporter who later worked in children's publishing. In the 1980s, Rowland visited Colonial Williamsburg and felt frustrated that the gift shop didn't seem to offer items oriented toward young visitors. She pitched the historical site on a printed children's guide to Williamsburg, which proved successful beyond initial expectations. She then combined her interest in making history accessible and engaging to children with her desire to see something "beyond Barbies" on the shelf for young girls. This is the core mythos of American Girl—rarely challenged. "In a version of a story she'd recall in virtually every interview she'd later give," Amanda FitzSimons writes in *Bustle*:

> She sat on a bench in the historical reenactment village and asked herself: "Was there some way I could bring history alive for [children], the way Williamsburg had for me?" A few months later, while Christmas shopping for her 8- and 10-year-old nieces, she found her answer: dolls. Cabbage Patch Kids—all the rage at the time—"were ugly, and Barbie wasn't what I had in mind either," Rowland later told CNN. "Here I was, in a generation of women at the forefront of redefining women's roles, and yet our daughters were play-ing with dolls that celebrated being a teen queen or a mommy."[2]

In 1986, Rowland launched Pleasant Company, as well as the American Girl brand, with three doll models: Kirsten, a Midwestern farm girl of Scandinavian extraction; Molly, a girl growing up in Illinois during WWII, and Samantha, a wealthy turn-of-the-century orphan living in upstate New York. Pleasant Company launched as a mail-order catalog for the Christmas season in 1986, and by 1993 they had added three more dolls to their lineup: Addy, Felicity, and Josefina. From the jump, the dolls and their collection of clothing, accessories, and furniture were unabashedly high-end. In 1986, the dolls retailed for $75 each (which only netted the purchaser the basic doll model with the first book in that particular doll's series). But price hardly seemed a deterrent. In 1989, just three years after launching, Pleasant Company was raking in close to thirty million dollars in annual sales. From there, American Girl expanded in all directions: a publishing arm, American Girl Library, which published a bimonthly magazine, guides, and books, including *The Care and Keeping of You*, their enduring guide to puberty; the Just Like Me doll line, which allowed buyers to customize a doll's hair, eyes, and skin tone to look like their owner; and the first American Girl storefront, American Girl Place, which opened in Chicago in 1998.

Meet the *An American Girl Anthology* Authors

Part of the expansion into publishing also allowed American Girl to make inroads in schools, introducing the characters of Molly, Kirsten, etc. to children who might not have had access to the dolls and AG "universe" otherwise. Some schools even purchased dolls to loan, allowing kids to check out a doll with its accompanying book. In her essay "Teaching Girl(')s History," Tara Strauch argues in this collection that American Girl's presence in K–12 classrooms and curriculums gave rise to what could be called the "Felicity Generation": "a cohort of scholars and other adults who learned to think with and through American Girl stories." Strauch, a historian who grew up learning from American Girl materials, notes that girls like herself "drove the future of historical research as a generation of female historians who were raised on American Girl stories asked new historical questions."

Similarly, in "The Care and Keeping of Me," Hannah Matthews describes *The Care and Keeping of You*, American Girl's bestselling guide to puberty, as existing somewhere between textbook and sacred text. And Mary Berman, reflecting on the legacy of the American Girl's guide to manners (*Oops! The Manners Guide for Girls*), reminds readers "of the ways in which American women and girls are encouraged to think of themselves as powerful, in spite of the glaring evidence of the ways in which they're not, not only in terms of things like a gender pay gap, antiabortion legislation, and disparity in leadership representation, but the more elementary-school realities of the fact that girls are expected to behave a certain way in order to be respected or taken seriously."

Of course, American Girl was not immune to well-earned controversy. The first major criticism and public backlash for the company revolved around the creation of their first Black historical doll, Addy, in 1993. Though the company did collaborate with Black historians to design her narrative and book line, many would-be buyers were still frustrated that the only Black historical doll available at the time had a backstory so radically different from the white lineup of dolls. For *Slate*, Aisha Harris writes:

> For almost two decades, generations of young black girls turning to the American Girl series for stories about characters who looked like them only had one choice: Addy Walker, a 9-year-old girl born into slavery who (in the accompanying books) eventually escapes to freedom alongside her mother. Ever since she arrived as the fifth doll in the company's incredibly successful collection of mail-order dolls, Addy has been a polarizing figure, revered by many as an inspiring character and an important educational tool and criticized by others as a vehicle for wallowing in black suffering. Much has been written about the painful memories she conjures up—I've had my own difficulties wrestling with how Addy made me feel as a child. A lot of these feelings are rooted not in a disdain for Addy herself but for the clear-cut lack of choice: While my white peers could pick from any number of varied characters made in their likeness, I could not.[3]

Cary Tide ("Nothing but Each Other and Hope") investigates not just the limitations of representation embodied in Addy but also questions of consumption and whiteness: "The problems with the Addy doll are nothing new: white desire for possessing Black people (or—sublimated—their images) is fundamental to racial capitalism. Pleasant Company merely capitalized upon the 1990s multicultural moment to frame their doll as a contribution to social justice."

Addy is not the only character that suffered from an incomplete engagement with difficult histories. In "How the Irish (Doll) Became White," Mary M. Burke invites us to consider American Girl's "best friend dolls" (dolls sold as limited edition—and limited—companions to an established character's story and collection) and the portrayal of Nellie O'Malley as such from the *Samantha* series. "Even the seemingly stereotype-busting arc of the Nellie stories, from immigrant poverty to final arrival in genteel Anglo-America, reflects the mainstream and ultimately conservative narrative of the 'inevitable' assimilation ('whitening') and entry into normative WASP values and society of Irish America itself."

Indeed, it is within Burke's essay that we are first introduced to depictions of racial phenotypes in American Girl, as articulated by the facial molds used in different doll designs:

A further indication that pale coloring was a racial marker that links Nellie to the wider Americas is that she was the first non-Latina American Girl doll to use the mold originated for the 1997 Josefina, who is represented in the accompanying book as living on a Mexican rancho in the 1820s.[4] This mold used a more pronounced philtrum, fuller lips, and a wider nose than that of the so-called "classic" mold used for the white character dolls. . . . In light of a history of Jewish "off-whiteness" in American culture that is shared with Irish America,[5] it is notable that this patently "ethnic" mold was also used for the 2009 Rebecca Rubin, the first Jewish doll/historical character in the line's representations.[6]

Samantha Pickette, writing about Rebecca Rubin in an expansive essay about American Jewish identity as presented by Pleasant Company ("Caught Between 'Jewish' and 'American'"), agrees: "The interchangeability of Rebecca and Josefina as two 'ethnic' dolls who share the same face suggests a flattening of the cultural pluralism inherent in American Girl's mission and a visual insistence on the 'sameness' of each character, even as their differences are celebrated within the context of their stories."

And of course, there is room to discuss what many fans feel was left out of American Girl's considerations entirely. Marissa J. Spear unpacks the profound lack of engagement with disability studies and disabled characterizations in "Where Is My Disability Community?" "As a disabled historian and writer, I owe my love for history to AG's historical collection," she writes. "My desire to see my disabled self represented in AG is 'not a mere desire for disability representation, but rather a longing to find a political identity of disabled people like me.'"

Similarly, Mackenzie Kwok ("Ivy Ling, Corinne Tan, and Chinese American Misrepresentation in American Girl") laments the one-dimensional notes American Girl has frequently struck in attempting to create Asian American characters and dolls. Kwok scrutinizes Ivy Ling and Corrine Tan through the lens of the Yellow Power movements of the late 1960s, surmising that "Ivy represents a missed opportunity for interrogating progressive politics, while maintaining a white-centric status quo, while Corinne underscores the harm of using COVID-19 as a *reminder* to engage with Asian American girls."

And Sheena Roetman-Wynn ("Belonging and Indigeneity in the American Girl Universe") strikes at an inescapable contradiction in the entire Pleasant Company universe: Who gets to be an *American* Girl in the first place? "Both Pleasant Company and Mattel were (literally) founded and operate on Indigenous land," she writes. "In taking on the role of teaching history to children via play, and in self-proclaiming that history's specific focus as 'America,' the argument could be made that both companies knowingly took on the responsibility of accurate storytelling when it comes to *all* American history, including the ugly bits." In 2002, American Girl released Kaya, a Nimíipuu character whose story is set in 1764. Roetman-Wynn leads us to ask whether it's right to categorize a precontact Indigenous child as American, by any definition.

In 1998, Rowland rather abruptly sold American Girl to Mattel, making the company a subsidiary of the giant toymaker responsible for Barbie, among other juggernauts. Immediately, questions were raised about what this would mean for the elements of American Girl that had made it unique amongst other companies, particularly against other dollmaking competitors. Sales were no longer driven by competition with Barbies but in direct *comparison* to them as part of a larger, shared conglomerate.

It's hard to speculate which changes American Girl experienced in the late nineties and early aughts were simply the natural evolution of a company experiencing the internet revolution at the same time as the rest of us, and which were suggestions that would have been dismissed by Pleasant Company of the late eighties. In *Playing with America's Doll* (a scholarly work to which this anthology is much indebted), Emilie Zaslow asks:

> How does a commercial product that is both profit-driven and socially and politically motivated negotiate its offerings to balance mission and revenue? What do feminist-inspired dolls and stories look like when they are for sale and when they are packaged by the Mattel machine, and how do thoughtful consumers understand their consumption of these products? What do American Girl books and dolls communicate to consumers about gender, race, ethnicity, and what it means to be an American? Whose American stories are told and whose are not told, what do they tell us about the gendered and raced relations of power in this country and how is citizenship characterized by this brand that owns the name "American Girl"?[7]

Juliette Holder ("Places, Parties, and Purchases"), writing here about the intersection of consumerism and American Girl, notes that the last decade or so has collapsed much of what made American Girl unique into branded monocultural cash grabs: "As the historical girls move closer to our own time, their accessory collections take on real-world brand names. Rather than Samantha's generic needlepoint kit, Kit's baseball glove, or Felicity's Noah's Ark play set, Courtney (of the 1980s) plays with PacMan arcade games and attends sleepovers in a Care Bears sleeping bag."

Abigail C. Fine ("Breeches, Silks, and Flowered Hats") also investigates an aspect of American Girl material culture by teasing apart sartorial styling as a crucial expression of self-identity—even when mediated through the Mattel Corporation: "Although as playthings these items can serve as opportunities for children to figuratively 'try on' new identities," she writes, "their means of production point to the inherent complexities of Mattel's commodity activism."

KC Hysmith and Esther Martin ("'Eating Breakfast Like It's 1774'") tease apart similar complications of consumer culture through the AG universe's creation of food-and-drink-themed accessories. With a veritable cornucopia of edible options from a wheatgrass juice bar to "Nanea's Luau Set" (each of which sells for $80 at the time of writing on the American Girl online store), these "examples are important aspects of the larger foodways created by the American Girl universe and marketed to the fan base, but were and continue to be largely exclusive to those only with the financial means to afford them."[8] To better understand the impact of food history on consumers, Hysmith and Martin focus, instead, on the role of American Girl cookbooks.

Laura Traister ("Interpreting, Imagining, and Inventing Queer Pasts and Futures through American Girl") illuminates the joyful and prophetic world of queer American Girl fandom in her essay, writing: "You can witness AG fans' delight in recognizing their younger selves in the characters, and in connecting with other strangers who are doing the same. Together, these fans are engaged in 'the work of making historic queerness visible in the present,' which allows them to 'make for themselves another version of history.'"[9]

Similarly, Rebekkah Rubin ("'Maybe I Could Be Part of the Story Too'") writes beautifully about the joys (and frustrations) of creating (and recreating) for oneself the kind of characterizations that would have been life-changing in childhood. "I created my own 1990s historical character, Rivkah, based on my experiences as a Jewish girl growing up in Ohio in the 1990s," she writes. "When I introduced her on Instagram, I drew upon my longing for a Jewish American Girl doll as a kid: 'It's 1999 and Rivkah is dreaming about visiting the American Girl Place in Chicago and picking out her own American Girl of Today doll. When she was younger, her parents gave her Samantha for Hanukkah. Although she loves Samantha, Rivkah doesn't have a doll like her. Because Samantha, like all the other character dolls sold by American Girl in 1999, celebrates Christmas, and Rivkah is Jewish.'"[10]

Tips and Tricks for Reading *An American Girl Anthology*

Inspired by all of the publications, imaginative play materials, and the recurring invitation to find *ourselves* in the American Girl universe, this anthology encourages readers to start with whichever essay or thematic section they think best fits their experience. Did you dog-ear all the latest and greatest accessories in every issue of the American Girl catalog? Start with the section "Consuming American Girl." Maybe you never had an American Girl doll or didn't grow up with a character that made you feel seen; then the section "Who Gets to Be an American Girl?" is for you. Fans of the main-character-learns-a-lesson trope will enjoy the section "American Girl Teaches a Lesson," which is full of essays expanding on lessons we were taught, lessons we never got, and lessons that need unlearning. And for readers new to American Girl and unclear on why it matters to its fans and how it serves as a powerful influence on contemporary culture, there's "Making American Girl Our Own," featuring an interview between editor Justine Orlovsky-Schnitzler and the creators of the American Girl meme account Hellicity Merriman—which might just inspire you to find yourself once again (or for the first time!) in the complex, captivating, and ever-expanding Pleasant Company Universe.

Notes

1. Ruth Etiesit Samuel, "The Resurgence of American Girl Doll-Core," *Huffpost*, July 10, 2022, https://www.huffpost.com/entry/resurgence-american-girl-doll core_n_62c50476e4b0aa392d37abcd.

2. Amanda FitzSimons, "She Founded American Girl to 'Bring History Alive.' Then She Made Over a Town," *Bustle*, September 21, 2022, https://www.bustle.com/entertainment/american-girl-founder-pleasant-rowland-aurora-controversy.

3. Aisha Harris, "The Making of an American Girl," *Slate*, September 21, 2016, https://slate.com/culture/2016/09/the-making-of-addy-walker-american-girls-first-black doll.html

4. "Josefina Mold," American Girl Wiki, Accessed January 14, 2024, https://americangirl.fandom.com/wiki/Josefina_Mold.

5. M. Alison Kibler, *Censoring Racial Ridicule: Irish, Jewish, and African American Struggles over Race and Representation, 1890–1930* (Chapel Hill: University of North Carolina Press, 2015).

6. The Rebecca narrative has been criticized for presenting an idealized, tolerant America into which Jewish identity "fits comfortably." Lisa Marcus, "Dolling Up History: Fictions of Jewish American Girlhood," in *Dolls Studies: The Many Meanings of Girls' Toys and Play*, ed. Miriam Forman-Brunell and Jennifer Dawn Whitney (New York: Peter Lang, 2015), 16–17.

7. Emilie Zaslow, *Playing with America's Doll: A Cultural Analysis of the American Girl Collection* (London: Palgrave Macmillan, 2017).

8. "Nanea's Luau Set," American Girl, accessed January 14, 2024, https://www.americangirl.com/products/naneas-luau-set-frh25.

9. Ellie Turner-Kilburn, "Reimagining Queer Female Histories through Fandom," *Transformative Works and Cultures* 37 (2022): para. 5.11, 5.3.

10. Rebekkah Rubin (@iamexcessivelydollverted), "It's 1999 and Rivkah . . . ," Instagram, February 21, 2023, https://www.instagram.com/p/Co78z_OOzzW.

PART 1

CONSUMING AMERICAN GIRL

Breeches, Silks, and Flowered Hats
Aspirational Clothing, Sartorial Labor, and Mattel's American Girl Brand

Abigail C. Fine

In the historical American Girl novel *Meet Rebecca* (2009) by Jacqueline Dembar Greene, Rebecca Rubin admires her grandmother's brooch, which depicts a running hare from the folktale "Clever Karina." Later that night at Sabbath dinner, Rebecca's cousin Max begins to tell the tale to the family as entertainment. Rebecca, who aspires to become an actress, joins him by imagining herself as the heroine of the narrative. Max drapes her mother's flowered shawl over Rebecca's head, which makes Rebecca "truly [feel] as if she was in a play, acting the role of Karina."[1] Sartorial items take center stage in this scene: both Rebecca's grandmother's brooch and her mother's scarf serve multiple functions. First, they connect Rebecca to her matrilineal forebears. Additionally, the items speak to her Russian-Jewish heritage. Most importantly, these pieces illustrate that dress has the power to shape the way we perceive ourselves and allows us to communicate these stories to others.

Sartorial styling plays a pivotal role for the young female protagonists of the American Girl brand's historical narratives. The garments that these characters wear, or aspire to wear, serve as more than markers of their historical milieu, but also convey ideas regarding the characters' gender identity, race, class, age, and even political stances. In *Styling Texts: Dress and Fashion in Literature*, editors Cynthia Kuhn and Cindy Carlson write that "attention to literary fashioning can contribute to a significantly deeper understanding of texts, their contexts, and their innovations."[2] Yet little scholarship engages with fashion in children's literature in general, and much of the scholarship on the American Girl brand, specifically, treats the inclusion of clothing in the novels and retail stores as incidental, or even insidious.

The business model of American Girl relies on sale of material items tied to the literary texts, which scholar Emily Zaslow argues "can be conceptualized not only as narratives but also as marketing tools for the dolls and their accessories."[3] Zaslow calls attention to American Girl's efforts to present characters who engage in political work and thus counter "the prescriptive femininity of the times in which they live."[4] Yet, she contends that the brand's choice to sell primarily clothing and other "beauty" products for dolls and children means that the brand is still negatively "steeped in the normatively feminine activities of grooming, dressing, styling, and consuming."[5] This attitude towards dress and fashion, however, belies the meaningful work that sartorial motifs accomplish within the American Girl books. It also discounts the importance of clothing, including doll clothing, in children's self-development through imaginative play.

In this chapter, I aim to draw attention to the importance of apparel within the American Girl narratives and to argue that dress (both literary and real) functions as more than mere frivolity. Although dress plays an important role in the narratives of all of the historical characters, in this chapter I will focus on Felicity Merriman, Addy Walker, and Rebecca Rubin as representative samples to analyze how dress informs ideas of gender, race, and class within the American Girl novels. I will then examine how these garments function when reified as material objects available for purchase through Mattel: although as playthings these items can serve as opportunities for children to figuratively "try on" new identities, their means of production point to the inherent complexities of Mattel's commodity activism.

Dress in American Girl Historical Narratives

Philosopher Lars Svendsen argues that, as a general principle, "clothes are a vital part of the social construction of the self"[6] and Kuhn and Carlson assert that in literature "the vestimentary frame enacts a site of aesthetic, social, and political inscription.... While sartorial performativity is at issue, so is the employment of apparel or accessory as symbol, image, motif, or metaphor."[7] This holds especially true in media for children and adolescents. Scholars of children's literature, including Peter Hunt and Seth Lerer, have demonstrated that childhood reading—even material read for leisure—is always inherently pedagogical and intimately connected to political, social, and cultural education (and it is worth noting that the American Girl novels, in particular, were developed with pedagogical intent).[8] Similarly, in her work on the radical potential of children's literature, Kimberley Reynolds argues that "growing up involves making choices and shaping an identity,"[9] and she further asserts that "young people construct and perform their cultural identities through . . . fashion."[10] Novels, then, serve as guide books for children to learn cultural codes, or a set of shared practices and expectations in a society. Importantly, these include sartorial codes.

Items of apparel have traditionally played a key role in children's literature: for example, Dorothy Gale famously dons a pair of metaphorically laden silver shoes in L. Frank Baum's *The Wizard of Oz* (1900),[11] and in Neil Gaiman's *Coraline* (2002) a critical conflict between the protagonist and her mother is sparked by a pair of neon green gloves. In the narratives that accompany the historical American Girl characters, dress takes an even more central role in shaping the plots. Although this is perhaps (somewhat problematically) due to the brand's commodification of the fictional garments as material goods, the use of clothing within these novels is often creatively nuanced. The outfits worn by the historical characters lend insight not only into historical fashions but into larger historical understandings of gender, race, political movements, and—most interestingly—the provenance of apparel. Zaslow rightly describes these characters and their collections as "neo-historical,"[12] meaning they reflect not only historical realities but cultural attitudes towards the past at the time of their writing (the late 1980s to the present); thus, these outfits have the power to shape a child's understanding of both past and present social norms.

For Felicity, a girl growing up in Williamsburg, Virginia, at the cusp of the American Revolution, dress serves as a clear marker of gender identity and functions to highlight Felicity's own discomfort with eighteenth-century Anglo-American gender norms (as understood by the author in the late 1980s). The character debuted in 1991, and her initial six books were written by Valerie Tripp. In *Meet Felicity*, Felicity tells her father's apprentice, Ben, that she wishes she could wear breeches (a form of short trousers)

Felicity wears Ben's breeches while winning the trust of her horse, Penny; image from *Meet Felicity* (1991) by Valerie Tripp, illustrations by Dan Andreason, p. 37.

like a boy: "Gowns and petticoats are so bothersome.... In breeches your legs are free. You can straddle horses, jump over fences, run as fast as you wish."[13] She continues, "It's very tiresome to be a girl sometimes.... You're lucky to be a lad."[14] Throughout the novel, Felicity dislikes traditionally female items of apparel, including her stays (eighteenth-century corsetry) and her wide-brimmed straw hat. In practice, these latter two items were important: stays, unlike later corsets, offered necessary support rather than physical alteration, and hats were one of the few methods available to stave off sunburns in the hot Virginia summers. But in literature, these garments work as metaphors. Felicity's discomfort with these items marks her discomfort with what she feels are stifling gender norms.

In *Felicity's Surprise*, however, Felicity covets a new blue silk gown to wear to a ball held by the Royal Governor. Her friend Elizabeth tells Felicity that the governor's wife, Lady Dunmore, is one of the most fashionable women in Virginia: "Felicity knew Elizabeth thought it was very important to wear a wonderful gown to the Palace."[15] The next day Felicity sees a fashion doll dressed in a blue silk gown—based, the shopkeeper says, on a gown worn by Lady Dunmore herself. Felicity's mother, pleasantly surprised by Felicity's sudden interest in feminine clothing, buys bolts of blue silk and promises to make her a new dress. Ben, however, finds Felicity's desire to wear a new gown while dancing at the Palace with the children of Loyalists (those who wanted the colonies to remain British) a betrayal of her family's revolutionary political beliefs. Then, Felicity's mother becomes ill and unable to finish the dress; in the face of her mother's serious illness, Felicity herself finds the idea of wanting a new dress trivial. On the day of the ball, however, her mother begins to get well and Felicity discovers that Elizabeth and her sister have finished the gown. Despite his earlier anger, Ben offers to take her to the Palace to dance in her new dress.

Apparel in *Felicity's Surprise*, then, underscores the political potential of clothing. Felicity's father opines that if Felicity can dance with the governor's children "then perhaps we adults can settle our differences without fighting."[16] Sending Felicity to the ball in a new gown modeled on one worn by the governor's wife sends a message: Felicity's family still respects the crown and they are willing to negotiate their differences. The book also implies that Felicity's father may hope that Felicity's appearance at the ball will persuade Loyalists to return their custom to his shop. Felicity's desire for the gown, too, contrasts with her earlier dislike of traditionally feminine clothing and pursuits: "The blue gown seemed to help her swoop and swirl and stay light on her feet. *Why, dancing is fun!* she thought with surprise."[17] Felicity's novels, then, plant the radical seed that clothing—rather than biological sex—dictates how a body can move and how others will perceive it.

The novel also makes explicit the material conditions behind the creation of garments in the eighteenth century. Felicity sees a doll-sized model of the dress she wants in a millinery shop, then the fabric is purchased. Her mother measures her, cuts the fabric, and begins the stitching; the work is laborious and, on top of her preexisting illness, the hours needed to sew the gown leave Felicity's mother exhausted. The completion of the gown by her friend takes on deeper meaning when the work behind its creation is made apparent. For girls in America in the late twentieth and early twenty-first centuries, many of whom purchase ready-made clothing, Felicity's books may constitute their first exposure to the labor of garment making.

A blue dress plays a role of desire for American Girl Addy Walker, too. Addy debuted in 1993 and her initial six-book series was written by Connie Porter. In *Addy Learns a Lesson*, Addy, a Black girl who has escaped enslavement in the American South and made a home with her mother in Philadelphia, longs to wear the fancy dresses that her smugly arrogant, but rich, classmate Harriet sports at school: "'Did you see that blue dress Harriet had on yesterday?' Addy sighed. . . . Harriet had everything that Addy had dreamed freedom would bring *her*. Harriet had fancy dresses. . . . Her friends wore fancy dresses and matching hair ribbons."[18] Addy had

Addy wearing her Christmas dress on the cover of *Addy's Surprise* by Connie Porter, illustrated originally by Melodye Rosales, with updates by Dahl Taylor (third cover, 2000–2004); image from American Girl Wiki, uploaded by user Nethilia.

imagined that freedom would bring equality: she discovers that is not the case as Philadelphia is still segregated and Black people cannot ride the streetcars. The novel, however, focuses more on Addy's disappointment that Harriet owns more dresses than herself than on the segregation of public transport and utilities.

Clothing, then, represents a site of class comparison. Addy learns that freedom does not mean equality for all, but the book suggests that Addy's desires should be the readers' desire: freedom *should* mean equality—and *quality*—for everyone. At the end of the novel, Addy's mother, Ruth, presents Addy with a new blue school outfit so that Addy will look her best for the spelling bee. Ruth tells her she looks like a city girl in the outfit, but Addy worries she does not deserve her new clothing. After she wins the spelling bee, however, another girl comments on Addy's pretty new outfit. Although ostensibly the novel carries the message that fancy clothing means little without a kind heart, Addy does feel more confident and intelligent in her new outfit.

In *Addy's Surprise*, too, Addy receives a new dress. Ruth works as a seamstress in a dress shop that caters to wealthy white clients. A few days before Christmas an angry client returns a beautiful plaid dress that Ruth had laboriously sewn, claiming that it had been shoddily made. The owner of the dress-shop, a white woman named Mrs. Ford, defends Ruth's work against the client's wrath. Later, after refitting the dress, Mrs. Ford gives it to Addy as a Christmas gift, along with the extra fabric that she cut from the hem when resizing the gown. Addy, in turn, creatively uses this fabric to sew a scarf for her mother. Although Addy had been planning to buy her mother a new red scarf, she instead decides to give her money to a fund to help newly freed people resettling in Philadelphia.

Here, the literary garment intersects with race relations and operates as a metaphor: the dress was originally made by Addy's mother, a Black woman, for a white girl. The dress was then returned in anger. Mrs. Ford, another white woman, takes that anger, neutralizes it, and reshapes it into a beautiful gift for Addy. The book does not make explicit the return of the dress as racially motivated, but metaphorically the gown operates as a complex piece of interplay between parties of different races, ending as a beacon of hope for racial understanding. Addy's dress was made by her mother *and* Mrs. Ford, working together to bring joy to a child. Although the Addy doll and her books have a complicated legacy, especially in light of the Black Lives Matter movement and current conversations on race in the United States, in 1993 Addy's novels were some of the first mainstream books for children to open a conversation on race.[19] Notably, some of the novels' most interesting observations on race are made through sartorial items.

Like in Felicity's and Addy's stories, dress in the books of the American Girl character Rebecca Rubin, a Jewish American girl living in New York City in 1914, plays an important role. Rebecca debuted in 2009 with a six-book series, and she is only the second historical American Girl character (after Kaya, released in 2002) to have a non-Christmas holiday story in her series: a fact highlighted in her clothing collection. In *Candlelight*

"Rebecca's Winter Coat" (2019 version) sold by American Girl for 18-inch dolls; image from American Girl Wiki, uploaded by user Nipasu.

for Rebecca, Rebecca's family celebrates Hanukkah, and the accompanying "Rebecca's Hanukkah Dress" was the first specifically Jewish sartorial item sold for a historical American Girl doll. The inclusion of a Hanukkah dress (when most of the other historical dolls have Christmas dresses) underscores the importance of clothing to the construction of religious and ethnic identities.

Throughout her book series, Rebecca feels drawn to acting and the magic of cinema. In the fourth novel in the series, *Rebecca and the Movies*, Rebecca's cousin Max gives her an ornate cream-colored hat adorned with flowers: "'Oh, Max,' Rebecca sighed, 'I feel just like a movie star.'"[20] Later, while wearing the hat, Rebecca accompanies Max to a film studio where she is chosen to act in a film. The hat becomes part of her costume, along with a fancy silk gown from the studio's wardrobe division. She learns, too, that most of the clothing used in the movies is custom made by the costume designer or else bought in secondhand stores. For Rebecca, dress and costuming allows her to glimpse a version of herself and her future that seems out of reach in her everyday life.

Yet, garments play another, darker role in Rebecca's narratives, too: Rebecca's uncle and cousin work in a coat factory where the conditions of labor are abysmal and the pay keeps workers below the poverty line. In *Changes for Rebecca*, Rebecca witnesses the toxicity of the environment firsthand when she delivers a lunch basket to the factory. When the workers decide to strike, Rebecca supports them. Although her aunt tells her to stay away from the picket line, Rebecca attends anyway. There, she sees women using sartorial accessories, like hatpins, to fight against strikebreakers, and she realizes that the police serve the interests of the factory owners, rather than the workers. Rebecca's stories, then, illustrate the positive, aspirational aspects of clothing while also drawing attention to the horrific human rights abuses perpetrated in the name of fashion.

For Felicity, clothing communicates her conflicting view of her society's gender norms. For Addy, the apparel she aspires to wear represents her understanding of freedom and metaphorically speaks to race relations. For Rebecca, dress and costume are both the provenance of dreams and the cause of despair for those who labor over sewing machines enduring unfair working conditions. For each of these American Girl characters, the vestimentary frame represents an entanglement of political statements and social performativity, bound together with manual labor. The duality of clothing—creative and ambitious, yet labor intensive and potentially exploitative—is evidenced clearly in these books.

Literary Dress as Material Object:
Imaginative Play and Fast Fashion

Importantly, American Girl clothing does not remain strictly fictional: indeed, actual children yearn for and purchase miniature versions of these garments for their dolls—and sometimes for themselves—which then factor into the children's own imaginative play and development. Maria Tatar asserts that "when children dress up as favorite characters, it is rarely because they want to surrender their own identities but because that character has specific traits they want to imitate."[21] Kiera Vaclavik further demonstrates that for children engaging in "fancy dress" or playing games of dress-up, embodying fictional characters often involves "annexation, rather than elimination" of a child's own identity.[22] The use of dress or costume, then, plays an important role in how children develop their own sense of self, their own value systems, and their own aspirations.

Zaslow notes the centrality of fashion within the American Girl historical narratives, but she sees the focus on clothing and beauty items in the material accessories produced for the dolls as problematic: she writes, "Rather than producing material objects that represent the series' historical and cultural specificity and narratives of resistance, American Girl relies on stereotypical tropes of femininity and doll play."[23] Yet, as demonstrated by the examples above, dress is intimately woven into the narratives of resistance within the texts. Additionally, research shows that the use of apparel in imaginative play reinforces character traits that a child admires. American Girl fashion, then, functions as an important component of the brand's socially progressive messaging and pedagogical imperatives.

Moreover, outside of the American Girl historical narratives, sartorial styling has factored into political movements for centuries. For example, during the American Revolution (and thus adjacent to Felicity's narratives) those who supported independence from Britain boycotted imported fabrics and wore "homespun" as a political statement. This boycott worked *because* of female participation and female labor.[24] To trivialize fashion and beauty items as "stereotypical tropes of femininity" feels shortsighted in light of the way women have historically used sartorial power.

Zaslow, however, sees a contradiction in the sales of sartorial items vis-à-vis the novels' participation in progressive political action. She writes that Rebecca's books, for example, demonstrate the brand's "commitment to stories about girls' leadership, the power of girls' voices, standing up for strong beliefs, and working with others to make change," yet "paired with the collections material consumer goods, it also exemplifies the contradictory portrayal of girlhood . . . which requires both participation in and acts of opposition to normative femininity."[25] She later asserts, "In American Girl, the cult of beauty is maintained and reinforced while a resistive feminist voice that participates in social change is promoted and presented as a model of ideal American girlhood."[26] I disagree with this framing, and instead argue that a focus on sartorial styling is not incompatible with social change; indeed, it can complement and even spearhead social change. For children, the use of dress in imaginative play can even help with a child's sense of awareness as an embodied, political actor as they develop their own identity.

What I *do* see as complicated and contradictory, however, is the American Girl brand's promotion of social change with Mattel's complicity in the fast-fashion industry. When American Girl launched as an independent start-up in 1986 under founder Pleasant Rowland, initial manufacture occurred in a rented warehouse space, while the dolls themselves were produced in West Germany. As the company grew, even before Mattel purchased the brand in 1998, production began to be outsourced to multiple Asian and European countries, along with retaining some manufacture in the United States. Today, however, "approximately 20,000 people in China, Thailand, Indonesia, Malaysia, and Mexico are working on Mattel's Barbie and American Girl products for low wages and in poor working conditions."[27]

Interestingly, the brand's takeover by Mattel almost perfectly coincided with the rise of the fast-fashion industry and cheap production in China. The NGO *China Labor Watch* "launched an undercover investigation of Mattel toy factories and found that workers were often forced to stand for over ten hours, were housed in dirty congested dormitories, and worked in factories where emergency egresses and fire escapes were blocked or locked."[28] This description is chilling, especially in light of the "Looking Back" section in *Changes for Rebecca*, which recounts the horrific treatment of women in garment factories and the 1911 Triangle Shirtwaist Factory tragedy, in which 146 workers died trapped in a garment factory after owners locked the exits.[29] Grievously, it now also recalls the much more recent Rana Plaza collapse in 2013 in Bangladesh, in which more than one thousand people, many of them garment workers laboring for low wages, were killed due to unsafe working conditions—a disaster that had not yet occurred when *Changes for Rebecca* was published in 2009.

Fast fashion is a growing global problem. Scholar Andrew Brooks writes that as clothing prices decreased in the early 2000s due to the expiration of various trade agreements on import controls, consumption in the global north boomed: "Exports of Chinese clothing to the USA increased by 18 percent per year, and to the EU by 21 percent per year, between 2000 and

2007."[30] This rise in consumption has an environmental cost, with more than three hundred thousand tons of clothing ending up in landfills each year from the United Kingdom alone.[31] Worse, perhaps, is the human cost of conspicuous consumption. Brooks writes that "one can choose to give Gap $50 and get a pair of new jeans; whereas if one 'chooses' to work sewing jeans in eastern China for eight or even ten hours a day one receives $1.80 a day."[32] Remarkably, given the narrative centrality of the plight of garment workers at the Uptown Coat Company in *Changes for Rebecca*, "Rebecca's Winter Coat" was an item sold by American Girl from 2017 to 2018, then redesigned and relisted from 2019 to 2023; it cost $42, which was later raised to $44. Who made the simulacra of "Rebecca's Winter Coat"? How much were they paid? What were their working conditions?

My intent is not to condemn Mattel wholesale. It appears that Mattel does attempt to take seriously the conditions in its overseas factories; moreover, in its corporate offices in the global north, between 2020 to 2022, Mattel has received a score of 100 from the Human Rights Campaign, which monitors the treatment of LGBTQ+ employees. Still, correspondence between the United States Securities and Exchange Commission and Mattel's lawyers in 2017 shows that despite shareholders asking management to prepare a report on its subcontractors in overseas apparel procurement (in part due to events like the Rana Plaza collapse), Mattel filed a motion to exclude these proxy materials. Instead, Mattel's lawyers referred shareholders to Mattel's "Citizenship" webpage, which it claims already addressed concerns over workers' rights and supply chain standards, and they further claimed exemption under a rule that this report related to ordinary business operations.[33]

Unfortunately, with the rise of globalization, successful participation in a capitalist economy requires inescapable compromise on the part of both producer and consumer. Sarah Banet-Weiser and Roopali Mukherjee describe corporations and consumers as participating in "commodity activism," and Brooks writes that "as consumption has grown and diversified, new politicized ways to exercise consumer choice have developed."[34] He further contends that "capitalist social relations are fundamentally ill-suited to resolving the problems of uneven development and environmental degradation fostered by economic globalization,"[35] and for Mattel to continue the promotion of its messages of social change and female empowerment on its current scale, the company needs to be financially profitable. This inherently means that it needs the ability to mass-produce dolls, clothing, and accessories. The success of American Girl requires a compromise somewhere in order to ensure their stories reach the children who need them, because perhaps paradoxically, commodity activism cannot work without commodity success and availability.

Conclusion

In *Orlando*, novelist Virginia Woolf writes that though clothes may seem "vain trifles," they have the enormously impactful ability to "change our view of the world and the world's view of us."[36] This precept is repeatedly illustrated in American Girl narratives. After filming her scene in *Rebecca and the Movies*, Rebecca tells Max that while acting in costume, "'It seemed as if I actually became someone else. It's such fun pretending to be a different girl leading a completely different life!'"[37] Similarly, in *Meet Felicity*, Felicity feels a new level of bravery and freedom wearing breeches instead of petticoats, and in *Addy Learns a Lesson*, Addy's smart blue dress gives her the confidence to demonstrate her knowledge to win the school spelling bee. The type of dress these protagonists don helps them access different parts of their own personalities, which in turn changes how they act in the world.

Ultimately, instead of denigrating the prevalence of sartorial items in American Girl historical narratives or in their retail stores, scholarship needs to recognize that the vestimentary frame plays an important role within the brand. This holds true not just for the protagonists of American Girl novels, but for the real children who interact with American Girl content and who may imaginatively enact their own stories using material garments purchased from the brand. As Roland Barthes postulates in *The Fashion System*, fashion has its own "grammar." Within children's literature sartorial items speak metaphorically, but the narratives teach girls to speak and understand the language of dress in real life, too.

Yet, I want to remark upon a danger in American Girl's consumerist success. Scholar Molly Rosner writes that her grandmother gifted her as a child with handsewn clothing for her American Girl dolls instead of purchasing items from the catalogue: "I politely thanked her . . . but really, I was disappointed. . . . While touting the importance of family, tradition, and gift-giving, the American Girl company had turned me into a loyal consumer devoted to their brand."[38] Although, as Rosner points out, hand-sewn doll clothing fits the ethos of the brand's historical narratives more than the store-bought garments, the brand loyalty American Girl instills in their young fans may prime them to enter their teen and adult years as ardent consumers of branded clothing; that is, fast fashion.

American Girl narratives, though, also teach children to think critically about the material realities of the past and the present. Thus, perhaps optimistically, I have hope that Mattel's dubious position in the supply chain will teach the next generation a lesson Mattel did not expect: to question the rising human and ecological costs of fast fashion.

Notes

1. Jacqueline Dembar Greene, *Meet Rebecca* (New York: American Girl, 2009), 18.

2. Cynthia Kuhn and Cindy Carlson, eds. *Styling Texts: Dress and Fashion in Literature* (Youngstown, NY: Cambria, 2007), 3.

3. Emily Zaslow, *Playing with America's Doll: A Cultural Analysis of the American Girl Collection* (New York: Palgrave Macmillan, 2017), 21.

4. Zaslow, 5.

5. Zaslow, 88.

6. Lars Svendsen, *Fashion: A Philosophy*, trans. John Irons (London: Reaktion Books, 2006), 19.

7. Kuhn and Carlson, 2.

8. Pleasant Rowland, the founder of American Girl, worked as both an elementary school teacher and textbook author before starting American Girl. She said, "I dedicated my third career to teaching American history to young girls through books, dolls, and related playthings." For more on Rowland's pedagogical aims and the founding of American Girl, see Laura Lattimore, "A Girl's Window into History," Journeys of Innovation, USPTO, March 1, 2023, https://www.uspto.gov/learning-and-resources/journeys-innovation/field-stories/girls-window-history.

9. Kimberley Reynolds, *Radical Children's Literature: Future Visions and Aesthetic Transformations in Juvenile Fiction* (New York: Palgrave Macmillan, 2007), 2.

10. Reynolds, 68.

11. These shoes famously became deep red "ruby slippers" to show off the wonders of technicolor for the iconic 1939 film of *The Wizard of Oz*.

12. Zaslow, 41.

13. Valerie Tripp, *Meet Felicity* (Middleton, WI: Pleasant Company, 1991), 20.

14. Tripp, *Meet Felicity*, 21.

15. Valerie Tripp, *Felicity's Surprise* (Middleton, WI: Pleasant Company, 1991), 22.

16. Tripp, *Surprise*, 10.

17. Tripp, *Surprise*, 59.

18. Connie Porter, *Addy Learns a Lesson* (Middleton WI: Pleasant Company, 1993), 36.

19. See Aisha Harris's article on the complex legacy of Addy Walker: "The Making of an American Girl," *Slate*, September 21, 2016, accessed June 14, 2022, https://slate.com/culture/2016/09/the-making-of-addy-walker-american-girls-first-black-doll.html.

20. Jaqueline Dumbar Greene, *Rebecca and the Movies* (New York: American Girl, 2009), 13.

21. Maria Tatar, *Enchanted Hunters: The Power of Stories in Childhood* (New York: Norton, 2009), 18–19.

22. Kiera Vaclavik, "Dress of the Book: Children's Literature, Fashion, and Fancy Dress," in *Beyond the Book: Transforming Children's Literature*, ed. Bridget Carrington and Jennifer Harding (Cambridge, UK: Cambridge Scholars, 2014), 69.

23. Zaslow, 94.

24. T. H. Breen, "'Baubles of Britain': The American and Consumer Revolutions of the Eighteenth Century," *Past & Present*, no. 199 (May 1988): 93.

25. Zaslow, 73.

26. Zaslow, 100.

27. Zaslow, 47.

28. Zaslow, 47.

29. Jacqueline Dembar Greene, *Changes for Rebecca* (New York: American Girl, 2009), 74–77.

30. Andrew Brooks, *Clothing Poverty: The Hidden World of Fast Fashion and Second-Hand Clothes*, 2nd ed. (London: Zed Books, 2019), 99–100.

31. Brooks, 119.

32. Brooks, 322.

33. Correspondence between the SEC and Mattel Lawyers, 2017, accessed August 24, 2023, https://www.sec.gov/divisions/corpfin/cf-noaction/14a-8/2017/nyscrf022117-14a8.pdf.

34. Sarah Banet-Weiser and Roopali Mukherjee, "Introduction: Commodity Activism in Neoliberal Times," in *Commodity Activism: Cultural Resistance in Neoliberal Times*, ed. Mukherjee and Banet-Weiser (New York: NYU Press, 2012), 13; Brooks, 319.

35. Brooks, 322.

36. Virginia Woolf, *Orlando* (London: Penguin Vintage Classics, 2016; originally published 1928), 132.

37. Greene, *Movies*, 57.

38. Molly Rosner, introduction to *Playing with History: American Identities and Children's Consumer Culture* (New Brunswick, NJ: Rutgers University Press, 2021).

"Eating Breakfast Like It's 1774"

American Girl Cookbooks, Gender, and Identity-Making through Food History

KC Hysmith and Esther Martin

"I would probably never eat it again, [to be honest]," said Seth Workman, then a Purdue University senior, referring to a plate of breakfast items including johnny cakes, fried ham with coffee gravy, breakfast puffs, and apple butter made using historical recipes from the *American Girl Felicity's Cook Book*.[1] While bored during the COVID-19 pandemic, Workman bought four of the original five American Girl cookbooks, published by Pleasant Company between 1994 and 1998, from an online used bookstore and planned to recreate the recipes in his dorm room kitchen. Workman's first video instantly went viral on TikTok, gaining nearly one million views and thousands of comments from other American Girl doll fans on the app. Between comments of support and excitement, in addition to the praise of Tad Stoermer (former historian at Colonial Williamsburg and lecturer at Johns Hopkins who served as an advisor to AG author Valerie Tripp), one user commented, "Imagining felicity [*sic*] drinking oat milk is hilarious" to which Workman responded, "Felicity (Republican) would hate me for using a non dairy milk." In the video, Workman poured soy milk into the cake batter, the same recipe that caused him to admit his disdain for the historical dishes. The same user replied that "her [Felicity's] spirit cursed the johnny cakes."

Would Felicity, a fictional and arguably romanticized character from the eighteenth century, care about the use or even comprehend the concept of nondairy milk? Would her johnny cakes taste better if made on a more traditional cast-iron griddle instead of the nonstick pan Workman used? How would she interpret her recipes being cooked by a young man? And how would she react to Workman's contemporary food-related technologies (let alone the current human obsession with making and watching cooking videos on a social media app)? These are all questions running through our food scholar minds as we think about American Girl cookbooks, the historical foodways they aim to represent, and the contemporary food studies moments they create. Workman, despite having only recently picked up the historically themed cookbooks, is part of a larger American food identity. So is Felicity—or, at least, the same is true of the historical foodways constructed for her by food scholars, historians, and other members of Pleasant Company.

This essay analyzes the use of food in the American Girl universe—specifically in publications such as character cookbooks and, later, themed food-and-drink-related books—as part of the brand's interpretation of history and construction of American girlhood and identity. The inclusion of food and drink in addition to instances of cooking or preparing meals provides opportunities for historical and cultural contextualization within each American Girl era. These same opportunities, however, also risk the flattening of cultural identities and the reaffirmation of heteronormative gender roles that have historically, and often disparagingly, associated women (and girls) with food-related labor. While most American Girl stories do not center around food or drink, such as Pleasant Company's historical birthday party kits and craft books, similar to everything else in the AG universe, their inclusion isn't accidental but rather carefully constructed and part of a broader (and importantly: corporate) strategy of character and world building. AG's use of food, while purportedly intended to add rich historical context and to help inform sociocultural aspects of a character's everyday life, actually serves to reaffirm heteronormative gender roles and create profit. In other words, we idealistically hope the inclusion indicates a commitment to historical accuracy and learning, but acknowledge the capitalistic underpinnings of American Girl.

While this essay focuses on food in American Girl publications, the Pleasant Company universe is full of other important examples of food and drink. In addition to mentions of food throughout the character novels, such as the traditional saffron buns for Saint Lucia Day in *Kirsten's Surprise: A*

Christmas Story (1986) and a trip to the soup kitchen in *Kit Learns a Lesson* (2000), the brand has created dozens of food-themed doll accessories over the past three decades. Each historical character had their version of a "lunch box," and an iconic nineteenth-century-styled hand-turned-crank ice cream freezer was first marketed with Addy's original collection in 1994 and then switched to Samantha's Birthday collection in 1998 (retailed for $22).[2] The ice cream freezer was one of the only accessories to ever be functional, and early versions came with instructions for how to make a small amount of ice cream using whipping cream. On the American Girl website today, you can buy a nonfunctional "American Girl Coffee Shop" ($280), a branded "American Girl x Jeni's Full of Flavor Ice Cream Truck" ($325), a "Snack & Snooze Sleepover Set" with a heart-shaped pizza and box of doughnuts ($36), a tiny "Chinese Takeout Set" ($26), "Rebecca's Sabbath Set" with challah and a gold samovar ($70), and even "Craving Carryout Mystery Packs" with items such as a sandwich, sushi, falafel, and burritos.[3] In the early aughts, American Girl partnered with Hallmark to create a holiday line of products including a cookie tin filled with thematic cookie cutters, treat boxes and bags, and note cards. And perhaps the most well-known American Girl food connection is the American Girl Café, which gained renewed interest in recent years as a trendy dining location for influencers and adult doll enthusiasts alike.[4] The first American Girl Place, a department-store-size shop selling dolls, accessories, and services catering to dolls including a toy hospital and salon, also included a full-service (albeit dessert heavy) restaurant complete with a liquor license.[5] Guests dine with their dolls and can even order them pretend food alongside their real meals. While options vary from store to store, most locations offer dining for all ages starting at $25 per person, with more elaborate choices including Teatime at American Girl and themed birthday parties.[6] Alternatively, if you don't happen to live in a major US city with an American Girl Place, you can buy the "Day at AG Cafe Set" with a pink plastic table and booth, tiny menus, silverware, and even tinier tableside doll seats for your American Girl doll's even *tinier* doll ($180). All of these examples are important aspects of the larger foodways created by the American Girl universe and marketed to the fan base, but were and continue to be largely exclusive to those only with the financial means to afford them. This exclusivity is one reason this essay focuses on the American Girl cookbooks. Although prescriptive, as all cookbooks are, the American Girl food-focused publications provide not only a more food history–themed lens on food in the AG universe, but they are also more affordable, shareable, and available at local libraries.

Between us we bring to this essay years of research and teaching experience with historical cookbooks and manuscripts in archives, expertise in gastronomy and foodways, public history and historic interpretation, and qualitative ethnographic research experience looking at how society interacts with food in the digital landscape. Esther's oldest memory of historical cooking is what she believes is the first cookbook she ever owned: *American Girls Pastimes Felicity's Cook Book*. Felicity and the other American Girls began Esther's obsession with historical costume, crafts, and, of course, food. The use of the word "historical" in this context is intentionally flippant, keeping in mind that all the information gathered from the AG books was filtered through the lens of a major toy corporation. Looking critically at the cookbook now, we can see plenty of plot holes: missing information about the time period, glossing over less pleasant aspects about food and food-related labor, and information that is pure fabrication. Esther still uses *Felicity's Cook Book* for using up leftover rotisserie chicken in the eighteenth-century recipe for chicken pudding and whipping up breakfast puffs (essentially Yorkshire puddings). She even keeps a bottle of rosewater on hand "just in case" she needs to make Felicity's queen cakes, like those served at her American Girl doll–themed ninth birthday party. Esther's obsession led her to acquire all of the Pleasant Company historical cookbooks, including the later published *Cooking Studio* books complete with cooking accessories such as cookie cutters and reusable place cards. She also now has the context to see and analyze the gaps these books all contain when it comes to using food history as a lens to understanding the construction of American culture and identity.

KC never owned anything related to American Girl as a child, but eagerly ate up the long row of books at the library, eventually finding the historical cookbooks much to her mother's chagrin. She remembers begging for ingredients to make Samantha Parkington's Lemon Ice, a recipe from the nineteenth century, despite her mother's insistence that it would melt almost instantly in the Texas heat. Early in her childhood, KC lived on a ranch in central Texas and helped her dad (the ranch hand) with various chores including milking cows, feeding sheep, and tending to a large wood-burning stove in the dining room. Skimming thick cream off the top of a fresh pint of milk and the cast iron skillets that her parents used to cook reminded her of the ingredients and cooking techniques frequently used in the historical AG cookbooks. This early connection to food initially guided KC towards culinary school, but a last-minute decision redirected her to studying food instead and finding the connections between historical recipes and our contemporary approaches to food.

Much like many of our fellow contributors in this anthology and countless American Girl fans across the world, these fictional characters and their historically based lives were integral aspects of our upbringings and arguably influential to our chosen paths of research and careers. Historical food texts possess powerful cultural context, and Pleasant Company recognized the opportunities for additional meaning- and identity-making by creating historically themed cookbooks for their characters. Now equipped with years of training and experience understanding the critical context surrounding food and cooking, we turn to these texts again to analyze the food of the American Girl universe and how American Girl has influenced food in our everyday lives, too.

In 1990, Pleasant Company released *The American Girls Cookbook: A Peek at Dining in the Past with Meals You Can Cook Today* under their Portfolio of Pastimes series that also included books on historical crafts and other activities.[7] This spiral bound book featured recipes from the three original historical characters (first launched in 1986), Kirsten, Samantha, and Molly, the only dolls available at that time. Readers were quickly shown the importance of food and cooking as the introduction explains how "cooking, dining, and kitchen cleanup were more than pastimes for American girls in times past" but actual jobs and responsibilities that people and even young girls had to navigate in their respective eras.[8] The book reinforces the notion that "learning about kitchens and cooking in the past will help you understand what it was like to grow up the way American girls like Kirsten, Samantha, and Molly did. Cooking the meals they ate in your own kitchen will bring history alive for you and your family."[9] Readers learn this context through the modernized historical recipes, short chapter intros for each character and their foodways, and numerous side bars with illustrations covering everything from butchering and Swedish table grace to finger bowls and food fashions. *The American Girls Cookbook* also tiptoed into more complex aspects of food history including servant labor and wartime rationing practices that introduce issues such as class and even race. For all the "good" the cookbook did, it largely ignores one of the biggest issues

American Girls (and girls) dealt with on a daily basis: gender stereotypes related to food and food labor. Aside from a brief mention in the book's introduction about how nowadays "men and boys cook, too," the book consistently reinforces the age-old historically gendered connection between women's social roles and food production.

In hindsight, we now know the early 1990s were hardly a moment of women's progress. Despite a plethora of messaging to the contrary, "radical" Lilith fairs, and a smattering of male-dominated careers–themed Barbies, late twentieth century women (the demographic that young American Girl readers observed and learned from every day) were still largely expected to shoulder the majority of food-related labor (usually in addition to working full-time jobs). It was an era known as "The Highly Anticipated Decade of Women," according to journalist Allison Yarrow, who argues that the 1990s put women in an impossible situation balancing the need to display both competence and femininity.[10] Thanks to deep gender divides in professional kitchens, this labor was almost always relegated to home kitchens or gender-appropriate sectors of the food industry such as baking or event planning. Mattel's Barbie, another popular toy marketed to girls at this time, launched a variety of food-related dolls in the early 1990s, including a McDonald's Birthday Barbie (1993) and a Little Debbie Barbie (1995); the first dedicated food-*career* doll, I Can Be . . . Barbie TV Chef didn't arrive until 2008. After being acquired by Hasbro in 1993, Easy-Bake Oven, first launched in 1963, doubled down on gendered stereotypes with girly pink and purple packaging (the Queasy Bake Cookerator, a green and black version that made "gross-looking" snacks was marketed to boys a decade later).[11] While American Girl clearly wasn't the only toy company struggling with gendered marketing, it was one of the few that dedicated time and energy into creating additional context—in the form of books, magazines, and detail-heavy package descriptions—for its products. Despite its mission to use the character dolls to educate young consumers about a shared history, American Girl passed up on the opportunity to disrupt centuries of gendered stereotypes to sell a half-baked historical cookbook.

A few years later in 1994, Pleasant Company Publications released five historical cookbooks based on the "original" historical dolls—Kristen Larson, Samantha Parkington, and Molly McIntire, dolls released in 1986; Felicity Merriman, doll released in 1991; and Addy Walker, doll released in 1993. One more historical cookbook was released in 1998, after Josefina

Montoya's introduction in 1997. These books pulled from food and cooking references woven into the plots of each character's book series in addition to researched food habits and recipes more or less historically accurate to their individual eras. While unique to each character, all of the recipes are adapted for the modern kitchen, using accessible ingredients and contemporary kitchen tools and technologies. Considerable time, effort, and financial resources went into the production of each cookbook made plain through the list of contributors featured in the front matter including multiple editors and authors, an art director, producers, cover and inside illustrators, photographers, historical artifact (displayed as photographs and scans throughout the books) researchers, recipe testing coordinators, food stylists, and prop researchers. The books also included a special thanks to the external recipe testers: all girls and their mothers.

These historical cookbooks were originally released as part of the American Girl Pastimes collection, which also included separate books on crafts, theater kits, and paper dolls. The series title served as both a verbal play on a *time past* but also a reference to the hobbies and activities the historical characters would have enjoyed. Aligning cooking and food production with other acts of leisure and, most importantly, choice, skews the historical perception of women's tasks and domestic duties.

After Mattel acquired the American Girl brand in 1998, just before the release of Kit Kittredge, all of the original historical cookbooks were phased out. A brief revival of historical recipes came in the form of the Cooking Studio series that repackaged bits and pieces of the original character cookbooks. A few years later in the early aughts, Mattel partnered with kitchenware retailer Williams-Sonoma to create a new line of American Girl cookbooks on subjects including baking, cookies, global dishes, summer treats, and general cooking. Contemporary cookbooks are displayed under the "Advice and Activities" section on the books page of the American Girl website. Repetitive cookbook titles including *Tea Parties: Delicious Sweets & Savory Treats to Share* and *Cookies: Delicious Recipes for Sweet Treats to Bake & Share* reproduce the language and themes used in late nineteenth- and early twentieth-century women's pages found in newspapers and specialized magazines across the nation.[12] The highly regarded *The Care and Keeping of You* and its various iterations has its own dedicated header on the books page, while cookbooks, party guides, and sticker journals make up the bulk of all other important and relevant information for a young girl's "how-tos and to-dos featuring fun to grown on" (to use the company's words).

Sweet & Savory Treats Cookbook: Delicious Recipes Inspired by Your Favorite Characters is perhaps the most historically inclusive cookbook featuring seventeen American Girl characters including five of the original six historical American Girl dolls (for reasons unknown, Samantha is not mentioned in this book). Published in 2021 by American Girl and Weldon Owen (an imprint of Simon & Schuster), *Sweet & Savory Treats* invites readers to celebrate and connect with the "girls who came before you" with recipes including "challah that Rebecca's family would have baked for Shabbat," anachronistic homemade hummus served with "fresh veggies that Molly would have grown in her victory garden," and fruit leather that Blair (the 2019 Doll of the Year) "would have shared with visitors to her family's farm."[13] While the cookbook references the importance of food in American Girl stories and in American history, the company takes care to absolve itself of possible misinterpretation by stating that the recipes are "inspired by the time and places each [girl] represents."[14] Real-life versions of Kirsten would have likely made Swedish Meatballs with Sour Cream Sauce in mid-nineteenth-century Minnesota and the Kit Kittredges of Depression-era Ohio would have also been familiar with well-known Americanized recipes for Mac-&-Cheese and Apple Bread Pudding. However, American Girl's entire foundation is built upon an intentional blurring between fact and fiction, and its handling of food and food history is no exception. Recipes are, in many ways, fictionalized any time a recipe developer, food historian, or home cook takes a historical recipe and adapts it for modern or new technologies, available ingredients, and contemporary tastes. With this process in mind, some fictionalization of historical recipes for historically inspired fictional characters makes sense and is expected. Much of the responsibility to adhere and accurately represent historical foodways, however, is reinforced by society's understanding and normalization of a white hegemonic foodways. Even Rebecca Rubin's early twentieth-century recipe for challah, a traditional Jewish bread, exists (or rather has been appropriated) in our American culinary hegemony.

Rather than trusting young readers to be equally curious and understanding of new-to-them historical foodways as they are about fashion, games, and larger societal concepts like class and race, American Girl opts for the easier route of *ahistoricalization* when it comes to foods and recipes from characters and stories that exist outside the American culinary hegemony. For example, instead of developing a recipe with salmon or berries, two staple ingredients to Kaya's Nez Perce (Nimíipuu) Indigenous community, she gets Spiced Applesauce Muffins.[15] According to *Sweet & Savory Treats*, since the Nez Perce people "lived throughout the Pacific Northwest, including present-day Washington," applesauce muffins make sense because "Washington state is the largest producer of apples in the United States."[16] Kaya's story is set in 1764; white settlers moving from the east introduced apples to the Washington State region starting around the 1820s. Early waves of colonists brought apple trees with them to the east coast where local Indigenous groups, including the Cherokee, worked to further establish the fruit with their intimate knowledge of the local growing environment. While the Nez Perce and other Indigenous groups are credited with shaping the Northwest apple industry as we know it today, this influence would not have started until over half a century after Kaya's time. Interestingly, this same geographic region was known for a native cousin to the imported apple (*Malus domestica*) known as the crabapple (*Malus fusca*), a wild-growing fruit that served as a staple ingredient for local Indigenous groups. While contemporary readers, especially those living outside of the Pacific Northwest, would have required a domesticated apple substitute, this small but important point of Indigenous food history would have radically changed Kaya's recipe narrative. Apples aside, the use of other colonized ingredients, as Indigenous food scholar Courtney Lewis calls them, including wheat flour, refined sugar, baking powder, and spices imported from the spice trade empires further fictionalizes and deemphasizes the importance of Kaya's Indigenous foodways.[17] *Sweet & Savory Treats* introduces readers to each historical character, including Kaya, on separate pages featuring short bios and notes about popular foods during their respective eras. In this short summary, American Girl notes the importance of camas plant (a wild lily variety), huckleberries, and salmon in the traditional Nez Perce diet.[18] The fact that these Indigenous ingredients, or readily available acceptable substitutes, still exist is never mentioned.

Acknowledging the difficulties of writing and adapting recipes for home cooks, let alone an audience who likely still requires adult supervision when opening the oven, taking the easy route with historical food interpretations is understandable. Nevertheless, and despite the evolution away from American Girl's original mission of historical education, these food-focused books continue to prescribe a flattened version of American food history and fail to distance the universe from gendered stereotypes, especially as they relate to food and food labor.

Perhaps we should look at a different group of American Girl fans, older ones who don't necessarily need step stools and their mother's help. As much as we food scholars would like for young children to learn about the importance of their foodways and food history from an early age, maybe the true barometer for the success of these books exists in their ability to lure grown-ups back into learning about history through the guise of recipes and food fun facts. That is, after all, why Seth Workman created his TikTok series and the impetus for food writer Tabitha Blankenbiller's Great American Girl Doll Cook Off historical recipe showdown for *Serious Eats*.[19]

The allure works the other way, too, as Gwen, the author behind American Girl themed food history blog *A Peek into the Pantry*, explains how she used her "love of history as a way to trick" herself into "learning how to cook. [20] While each new cook questions apparent omissions and cautiously approaches the historical authenticity of the recipes, they use the American Girl cookbooks as launching points for new avenues of food history discovery. The act of preparing a recipe and using even more contemporary ingredients than originally devised in the first run of historical cookbooks provides new opportunities for critical inquiry about the food we ate then and the way we eat now. Sure, Felicity wouldn't have used alternative milks in her breakfast prep, but until you've made eighteenth-century-inspired johnny cakes with oat milk you've probably never considered why dairy milk was so prevalent in a place where cows weren't native *or* why twenty-first-century alt-milks now have a political leaning. The American Girl cookbooks leave plenty to be desired, but they still do what food history does best: give you something to chew on.

Notes

1. Seth Workman (@arenclelle), "Eating breakfast like it's 1774," TikTok, April 15, 2022, https://www.tiktok.com/@arenclelle/video/7086937030160223534?is_copy_url=1&is_from _webapp=v1. "Breakfast puff" refers to a kind of popover.

2. Historical character Kaya instead has a "Trading Feast and Tule Mat" with huckleberries, camas roots, and dried salmon; see https://www.americangirl.com/products/kaya-trading -feast-and-tule-mat-ghr29. "Ice Cream Freezer," American Girl Wiki, accessed January 14, 2024, https://americangirl.fandom.com/wiki/Ice_Cream_Freezer.

3. Samovars are traditionally used to make and keep warm large servings of tea. "Food & Dining," American Girl, accessed January 14, 2024, https://www.americangirl.com /collections/food-dining.

4. Shane O'Neill, "Dolls and Drinks for Likes and Clicks," *New York Times*, February 18, 2022, https://www.nytimes.com/2022/02/18/style/american-girl-cafe-harry-hill-serena -kerrigan.html; Alana Bracken, "My Afternoon at the American Girl Cafe," *Bustle*, April 21, 2022, https://www.bustle.com/life/american-girl-cafe-new-york-review.

5. O'Neill, "Dolls and Drinks," 2022.

6. American Girl Place, Dallas, Dining Menu, accessed January 14, 2024, https://www .americangirl.com/pages/retail-dallas.

7. *The American Girls Cookbook: A Peek at Dining in the Past with Meals You Can Cook Today* (Middleton, WI: Pleasant Company, 1990).

8. *The American Girls Cookbook*, 1.

9. *The American Girls Cookbook*, 3.

10. Allison Yarrow, *90s Bitch: Media, Culture, and the Failed Promise of Gender Equality* (New York: Harper Collins, 2018).

11. Mayukh Sen, "How the Easy-Bake Oven Has Endured 53 Years and 11 Designs," *Food 52*, September 29, 2016, https://food52.com/blog/18007-how-the-easy-bake-oven-has -endured-53-years-and-11-designs; "Queasy Bake Cookerator," The Strong National Museum of Play, accessed January 14, 2024, https://artsandculture.google.com/asset/oven-queasy -bake-cookerator-hasbro-inc/EAGAnW_bfiaP1A.

12. Kimberly Wilmot Voss, *The Food Section: Newspaper Women and the Culinary Community* (Lanham, MD: Rowman & Littlefield, 2014).

13. Katie Killebrew, ed., *Sweet & Savory Treats Cookbook: Delicious Recipes Inspired by Your Favorite Characters* (San Rafael, CA: Weldon Owen, 2021), 6.

14. Killebrew, 8.

15. Killebrew, 24.

16. Killebrew, 24.

17. Courtney Lewis, "Native Food Sovereignty," in *Edible North Carolina: A Journey Across a State of Flavor*, ed. Marcie Cohen Ferris and KC Hysmith (Chapel Hill: University of North Carolina Press, 2022). Lewis is a member of the Eastern Band of Cherokee Indians. While the concepts of "Indigenous food sovereignty" and "colonized ingredients" are central to her research, other Indigenous scholars including Hi'ilei Julia Kawehipuaakahaopulani Hobart of Hawai'i and Native food professionals including Oglala Lakota Sioux chef Sean Sherman use these terms in their work.

18. Killebrew, 25.

19. Tabitha Blankenbiller, "The Great American Girl Doll Cook-Off," *Serious Eats*, June 20, 2019, https://www.seriouseats.com/the-great-american-girl-doll-cook-off.

20. Gwen, "About," *A Peek into the Pantry* (blog), https://apeekintothepantry.blogspot .com/p/about.html.

Places, Parties, and Purchases
Creativity and/against Consumerism
in the American Girl Experience

Juliette Holder

When I first began researching this project, I made a sojourn to the Los Angeles American Girl Place, a large department store that offers everything from the branded dolls to curated brunch menus with doll-size portions. I'd met my mom for dinner at the outdoor mall that serves as its host; afterward, I asked if she wanted to pop into American Girl Place with me.

The Los Angeles location opened in 2006, years past my own childhood American Girl era, so I'd never visited or even really been curious about it. But walking into the multistory building felt . . . electrifying. Mom and I moved from the doll displays and past the hair salon before we dead-ended at the cafe. Waiting for the elevator, we heard the excited clamor of a birthday party across the hall.

In the historical character wing, we admired Kit's scooter and Molly's Jack Russell terrier, whose name I'd forgotten (It's Bennett). My mom pivoted, picked up a doll-sized banana-seat bicycle, and exclaimed, "I had a real bike just like this as a kid!" I noticed a poster above. "This is Julie, the historical girl from the seventies." "Well, I don't know how I feel about them calling me historical, but it's fun to see all this," she said, as we moved down the museum-like display. I peered around the corner: "They've added a lot of historical girls since we last checked in, looks like." At this mention of time and its passing, my mom looked up and laughed, "Yeah, hold on. You're an adult now. Why are we here, anyway?"

It was a good question. Without realizing it, we'd both stepped back in time to my childhood, then hers—or at least some version of them. What about American Girl and its characters made me so quickly neglect my research questions, or remember that I had them at all? Why do I feel compelled to research and write about American Girl anyway? In essence, I hope to question what the American Girl experience is, how conspicuous consumption undermines the company's more laudable goals, as well as how "unofficial" engagements with American Girl, especially the historical characters, may provide a corrective to the company's shortcomings.

Through its historical line of books, dolls, and accessories, Pleasant Company constructs a version of history promoting not only female empowerment but also valuing family, advocacy, and community building.[1] These themes repeat across series, implying that they are deeply important ideas for American girls across time periods. More troublingly, these themes are presented parallel to encourage financial consumption. Here, contradiction starts to creep in.

Take Kit Kittredge, for example. In Kit's story (set during the Great Depression) her family takes in boarders to help with the rent. Kit is moved into the attic, which she gets to decorate herself—a moment both empowering and formative. She selects a Robin Hood theme, in honor of her favorite story. While discussing her new room, Kit and her mother share this exchange:

> "Good old Robin Hood," said Mother. "Robbing the rich to give to the poor." Kit propped herself up on her elbows and looked at Mother. "Too bad there isn't any Robin Hood today," she said. "If rich people had to give some of their money to the poor, it would make the depression better." "It would help," said Mother. "But I don't think it would end the Depression." "What will?" asked Kit. "I don't know," said Mother. "Lots of things, I suppose. People will have to work hard. Use what they have. Face challenges. Stay hopeful."[2]

This short scene reveals the text's conflicted state about where exactly responsibility lies for financial hardship: Is it personal action that makes the difference?

Kit's Uncle Hendrick seems to think so. Uncle Hendrick has managed to hang on to his wealth, despite the Depression. And despite his comfortable life, he won't help out Kit's family—*his* family—when they need it, not even a loan for one month's mortgage payment to keep them from being evicted. "Uncle Hendrick believes that money must be earned by hard work, not given away," Mother explains.[3] When Uncle Hendrick writes a letter to the local newspaper opposing a measure to open a new homeless shelter, Kit argues with him, saying his belief that unhoused populations are "worthless riffraff" and "men who have chosen to wander than to work" is untrue and unfair.[4]

Ultimately, Kit decides that "if Uncle Hendrick could write letters to the newspaper, she could, too."[5] She pens a letter—published the next morning—that supports the shelter and urges people to take care of one another and hold on to hope. It's not Robin Hood, per se, but it is a clear rejection of the "bootstrap" mentality that her villainous Uncle espouses. It shows Kit finding her voice, advocating for others, and being creative.

Yet, there is a parallel narrative about money developing through Kit's tale, one that overpowers more aspirational themes like generosity, resourcefulness, and grit. As an American Girl character, Kit cannot fully, outright reject Uncle Hendrick's perspective; after all, Uncle Hendrick is a great capitalist, and American Girl is a capitalistic enterprise (as is America itself). The American Girl Place is a very specific type of place: a retail store. At time of writing, a Kit doll with one outfit and one book costs $150. Kit's dog Grace is available for $28, as is her school lunch kit ($36), additional outfits ($34–38), and her "homemade" scooter ($50). While not currently available, a miniature version of Kit's *Robin Hood* book was included in various now-retired accessory sets that ran between $20–$50.[6]

Throughout her books, Kit is embarrassed that her dad lost his job and that her family is struggling financially. She feels it to be some sort of personal failing—and when she expresses this, the adults in her life do little to talk her out of it. She can't extend the same understanding she expresses in her letter to herself. All her discussion of Robin Hood is never considered something that may become real. In fact, Kit laments that her family doesn't have money; if they did her parents could afford to throw her a Robin Hood–themed birthday party.[7]

Later in the series, Kit learns that her family cannot pay the electric bill and may also be evicted. Working for change from Uncle Hendrick, Kit secretly saves up enough money to pay her family's bill for a month—for the express purpose of turning on the Christmas lights on the tree.[8] Her choice to focus on the Christmas lights rather than food or rent shows the perspective of a child (which Kit is), perhaps, but it also promotes the notion that being able to consume things to be seen by others—such as an illuminated tree through a window—is important.

Kit's story shows us how alongside themes of empowerment, questioning social systems, and finding one's voice, there is a theme of enhancing one's social standing by displaying signs of wealth. Unfortunately, American Girl has had a large stake in developing that theme of conspicuous consumption. That's the company goal that matters most: getting girls (and their parents) to *buy from them*.

This is, perhaps, one reason why American Girl has expanded its focus beyond the historical characters. In 2005, the company began offering more content focused on contemporary girls.[9] This, in turn, resulted in an uptick in doll accessories related to beauty, food, and bedroom culture, as opposed to accessories that are historically situated and related to specific characters' narratives.[10] Now, the books primarily serve to sell the dolls and have been shortened and otherwise deemphasized in the company's offerings.[11] On the day I walked into the American Girl store, I saw plenty of dolls in the foyer, but no historical characters. We had to make our way upstairs to locate the historical character wing. Even there, the books themselves were not featured prominently but rather tucked away amid displays of doll clothing, furniture, and food items. Many of the historical dolls had been retired by 2010, meaning contemporary doll options outnumbered historical ones. The six original dolls—Kirsten, Samantha, Molly, Felicity, Addy, and Josefina—were brought back in 2021 to celebrate American Girl's thirty-fifth anniversary. In 2023, Kit was brought back to mark what would be the character's one hundredth birthday. These rereleases are limited and include significantly reduced accessory options.

American Girl authors were always encouraged to "write in" dolls, accessories, and outfits that the company could then sell, and this meant that each doll's merchandise collections were never the best representatives of those characters' narratives.[12] The accessories are not designed to support the books as much as the books are carefully written to launch accessories. While many of the characters engage in social change activism, their accessories don't necessarily reflect that. Emilie Zaslow notes "With the exception of Kit's typewriter, there are not now, nor were there ever, accessories that alluded to the characters' social change activism; the accessories collections have not included protest signs, podiums, or eagle launches."[13]

Kit's typewriter is now out of production. The rereleased historical dolls demonstrate just how limited the scope of accessories has become. The more narrative and time-period specific accessories are still gone. The outfits, furniture, and food items that remain offer a distinct style, but could, technically, exist at any time period covered by American Girl. As a result, the historical characters primarily offer an aesthetic, rather than a story or a distinct perspective of history.[14]

Furthermore, as the historical girls move closer to our own time, their accessory collections take on real-world brand names. Rather than Samantha's generic needlepoint kit, Kit's baseball glove, or Felicity's Noah's Ark play set, Courtney (of the 1980s) plays with *Pac-Man* arcade games and attends sleepovers in a CareBears sleeping bag. Courtney doesn't just buy things—she buys *real brands*, including American Girl. In a meta-moment, you can buy your American Girl doll an American Girl doll of her own (Courtney is, I guess, a Molly fan). As the historical book series are deemphasized and aesthetics continue to rise in importance, the accessories that American Girl sells for each character are less and less attached to a narrative. We see that it's not just that consumerism undercuts the other themes of the books; it may be that consumerism is the only theme left at all.

As a result, American Girl promotes the idea that purchasing things, particularly things that give off a certain sense of status, is central to what American Girls *do*. And that actionable component makes the theme of consumerism all the more "sticky" for girls. It's something that they can really partake in. More than just presenting the idea that consumerism is important to American girls, the company presents girls with a chance to live out this idea.[15] While American Girl goes to great lengths to root material consumption in history, for girls, this theme becomes more *present* than it does *past*; it is an activity that they can participate in *now*. Other themes, like activism, lack this consumable, tactile element and remain mostly abstract and in the past; whereas consumerism, still rooted in and justified by the past, is able to move past history and into girls' experiences of today.

As American Girl opened up more American Girl Place destinations, there was a chance to provide more opportunities for girls to *do* something. There's no shortage of events held at American Girl Place locations. It's a doll-centric world, with hair salons and cafes offering doll-friendly seating and services. Special activities such as cooking classes or Grandparent's Day socials include dolls in the activities. But it's always just "dolls," not a specific doll or character. While it's likely that some attendees will bring their historical dolls, none of the activities or events are themed *around* American Girl characters themselves, at least not anymore. When Kit Kittredge was released in 2000, some nonprofits organized Kit-themed events that raised money and supplies for local food banks. American Girl approved of, but did not host, these events.[16] Molly Rosner reports on an early American Girl event that celebrated Felicity Merriman (a doll living through the Revolutionary War), which had attendees experience etiquette classes like Felicity does in the book. But Felicity despises those classes, so this reads as a bit of an odd choice for people familiar with the book series.[17] When the historical characters have shown up in American Girl Place events, the events have worked *against* the characters' own narratives.

The same holds true for American Girl birthday parties held on location at the American Girl Place. Rather than revolving around characters or historical periods, girls choose from different themes including "sprinkles," or "rainbows." An American Girl Place birthday runs sixty to ninety minutes and includes a meal, cake and ice cream, a goodie bag with doll tiaras, a crown for the "guest of honor," and personalized digital invitations. For an extra fee, attendees can complete a craft during the party. American Girl also offers cheaper "host at home" options with similar cake, goodie bags, doll tiaras, and doll-sized paper dishes. The American Girl Place does not provide space for girls to enact the stories, themes, or even settings of the historical collection. Rather, it provides an opportunity for dolls to consume things the way real people do. Instead of bringing girls into the dolls' worlds, American Girl parties bring dolls into our world, through consumer practices. This is noteworthy because birthday parties are important in American Girl culture; in the original book series format, each character has a book dedicated solely to birthday celebrations. In September 2000, Kit Kittredge debuted, and a few months before Kit swapped her Robin Hood birthday party dreams for a "penny pincher" party thrown by her aunt, I had an American Girl birthday party myself.

I was turning eight, or, rather, *we* were turning eight. My triplet sisters and I couldn't agree on a party theme, so my parents concocted a "marathon birthday" sleepover party, split into three parts, each with a different theme. My part of the party—Samantha-themed—was in the morning. I was one of the first ones awake, and I remember tumbling into the kitchen to see my mom and my "Aunt" Barbie hanging a banner over the patio door that said, "Welcome to 1904." A few weeks earlier, I'd helped my mom design the banner in Microsoft Word; I stood next to her, eye-level with the computer screen, pointing at which clip art pictures of flowers I liked best. Relying on *Samantha's Cookbook* and *Samantha's Craft Book* as our guides, we enjoyed a "Victorian" breakfast and then made "Fancy Fans" out of wrapping paper and popsicle sticks along with "Walnut-Shell Surprises."[18] "Walnut shells make perfect hiding places for tiny treasures," the *Craft Book* assured me.[19]

What made this party an American Girl party? I stacked my books up next to the cake to make it look "official," but did that do the trick? I wore a big pink bow atop my head (a nod to Samantha's own *iconic* birthday outfit), and my best friend, Megan, rocked Kirstin's looped braided look. Was that enough? We pulled from American Girl books, but nothing we used that day was bought from American Girl or branded in any way. There weren't even any dolls in attendance. I don't think any of us—or at least not most of us, certainly not all of us—had dolls to bring. It was a far cry from the American Girl parties the American Girl Place sells now. Was my party just a cheap knockoff? Or, in some ways, did it pay more tribute to American Girl by featuring the actual historical characters more? American Girl party culture raises questions about the very definition of American Girl and how the historical characters fit into that definition: Does the official version have to promote consumption so much that it loses its most defining feature of the characters themselves? Or is it the dolls and their participation, the location, the brand that matters?

It's a surprisingly complex question–one that carries through most of my experiences with American Girl. I did end up owning a Samantha doll, a Christmas gift from my grandparents. A year later, I got Samantha's school desk. To me, these were sacred objects, prized possessions. I knew that they *mattered*. But the rest of the clothes and accessories I got for my doll weren't from American Girl. We bought them from cheaper places or got hand-me-downs from friends. My mom picked up a wooden doll-sized bed frame on sale one day, and we painted it together, taping the floral stencil down and running the sponge-tip brush over it until it looked "old-fashioned" and "fancy" enough for Samantha. My mom even sewed bedding for the tiny bed, telling me stories about how she learned to sew from her mom, relaying stories of the generations of seamstresses and tailors I descend from. None of that is part of the official American Girl catalog—should I count them among my American Girl experiences? I do. I think many other American Girl fans do, too.

These unofficial engagements with American Girl and especially the historical characters have always been part of the American Girl experience. And it's a profound experience, one that women, in all sorts of ways, return to as adults. It's expected (and part of American Girl's corporate strategy) that girls who grew up with the dolls will want to share the brand with their own children. And that's certainly happening. But women who grew up with the brand return to it in other ways—ways that are unofficial and sometimes even critical of the brand. Consider Nana Osei-Kofi's "Breaking Free" art project, podcasts like *Dolls of Our Lives* hosted by Allison Horrocks and Mary Mahoney, or the play *In Sisters We Trust: My F*cked Up American Girl Doll Play* by Justine Gelfman.[20] All of these projects return to the American Girl historical characters to question social structures and call for change—inspired, perhaps, by the books and doll play we engaged in as children, furthered by the "off-market" accessories we found or made with the older women in our lives, by the conversations those playtimes brought about. Participating in American Girl culture has, for many, always included some "unsanctioned" engagement—committing to the better themes and our favorite parts of these characters' stories requires it.

This complicates the story of American Girl and what (along with how) it teaches girls about history. There is worthy scholarly debate about the version(s) of our country's history American Girl presents, which is, in part, complicated (and probably corrupted) by the company's overemphasis on consumerism. What's less discussed is how American Girl might connect us to our smaller, personal histories. Girls become part of intergenerational networks of women, through play and through finding ways around the often prohibitively expensive official avenues of play. Within those networks, girls learn not only that sometimes you do have to operate outside the lines of official pathways and provide some practice with learning how. In doing so, we're provided the chance to act out and reclaim American Girl's better themes and goals.

Notes

1. Emilie Zaslow, *Playing with America's Doll: A Cultural Analysis of the American Girl Collection* (New York: Palgrave Macmillan, 2017), 71–104.

2. Valerie Tripp, *Meet Kit* (Middleton, WI: Pleasant Company, 2000), 58.

3. Valerie Tripp, *Kit's Surprise* (Middleton, WI: Pleasant Company, 2000), 20.

4. Tripp, *Kit's Surprise*, 25.

5. Tripp, 39.

6. "Kit's Bedtime Extras," American Girl Wiki, n.d., accessed June 12, 2024, https://american girl.fandom.com/wiki/Kit%27s_Bedtime_Extras.

7. Valerie Tripp, *Happy Birthday, Kit* (Middleton, WI: Pleasant Company, 2000).

8. Tripp, *Surprise*, 65.

9. Zaslow, 27–28.

10. Zaslow, 9.

11. Anne Lesme, "The Historical Characters of American Girl Dolls: Spectacle and Visual Culture as Agents of Consumerism," *In Media* 7, no. 1 (2018), https://doi.org/10.4000/inmedia.1055.

12. Zaslow, 72–73.

13. Zaslow, 91.

14. Molly Rosner, "The American Girl Company and the Uses of Nostalgia in Children's Consumer Culture," *Jeunesse: Young People, Texts, Cultures* 6, no. 2 (2014): 35–53, https://doi.org/10.1353/jeu.2014.0019.

15. John F. Sherry, "The Work of Play at American Girl Place," *Social Psychology Quarterly* 72, no. 3 (2009): 199–202, https://doi.org/10.1177/019027250907200301.

16. "Come to 'Kit's Care and Share Party,'" *Dispatch Argus* (Moline/Rock Island, IL), September 23, 2000, https://qconline.com/life/come-to-kits-care-and-share-party/article_2e22e907-3446-5dd8-a419-9cb85b566623.html.

17. Rosner, 49.

18. Jodi Evert et al., *Samantha's Cookbook: A Peek at Dining in the Past with Meals You Can Cook Today* (Middleton, WI: Pleasant Company, 1998); Rebecca Bernstein et al., *Samantha's Craft Book: A Look at Crafts from the Past with Projects You Can Make Today* (Middleton, WI: Pleasant Company, 1998).

19. Bernstein et al., 28.

20. Nana Osei-Kofi, "American Girls: Breaking Free," *Feminist Formations* 25, no. 1 (2013): 1–7, https://doi.org/10.1353/ff.2013.0003; "About," Dolls of Our Lives, accessed June 12, 2023, https://podcasts.apple.com/us/podcast/dolls-of-our-lives/id1454139632; Justine Gelfman, *In Sisters We Trust, or My F*cked up American Girl Doll Play*, Department of Theatre and Dance—The University of Texas at Austin, 2022, https://theatredance.utexas.edu/event/sisters-we-trust.

PART 2

WHO GETS TO BE AN AMERICAN GIRL?

Where Is My Disability Community?

A Comparative Close Reading
of Children's Historical Fiction

Marissa J. Spear

Middle grade (MG) and young adult (YA) authors and readers continue to push the field of children's literature forward, widening the types of narratives that come alive in its pages, even in historical fiction. Malinda Lo and Nita Tyndall give us queer communities in San Francisco's 1950s Chinatown and Nazi-occupied Berlin. Randi Pink explores the Greenwood Tulsa Massacre of 1921 through a love story between two teens, and Traci Chee follows fourteen Japanese American teenagers incarcerated during World War II. Jewell Parker Rhodes depicts a twelve-year-old's perspective of New Orleans's Ninth Ward during Hurricane Katrina, and Rita Williams-Garcia's young characters transport us to Oakland in 1968 to visit their mother, a Black Panther. Disabled authors like Lillie Lainoff and Carly Heath incorporate protagonists with POTS and Waardenburg syndrome into seventeenth century France and twentieth century Norway.[1]

Similarly, scholars and fans of the almost forty-year-old American Girl (AG) brand have continuously pushed for the diversification of its collection. Since the release of its flagship historical characters, Black writers have questioned placing AG's first Black doll, Addy Walker, in slavery.[2] Jewish scholars and writers have critiqued the brand's exclusion of Jewish stories and the increasing dehistoricization of its Jewish characters.[3] Other scholars have critiqued the retirement of many of AG's historical characters of color

Screenshot of the Courtney Moore @PinkSaltCollective meme referencing the need for an American Girl doll who has POTS.

and the analogous retirement of characters' historical accessories in favor of "increasingly gendered objects."[4] Author Valerie Tripp credited letters from disabled girls asking to see themselves reflected in the historical collection with the release of Maryellen Larkin in 2015, a ten-year-old girl in 1954 with polio.[5]

As a disabled historian and writer, I owe my love for history to AG's historical collection. My desire to see my disabled self represented in AG is "not a mere desire for disability representation, but rather a longing to find a political identity of disabled people like me."[6] In this text, I analyze the role of disability in AG historical fiction in comparison to two MG and YA historical fiction novels featuring disabled protagonists. I argue that unlike these novels, the AG brand lacks engagement with the disability community at large. In addition, I assert that the reduction of AG's "Looking Back" sections (the postnarrative sections dedicated to historical context for each novel) since the launch of its BeForever line (a rebranding of its original historical collection) in 2014 has contributed to this lack of critical engagement with disability history and community building. By comparing and contrasting AG's representation of disabled characters in their historical collection with those in MG and YA historical fiction, we can better understand the importance of centering disabled authors in telling these

We need an American girl doll who moved back in with her parents at the age of 30 thanks to a disability

@PinkSaltCollective

We need an American girl doll who was an overachiever & is now chronically ill

@PinkSaltCollective

Screenshot of the Melody Ellison @PinkSaltCollective meme referencing the need for an American Girl doll who moved back in with her parents because of a disability.

Screenshot of the Molly McIntire @PinkSaltCollective meme referencing the need for an American Girl doll who is chronically ill.

stories. It is in AG's best interest to continue to stay relevant with a growing audience of disabled readers who want to see authentic stories portrayed by and about them. In this essay, MG novels (including AG) refer to those with ten- to twelve-year-old protagonists targeting eight- to twelve-year-olds and YA refers to those with sixteen- to eighteen-year-old protagonists targeting fourteen- to nineteen-year-olds.[7] For the purposes of this essay, I will focus on US-based MG and YA historical fiction by disabled authors that center disabled female protagonists with physical disabilities.

Disability in Children's Literature

The growth of disability representation in children's literature over the past ten years is in part due to disabled authors demanding more. Disabled authors have continued to combat harmful tropes and provide support for each other in an inequitable publishing industry. For example, in 2015 disabled author Corinne Duyvis coined the social media hashtag #OwnVoices to share recommendations for books that shared the identity of their protagonists. The hashtag quickly spread across platforms, becoming a widely used term in author, agent, and editor circles. The term resonated with ongoing conversations in the publishing industry about the lack of diversity and served as a way for authors and professionals to prioritize voices of those with lived experiences.[8] However, in recent years, authors have pointed out issues with the term's vagueness, particularly the pressure many LGBTQIA authors face to out themselves to prove #OwnVoices.[9] As a result, the term has fallen out of practice.[10]

Disabled authors have also contributed to the normalization of the use of sensitivity readers. The goal of sensitivity readers is to have another critical set of eyes on a manuscript and can include reading for disability, gender, sexuality, race, and class. For instance, if an author has a secondary disabled character but does not share that character's experience, they may hire a sensitivity reader from that lived experience to review their manuscript for potentially damaging tropes and stereotypes and to provide them with honest feedback to help make that character more authentic. Furthermore, disabled authors have established support networks for each other throughout the publishing process. In 2019, disabled author Lillie Lainoff created the Facebook group Disabled Kidlit Writers, a group designed for disabled authors of children's literature "to support each other, talk about writing, ask questions, get advice, and celebrate successes," which has amassed over five hundred members.[11] While the publishing industry has made strides, gaps still exist in children's historical fiction, particularly when it comes to disability. As Lainoff explains, the gap in disability representation in historical fiction is "partially because of the pervasive misconception that there weren't as many disabled people in the past as there are now. ([S]poiler: a lot of disabled folks were institutionalized and/or kept off the street via Ugly Laws.) But there was also a population of disabled people who spent their lives outside of institutions."[12]

History of Disability in American Girl

In recent years, scholars and fans alike have also critiqued the lack of disability in the AG franchise across its contemporary and historical collections.[13] For example, ten-year-old Melissa Shang garnered national attention in 2013 when she petitioned AG to release a disabled Girl of the Year, eventually self-publishing a book with her sister.[14] In 2017 AG released its first disabled Girl of the Year (although not marketed using that terminology),

Gabriela McBride, a Black girl with a stutter. A few years later in 2020, AG released another disabled Girl of the Year (again not marketed as such), Joss Kendrick, a character with congenital hearing loss who is deaf in her left ear and uses a hearing aid in her right.[15]

Secondary disabled characters had existed in the *contemporary* collection before 2017 (e.g., Josie, a wheelchair user in the McKenna series) in limited capacities, with "disability doll accessories" made available to consumers since the late 1990s.[16] However, AG has been comparatively slow going in placing disabled characters at the center of its historical collection. Up until the early 2000s, AG's historical collection only included disabled *secondary* characters.[17] In 2002, AG released Kaya'aton'my or Kaya (1764), a Nimíipuu girl, whose collection featured Speaking Rain, Kaya's adopted blind sister. In 2007, AG released Julie Albright (1974), whose collection featured Joy Jenner, a deaf classmate and friend. In 2015, after rebranding its historical collection to BeForever in the previous year to make the historical characters more relevant to their target audience, AG released Maryellen Larkin (1954), both the first new historical character of the BeForever collection and the first historical character with a disability—polio—although she was not marked as disabled.[18]

Since the inception of AG, the company has relied on a team of in-house historians and researchers to inform the development of each of their historical characters. Beginning with the creation of Addy, AG also began using advisory boards made up of historians, museum professionals, local activists or cultural workers, and community leaders. This process included finding an author that lent credibility, had the time to complete multiple books, and was open to the advisory board's feedback.[19] While the in-house historians and advisory boards are important in creating the historical characters, it remains to be seen why AG has not prioritized providing more authenticity to their characters by hiring writers who share their experiences. AG has been mixed on this account in the historical collection even in recent years. While Black authors were chosen for Addy, Melody, Cécile, and Claudie, Nimíipuu and Mexican authors were not chosen for Kaya and Josefina. Of the BeForever line, neither Nanea nor Maryellen was written by a Hawaiian and disabled author, respectively.

In 2020, the onslaught of American Girl memes from Instagram accounts such as @hellicity_merriman and @klit_klittredge brought a resurgence to the need for more diverse representation in AG in a tongue-in-cheek way. Themes built on the overwhelming nostalgia many millennials associate with the brand. Of particular importance were the "We Need an American Girl Doll" memes. @PinkSaltCollective on Instagram posted a series of memes connecting AG dolls and disability and chronic illness. For instance, one featuring Courtney Moore (1986) read: "We need an American Girl doll whose legs turn purple when she stands up bc POTS." Another featured Melody Ellison (1964) with the location marked as "American Girl Doll Hospital" and read: "We need an American Girl doll who moved back in with her parents at the age of 30 thanks to disability." Still another featuring Molly McIntire (1944) read: "We need an American Girl doll who was an overachiever and is now chronically ill."[20] These memes sparked new discussion and scholarship on reading disability back into the AG historical collection.[21]

Disability in American Girl Historical Fiction

In disabled historian Sami Schalk's close reading and analysis of AG's historical collection, she focuses on the three disabled historical characters mentioned above: Speaking Rain, Joy, and Maryellen. Schalk argues that these characters are written in "isolation," with no disabled community around them.[22] In contrast to other AG historical characters where protagonists "experience issues of race, class, and gender as collective concerns," disability "remains highly individualized."[23] For the purposes of this essay, I will focus on analyzing Speaking Rain and Maryellen's stories.

Speaking Rain

Speaking Rain is a blind Nimíipuu girl growing up in the 1760s and Kaya's slightly younger adopted sister. She appears in four of the six original Kaya stories, initially portrayed as a dependent character, often relying on Kaya and other community members for support. For example, she is not allowed to take care of Kaya's little brothers (about four years old) and is rescued by Kaya after falling into a river. The latter example falls into the ableist trope where a disabled character, in this case, Speaking Rain, only exists in the story to provide character growth for the protagonist, Kaya.[24] In the second book in the series, Kaya and Speaking Rain are kidnapped by raiders. Kaya notes how the raiders are upset that Speaking Rain is blind, often solely sending Kaya to perform tasks like gathering heavy loads of wood. Still, Speaking Rain has her own moments of defiance in captivity, singing their mother's lullaby as she and her sister fall asleep.[25]

In one instance, Kaya is able to name their captors' ableism, even if that language is not explicitly used. For example, the narrator describes how once at the raiders' camp, the older woman "[doesn't] bother to tie up Speaking Rain—a blind girl wouldn't try to escape."[26] Eventually, Kaya and Speaking Rain start to discuss an escape, but Speaking Rain tells her sister that she will never be able to keep up, that she must go on without her. Although Speaking Rain has a role in the initial *Kaya* books, the way she is perceived by Kaya and her community is often defined by her lack of agency, which is solely attributed to her blindness.

Ultimately, Kaya and Speaking Rain are reunited in book six, *Kaya Shows the Way*, when Kaya learns Speaking Rain has been living with an elderly woman, White Braids. White Braids found Speaking Rain and in return, Speaking Rain cares for White Braids, taking care of daily tasks the woman cannot accomplish. The narrator observes, "Her sister wasn't just helping White Braids—the old woman relied on her now in a way that Kaya and her family never had."[27] It takes Speaking Rain living in a different community with White Braids for Kaya to see her sister differently, as capable of being reliable and dependable. While Speaking Rain's (in)dependence shifts over the course of the novels, we never see Speaking Rain in community with other disabled children or adults. The elderly woman is the closest we come to this shared community, although White Braids is never named as disabled.

Indigenous scholars Doris Seale and Beverly Slapin's review of the *Kaya* books points out several inaccuracies in its portrayal of the Nimíipuu people. Slapin argues that Speaking Rain, "like all Native children, would have been taught to take care of herself. She would not have to hold hands while walking with someone, nor would she be constrained from picking berries or gathering firewood, nor would she ask questions about things she could figure out for herself."[28] The historical inaccuracies in Kaya's stories suggest that a blind Nimíipuu girl like Speaking Rain would have had more agency than the stories portray. These inaccuracies, and by extension, Speaking Rain's lack of agency may have been mitigated by having a Nimíipuu disabled author write Kaya's stories. As Seale and Slapin state: "It's almost impossible to tell another people's story in a believable way, no matter how good one's intentions may be and no many how many cultural advisors there are."[29]

Maryellen Larkin

In an interview, Valerie Tripp, the author of the Maryellen Larkin series, stated that she received letters from young disabled girls asking to see stories of themselves reflected, particularly ones where the "character's physical or developmental challenge is not what defines her."[30] She indicated that these letters were part of the impetus for Maryellen Larkin, a nine-year-old, white, middle-class girl growing up with polio in Florida in 1954. In the same interview, Tripp went on to say: "I know that my readers will understand that polio, rampant in the '50s, is a metaphor for any unfair wallop that life surprises you with."[31] From the outset, Tripp was naming polio as a metaphor for any "unfair" thing that happens to young readers. Invoking disability as a metaphor is an ableist trope all too common in literature that diminishes the experiences of disabled people.[32] As Schalk writes, Maryellen was "a prime opportunity for AG to finally engage with disability in its historical fiction, and yet disability is arguably even more avoided and occluded in the Maryellen books than in those that represent Speaking Rain and Joy."[33]

The first mention of disability occurs in Maryellen's first novel, *The One and Only* when Maryellen, her siblings, and friend Davy are running toward the beach. The narrator states that Maryellen "had a sickness called polio when she was younger, and one leg was a little bit weaker than the other. Sometimes Maryellen worried that Mom babied her because of her leg. But Maryellen never let her leg slow her down."[34] Immediately, Maryellen's narrative falls into the idea that disability is something to be overcome. Later in that same novel, Maryellen's friends are annoyed that she is hanging out with the new Italian student, Angela. When talking about how Angela stands out for a weird reason including her "long braids and *pierced ears*," one friend asks Maryellen if she likes to stand out because of her polio.[35] Maryellen is speechless; "it had never occurred to her before that her friends thought her polio made her *weird*."[36] This moment is an opportunity for the reader to see Maryellen grappling with the "othering" that often comes with disability identity and confront her friends about it, but this comment is not explored any further.

Maryellen's second novel, *Taking Off*, presents further opportunities to explore disability identity and history. The novel opens with a special school assembly announcing Dr. Jonas Salk's invention of the polio vaccine.[37] As the school reacts to the announcement, the narrator states: "But Maryellen had remembered very well how much polio had hurt. Sometimes in her dreams she had polio again, and the heavy, dark, frightened feeling of being lost in pain and worry came back."[38] This instance is the only interior look the reader receives at Maryellen's experience with polio, or as Schalk notes, the kind of disabling effects polio can have on people.[39]

Maryellen spends the second novel preparing a show for her birthday to encourage people to get vaccinated, often fielding fear and doubt from her friends about the effectiveness of the vaccine in the process. Maryellen prepares a short speech for the show she puts on with her friends, sends the money from the show to the March of Dimes, and appears in a parade alongside the mayor to celebrate the fact that children went to get vaccinated after attending her show. Similar to Speaking Rain, despite all this advocacy, Maryellen never encounters another child or adult with polio, nor another disability. There is no opportunity for Maryellen and by extension, the reader, to see that she's not alone in what she experienced, or understand the power of collective identity.

Like other AG historical characters, the model of girlhood promoted in Maryellen's story is overlaid with patriotism, constant reminders to be civically engaged and to *do your part*. Emilie Zaslow argues that AG's historical narratives post-2000 "normalize civic engagement and having a political voice . . . rather than featuring a heroic neoliberal subject who can save the day."[40] Zaslow writes that this civic engagement involves "raising awareness, petitioning, protesting, working collectively, and running for office."[41] However, Zaslow's reading obscures the fact that these stories "tend to underplay the legitimacy of negative emotions in girls or the possibility of more radical responses to injustice."[42] What if Maryellen, and by extension, the reader, learned about the continued institutionalization of disabled children like her in the 1950s? What if she were given the space to be angry at the institution, their poor conditions, and then used that anger to fuel a different form of activism? The traditional AG narrative of civic engagement coupled with disability in Maryellen's story perpetuates *ablenationalism*, using the exceptional figure of the disabled character to name the "superiority, morality, and exceptionalism of the United States."[43] In this case,

Maryellen is the accepted model of respectable American disabled girlhood, one who does not let her disability stop her, who uses her individual voice to bring awareness in a way that is nonviolent and, in turn, is celebrated for this civic duty, all tied together with the literal patriotic American flag waving in a Memorial Day parade.

Disability in Middle Grade and Young Adult Historical Fiction

As noted above, disabled authors have continued to push MG and YA forward in historical fiction. Below I present two examples of MG and YA historical fiction respectively published in the last five years that feature disabled protagonists. Namely, these novels are by disabled authors with disabled main characters and show disabled people in community with each other.

Show Me a Sign

Deaf author Ann Clare LeZotte's MG novel *Show Me a Sign* explores the Noepe's Deaf community in 1805 through the lens of Mary Elizabeth Lambert, its eleven-year-old deaf protagonist.[44] The Noepe land is on what is known today as Martha's Vineyard. Mary's great-great-grandfather arrived on the island in 1692 and was "the first recorded deaf person to settle" there, bringing sign language from England.[45] In many ways, Mary is the disabled AG character that could be. Similar to AG historical characters, she is a keen observer of the world around her and, after the recent tragic death of her brother, quick to question everything. This curiosity extends to critiquing the very systems that make up her world. She notes that her deaf father is "sympathetic to the Wampanoag" Tribe of Gay Head (Aquinnah) in contrast to her mother who "only socializes with English women."[46] She is curious, asking questions of her father's farm laborer, Thomas Richards, a formerly enslaved man married to Helen, a Wampanoag woman. Mary wonders why Thomas refers to Aquinnah instead of Gay Head for the land they live on, or how Thomas can be seen as part of the Wampanoag people even if he does not have "Indian blood."[47] As a Native youth reviewer of the book noted, Thomas "doesn't just exist to give Mary wisdom," which is in stark contrast to AG's Felicity (1774) books, where enslaved peoples remain "nameless, faceless, and voiceless."[48]

Unlike her disabled AG counterparts, Mary lives amongst a community of both hearing and deaf people, the majority of whom can communicate in sign language. Mary is surrounded by community on the one hand, yet still able to name the "careless" acts of her hearing peers, who "forget to slow down and include [her]."[49] It is not until a newcomer Andrew Noble arrives that she notices that the world outside her community thinks and treats deaf people differently than they do on the island. Mary's father is determined that "Mary need never have known that the deaf are treated as less than human on the mainland."[50] Noble is a young scientist, intent on finding the scientific origins of deafness on the island. Right away, Mary observes how Noble avoids making eye contact with her deaf father, only speaking directly to her hearing mother.[51] Though not having specific language for it, she is able to notice the discrimination her father faces from men like Noble because of his deafness.

In the latter half of the novel, similar to Speaking Rain, Mary is kidnapped. Mary becomes Noble's "live specimen," taken to Boston, forced to do housework and subject to medical experimentation.[52] In Mary's time under Noble's captivity, she is able to express solidarity for Helen Richards, Thomas's wife, who works as a housemaid in Mary's best friend's house. Mary describes, "I am too exhausted from housework. I remember nothing in the morning. Is this how Helen and [daughter] Sally feel working in homes like the Skiffes? How do they keep up good cheer?"[53] Still, the reader is able to understand Mary's privilege, her ability to go back to the safety of her home while the Richards family's Native land is being colonized.[54]

Throughout the novel, we see Mary's politics sharpen as she continues to interrogate land ownership and colonization in her community and the people it affects. Mary is able to make her own judgments without relying on the adults around her to form opinions, even questioning her own father.[55] This is clearly demonstrated in a final exchange between them. Her father points out that if not for their ancestors, they would not be in the New World, living in a deaf community. Mary signs in response, "Yes, but our New World is someone's old world, isn't it, Papa?" She continues: "The Wampanoag have lived here for a very long time. What about them? Look how they were affected by Grandpa Lambert's ways." Her father goes on to tell her that her grandfather worked on a slave ship, to Mary's surprise. Her father reminds her that they "can't hide from [their] ancestors' misdeeds," and Mary reiterates, "But we can make our own choices now."[56] Mary confronts and critiques the colonization of her ancestors, demonstrating to young readers the importance of wrestling personally with one's privilege and violent past.

The Degenerates

Though a number of additional MG novels center disabled protagonists, they do not fit my parameters of disabled authors writing US-based historical fiction featuring female protagonists with physical disabilities.[57] Because of this I will be discussing J. Albert Mann's YA novel *The Degenerates*, targeted towards ages fourteen and up; however the ages of its protagonists, thirteen and fourteen years old, place it in the crossover space between what is considered upper MG (twelve- to fourteen-year-old protagonists targeting eleven- to fourteen-year-olds) and YA. While the protagonists in *The Degenerates* may be older and dealing with more mature themes than those in AG, AG has never shied away from engaging in such themes in its historical collection.[58] As Schalk insists, "American Girl found a way to introduce age-appropriate representations of slavery, the New Orleans yellow fever epidemic, and the Great Depression, so why not some history of disability?"[59] I argue that *The Degenerates* is an essential comparison because it explores the typical experience for many disabled children in the US in the 1900s, institutionalization, and gives these protagonists dignity and community.

The novel is told through the alternating points of view of four queer and/ or disabled young girls living in the Massachusetts School for the Feeble-Minded in 1928: Maxine (fourteen), a queer girl doing her best to protect her younger sister; Rose (thirteen), the aforementioned sister and a curious and mischievous girl with Down syndrome; Alice (fourteen), a young Black girl with clubfoot who has feelings for Maxine; and London (fourteen), a young pregnant Italian immigrant who recently was brought to the school.

While her characters are institutionalized and subject to cruel working conditions, Albert Mann is able to give each of them full lives. London, in many ways, represents the antithesis of the prototypical AG historical character. Though not considered disabled in the context of today, her unwed pregnant status deems her unfit in 1920s America. London is stubborn, constantly trying to escape the institution, initially resistant to any kind of relationship with the other girls. Albert Mann's portrayal of London resists a common trend present in AG historical fiction—the need to make the young protagonists respectful, eager to be good and nice, even when situations reasonably call for anger or frustration.[60]

Later in the novel London works in the "Sick Ward," witnessing firsthand how the institution's cruelty and medical experimentation carries on after death. When she goes with an attendant to the morgue, she notices shelves of jars containing floating objects and labeled by numbers. London asks the attendant, "When they say we are incurable. Why would they cut us up? Are we that horrible that locking us away wasn't enough?" The attendant wonders if maybe they do it as a way to "prevent it." London responds, "We don't need to be prevented," and expresses her desire to smash all the jars to pieces, "whip[ping] [them] at the floorboards with all her might."[61] Alice has a similar expression of anger in the novel, recounting how unfair it is that the nurses, the doctors, the attendants are allowed "to feel" and "to become emotionally attached. . . . All of it somehow marking them as normal." Meanwhile, in sharp contrast, "for Alice to cry out in pain because of her aching foot, to reach out and touch Maxine's warm hand, to scream in anger at not being able to stop this next horrible thing from happening—all of it marked her a degenerate."[62] Albert Mann again here does not diminish the weight of violence inflicted on young disabled girls, and in doing so, allows the reader to see London and Alice's anger as legitimate, as a worthy response to the injustice around them.[63]

Although the girls, particularly Rose, are often bullied in the institution, the four still find community in each other. Their care for each other highlights the kind of disabled intimacy that comes with being able to recognize disabled needs, and the importance of being in disability community. The narrator describes how on some nights Maxine rubs Alice's bad foot until she falls asleep. The narrator goes on: "Alice would let the tears slide out of her eyes the entire time Maxine's warm hands kneaded the knots from her sole . . . and slowly, with each squeeze of her fingers around Alice's tired foot, everything began to feel better."[64] The intimacy Maxine and Alice share is reminiscent of what disability justice organizer Mia Mingus refers to as "access intimacy," that "automatic understanding of access needs" disabled people share because of similar lived experiences.[65] While their acts of courage and solidarity may not mirror those of their AG peers, the girls are able to empower each other through acts of care and collective action towards survival; in tangible ways, they make space, dignity, and community for each other while incarcerated.

"Looking Back" and Historical Sections

In the original AG historical collection, each book ended with a "Looking Back" section that provided more historical context and information about the time period and place specific to the characters in the book. These sections often contained pictures of archival materials such as letters, photographs, paintings, and maps, as well as a glossary of common words and/or pronunciations. Scholars have debated the historical accuracy of the AG historical collection; however, the "Looking Back" sections were significantly cut down in the BeForever line and renamed "Inside [character]'s World."[66] Only in the BeForever's rereleased abridged editions of the series in 2019 did this section contain archival materials and photos.

In both *Kaya's Escape* and *Kaya Shows the Way*, despite Speaking Rain playing a prominent role in both novels, there is no mention in the "Looking Back" sections about blind and/or disabled Nimíipuu children. Similarly, neither Maryellen's first BeForever book nor the abridged version contain information on polio or disabled children specifically. The BeForever and abridged version of *Taking Off*, however, does contain information on polio, describing how polio often started with "a fever, aches, and weakness, but it could . . . cripple or even kill the patient."[67] In addition to the use of an ableist slur ("cripple"), the section describes the response to the vaccine and how the US has been polio free since 1980.[68] The section also names the privileges of Maryellen's life as a white middle-class kid, discussing the segregation of Black families and *Brown v. Board of Education*. However, the section never mentions that *Brown* set the precedent for disability rights activists to fight for access to education for disabled children.[69] The "Looking Back" sections offer an opportunity for young readers to connect the stories of the past with the present day, naming (as Kaya's sections do) the ways historical events affect these present-day communities. However, the phrasing of Maryellen's section places polio (and disability) as a thing of the past, which overlooks the ways many people continued to live with the disabling effects of the virus for most of their lives.[70]

The reduced "Looking Back" sections at the end of the AG historical collections are in stark contrast to the MG and YA historical fiction novels by LeZotte and Albert Mann. Both contain at least four pages framed as historical notes or author's notes that provide more context similar to the intent of the AG "Looking Back" sections and recommendations for further reading. Although these sections do not contain archival materials, they are extensive. LeZotte's historical notes discuss hereditary deafness on Martha's Vineyard, Deaf education and American Sign Language, the naming of Martha's Vineyard, and the Wampanoag of Gay Head (Aquinnah). LeZotte's novel also contains an afterword section with an interview, sign language diagrams, and a history of the Chappaquiddick Wampanoag people from Penny Gamble-Williams, activist and Spiritual Leader of Wampanoag and African heritage who was a sensitivity reader for LeZotte. Albert Mann's sections discuss the institutionalization of disabled people, and a short history of eugenics, drawing the parallels between the past and the way eugenics continues today. She also discusses how each of the characters' experiences were pulled from archival documents, and what their present-day diagnoses might be. These kinds of sections that contextualize history are essential education for young readers. They provide an opportunity for readers to differentiate between primary and secondary historical sources, understand point of view, connect past events with present day realities, and gain access to supplemental education about a specific time period or historical event.[71]

As a disabled historian, naming the lineages of disabled ancestorship have been crucial to knowing my present. Rediscovering this lineage through children's historical fiction has been integral to healing younger versions of myself longing for disabled kinship. When we place disabled protagonists written by disabled authors like LeZotte and Albert Mann at the forefront of our children's historical literature, we provide authenticity and historical accuracy (in sections like AG's "Looking Back") for young readers looking to understand their place in the world. As disabled author Lillie Lainoff explains, "Disabled people didn't just spontaneously appear in the 21st century," and leaving them out of historical genres "further[s] the misconception that disabled people are not worthy or capable of thriving in different worlds and time periods."[72] If an AG disabled historical character had been available to me as a young reader, it may not have taken me nearly as long to understand my disability identity and its place in a larger historical narrative, to unlearn years of internalized ableism, and to find a disability community that grounds me in the midst of an increasingly ableist society. AG and the publishing industry at-large must do more to center authentic disabled historical characters by disabled authors. In doing so, we demonstrate to young readers how the disability community has and continues to be essential for survival, for care, and for collective action.

Notes

1. For a growing database of disability representation in MG and YA literature across genres, see YA Disability Database, https://yadisabilitydatabase.wixsite.com/home.

2. Brit Bennett, "Addy Walker, an American Girl," *Paris Review*, May 28, 2015, https://www.theparisreview.org/blog/2015/05/28/addy-walker-american-girl/; Aisha Harris, "The Making of an American Girl," *Slate*, September 21, 2016, https://slate.com/culture/2016/09/the-making-of-addy-walker-american-girls-first-black-doll.html.

3. Michelle Widgen, "The Rise of American Girl Rebecca Rubin," *Forward*, January 2, 2013, https://forward.com/culture/168334/the-rise-of-american-girl-rebecca-rubin/; for more on AG's representation of Jewish culture, see the work of public historian Rebekkah Rubin.

4. Emilie Zaslow, *Playing with America's Doll: A Cultural Analysis of the American Girl Collection* (New York: Palgrave McMillan, 2017), 90–91; Sami Schalk, "BeForever? Disability in American Girl Historical Fiction," *Children's Literature* 45 (2017), 164.

5. Valerie Tripp quoted in Jessica Harrison, "American Girl Book Honors Readers, Valerie Tripp Says," *Cracking the Cover* (blog), September 28, 2015, https://www.crackingthecover.com/11846/american-girl-books-honor-readers-author-valerie-tripp-says/.

6. Marissa Spear, "Reading Disability Back into American Girl," *Nursing Clio* (blog), November 1, 2022, https://nursingclio.org/2022/11/01/reading-disability-history-back-into-american-girl/.

7. Eva Langston, "Kidlit Genres Explained: Middle Grade, YA, New Adult, & More," August 16, 2021, https://evalangston.com/2021/08/16/kidlit-genres/; MG and YA classifications tend to differ based on sources; however, most classifications are set by the publisher and the industry more broadly.

8. Grace Lapointe, "What Happened to the Own Voices Label?" Book Riot, April 25, 2022, https://bookriot.com/what-happened-to-the-own-voices-label/.

9. Danika Ellis, "The Problem with #OwnVoices LGBTQ Lit," Book Riot, April 21, 2017, https://bookriot.com/the-problem-with-ownvoices-lgbtq-lit/.

10. Alaina Lavoie, "Why We Need Diverse Books Is No Longer Using the Term #OwnVoices," *We Need Diverse Books* (blog), June 6, 2021, https://diversebooks.org/why-we-need-diverse-books-is-no-longer-using-the-term-ownvoices/.

11. Disabled Kidlit Writers, Facebook, July 18, 2019, https://www.facebook.com/groups/622639168232657.

12. JoAnn Yao, "Q&A with Lillie Lainoff, One for All," *We Need Diverse Books* (blog), March 8, 2022, https://diversebooks.org/qa-with-lillie-lainoff-one-for-all/. From the late 1860s to the 1970s the US instituted "ugly laws" or ordinances that criminalized the presence of poor and disabled individuals in public. For more information, see Susan M. Schweik, *The Ugly Laws: Disability in Public* (New York: NYU Press, 2010).

13. Sami Schalk, "Ablenationalism in American Girlhood," *Girlhood Studies* 9, no. 1 (Spring 2016): 36–52, doi: 10.3167/ghs.2016.090104; Schalk, "BeForever?"; Sami Schalk, "De-politicized Diversity in the American Girl Brand," *Research on Diversity in Children's Literature* 2, no. 2 (2020); Melissa and Eva Shang, "American Girl: Release an American Girl with a Disability," change.org, December 28, 2013, https://www.change.org/p/american-girl-release-an-american-girl-with-a-disability; Spear, "Reading Disability Back." See also the work of Tiffany (@justdream_away on Instagram) on dolls and disability.

14. Melissa and Eva Shang, "American Girl."

15. Schalk, "De-politicized Diversity."

16. Schalk, "Ablenationalism," 43–46.

17. While not explicitly disabled, AG historical character Cécile Rey (1853) confronts New Orleans's yellow fever epidemic through the lens of her brother's infection. For a comparable (though white) MG novel with similar themes see Laure Halse Anderson's *Fever 1793*.

18. Polio or poliomyelitis is an infectious viral disease that predominantly affects children under the age of five. I name polio as a disability rather than a disabling disease as I am following other chronically ill individuals who have embraced a wide definition of disability, including myself.

19. Mark Speltz, "No Ordinary Girl: A Peek into the Creation of Civil Rights Girl, Melody Ellison," *Public Historian* 43, no. 1 (February 2021): 123–37.

20. See @PinkSaltCollective on Instagram

21. Marissa J. Spear, "Reading Disability Back."

22. Schalk, "BeForever?," 175.

23. Schalk, "BeForever?," 175.

24. Margaret Kingsbury, "9 Ableist Tropes in Fiction I Could Do Without," Book Riot, February 21, 2022, https://bookriot.com/ableist-tropes-in-fiction/; "Discussion: Disability Tropes," *Disability in Kidlit* (blog), July 25, 2013, https://disabilityinkidlit.com/2013/07/25/discussion-4-disability-tropes/.

25. Janet Beeler Shaw, *Kaya's Escape! A Survival Story* (Middleton, WI: Pleasant Company, 2002), 13–19.

26. Shaw, *Kaya's Escape!*, 23.

27. Janet Beeler Shaw, *Kaya Shows the Way: A Sister Story* (Middleton, WI: Pleasant Company, 2002), 38.

28. Doris Seale and Beverly Slapin, "American Girls Collection: Kaya," American Indians in Children's Literature, April 26, 2007, https://americanindiansinchildrensliterature.blogspot.com/2007/04/american-girls-collection-kaya-broken.html.

29. Seale and Slapin, "American Girls."

30. Tripp quoted in Harrison, "American Girl Book."

31. Tripp quoted in Harrison, "American Girl Book."

32. Angela Patel, "Disability Is Not a Metaphor," *FEM*, May 15, 2023, https://femmagazine.com/disability-is-not-a-metaphor/#:~:text=Ableism%20in%20our%20language%20goes,what%20those%20terms%20actually%20mean . . .

33. Schalk, "BeForever?," 176.

34. Valerie Tripp, *The One and Only: A Maryellen Classic*, vol. 1 (Middleton, WI: American Girl, 2015), 25.

35. Tripp, *The One and Only*, 112.

36. Tripp, *The One and Only*, 113.

37. Dr. Jonas Salk's successful testing of a polio vaccine was announced nationally over the radio on March 26, 1953, see: https://www.history.com/this-day-in-history/salk-announces-polio-vaccine.

38. Valerie Tripp, *Taking Off: A Maryellen Classic* vol. 2 (Middleton, WI: American Girl, 2015), 14.

39. Schalk, "BeForever?," 177–78

40. Zaslow, *Playing with America's Doll*, 87.

41. Zaslow, *Playing with America's Doll*, 87.

42. Molly Rosner, "Playing Not So Nicely: Respectability Politics and One Crazy Summer's Radical Black Girl Protagonist," *Public Historian* 43, no. 1 (February 2021): 183.

43. Schalk, "Ablenationalism," 36.

44. I use uppercase Deaf to describe the community and lowercase deaf here to describe the disability (which matches the author's use throughout the novel).

45. Ann Clare LeZotte, *Show Me A Sign* (New York: Scholastic Press, 2020), 127.

46. LeZotte, *Show Me A Sign*, 10.

47. LeZotte, *Show Me A Sign*, 41–42.

48. "Show Me A Sign, by Ann Clare LeZotte—A Group Review," *Indigo's Bookshelf: Voices of Native Youth* (blog), October 26, 2019, https://indigosbookshelf.blogspot.com/2019/10/show-me-sign-by-ann-clare-le-zotte.html; Zaslow, *Playing with America's Doll*, 144.

49. LeZotte, *Show Me A Sign*, 132.

50. LeZotte, *Show Me A Sign*, 138.

51. LeZotte, *Show Me A Sign*, 70.

52. LeZotte, *Show Me A Sign*, 153.

53. LeZotte, *Show Me A Sign*, 168.

54. "A Group Review."

55. Rosner, "Playing Not So Nicely," 190.

56. LeZotte, *Show Me A Sign*, 256.

57. See *The War That Saved My Life* by Kimberly Brubaker Bradley and *All He Knew* by Helen Frost.

58. In many ways AG "aged-up" their historical collection with the launch of their BeForever line. Before BeForever, AG historical novels were shorter in length with more illustrations, what is usually considered lower MG novels, and with the BeForever line, these novels became longer with less illustration, what is generally considered upper MG.

59. Schalk, "BeForever?," 182.

60. Rosner, "Playing Not So Nicely," 182; Zaslow, *Playing with America's Doll*, 71.

61. J. Albert Mann, *The Degenerates* (New York: Atheneum Books for Young Readers, 2020), 206.

62. Mann, *The Degenerates*, 215.

63. Rosner, "Playing Not So Nicely," 182.

64. Mann, *The Degenerates*, 109.

65. Mia Mingus, "Access Intimacy: The Missing Link," *Leaving Evidence*, May 5, 2011, https://leavingevidence.wordpress.com/2011/05/05/access-intimacy-the-missing-link/.

66. Schalk, "BeForever?," 165–66.

67. Tripp, *Taking Off*, 180.

68. For more on ableist language, see the work of disability activist Lydia X. Z. Brown at *Autistic Hoya* (blog), https://www.autistichoya.com/p/ableist-words-and-terms-to-avoid.html.

69. Tripp, *Taking Off*, 181; "The Right to Education," Disability Justice, https://disabilityjustice.org/right-to-education/.

70. Schalk, "BeForever?," 178.

71. "Common Core State Standards for English Language Arts & Literacy in History/Social Studies, Science, and Technical Subjects," Council of Chief State School Officers, accessed August 1, 2023, https://learning.ccsso.org/wp-content/uploads/2022/11/ELA_Standards1.pdf.

72. Lillie Lainoff email interview with the author, August 15, 2023.

How the Irish (Doll) Became White
The Nellie O'Malley AG Story Arc[1]

Mary M. Burke

The stereotype of the "off-white" Irish servant girl or woman saturates American culture at every level and age bracket, even into the current century. Since American Girl is a brand that has been credited with introducing American history to countless children, the version of the Irish American past marketed by the company is likely to be influential. This essay examines the earliest stereotypes of Irish America, to ask if American Girl queries or reinforces that narrative. Eighteen years after the release of the wealthy Edwardian-era New York doll/character, Samantha Parkington, American Girl created a sidekick doll: Nellie O'Malley, a poor Irish immigrant servant girl. Nellie had originated as a secondary character in the Samantha storyline (*Meet Samantha*) and featured in other Samantha-centered narratives. However, the Irish character was given her own book (*Nellie's Promise*) to coincide with the Nellie doll release. With red hair and freckles,[2] the Nellie doll possesses the coloring associated with the very earliest moment of Irish abjectness and stereotype in the seventeenth-century Americas, and a discussion of the mold used for Nellie's features will add weight to this reading of her deep contexts. Irish racialization continued in the nineteenth century with the "Bridget" ("off-white" Irish servant girl) stereotype, which is central to the Nellie narrative. Even the seemingly stereotype-busting arc of the Nellie stories, from immigrant poverty to final arrival in genteel Anglo-America, reflects the mainstream and ultimately conservative narrative of

"Little Mother" (1911) by Charles F. Clarke (b. 1865), a resident of Springfield, MA, a city with a huge Irish immigrant cohort. The unnamed subject may have been an Irish American girl.

the "inevitable" assimilation ("whitening") and entry into normative WASP values and society of Irish America itself.

In an appraisal of American Girl Doll books' historical accuracy, Fred Nielsen praises the Samantha series for providing young readers with a solid picture of early twentieth-century conflicts of class (child labor) and gender (women's suffrage).[3] Nielsen argues that AGD books are "worth taking seriously . . . because of their very success" and because they "are the way in which millions of young readers are introduced to many aspects of the nation's past."[4] (The books also deserve attention due to the fact that, as noted in a 2010 study, the company sells roughly seven times more books than dolls.[5]) This essay will deepen and enrich Nielsen's take on the Samantha narrative by delving into the social and racial contexts of Irishness in America in this period and before, suggesting that Nellie's "not-quite-whiteness" reflects the status of post-1845 Famine Irish immigrants in America, just as Samantha's high social status reflects a contrasting normative and unconditionally white Anglo-Americanness. The analysis will also go some way toward answering the question posed by Emilie Zaslow's chapter on ethnicity and AG in her foundational 2017 study, *Playing with America's Doll* (which does not otherwise give attention to Irishness or Nellie): "Why is Samantha the star and her orphan friend Nellie the understudy?"[6]

The Samantha (and Nellie) Stories: A Summary

A summary of Nellie's arc across *Samantha* books runs as follows. In the 1986 book *Meet Samantha*, which is set in 1904 in a fictional upstate New York town, Nellie O'Malley is introduced as an illiterate and exploited Irish immigrant orphan who has worked in a factory and now toils as a servant next door to the household of Samantha Parkington, a girl who befriends her.[7] Although Samantha kindly includes Nellie in her life, *Samantha's Winter Party* and *Samantha Learns a Lesson* audit the young servant girl's initial difficulty in fitting in with her elite friend's social set due to lack of time and money and their occasional snobbery.[8] *Samantha and the Missing Pearls* traces Nellie's trials with her employer, whose circle mistakenly believes the Irish child to be dishonest. Set in late 1904, the next Samantha AG book in which Nellie features is *Changes for Samantha: A Winter Story*. It opens with the return to New York City of Nellie O'Malley and her sisters Bridget and Jenny after the death of their parents. They have no option but to move into the run-down apartment of their drunkard manual laborer uncle, Mike O'Malley. After they arrive, Mike sells their belongings to fuel his alcohol habit, and then abandons them. Ultimately, the O'Malley girls end up in a cruel institution for children, which they eventually escape with Samantha's help.[9] The sisters are then informally adopted by Samantha's uncle and aunt, with whom she too is also now living in New York City. In *Nellie's Promise*, set in 1906, Nellie's uncle returns as an antagonist after she bumps into him as he is working with a road crew. Noticing the fine clothes that denote someone is taking care of her, Mike warns that (as the law would then have agreed), his relatives "belong" to him.[10] He will, he threatens, come find the O'Malley girls, take them with him, and put them to work in a factory and keep their wages.[11] Later, Mike attempts to obstruct the formal adoption of the O'Malley girls by Samantha's uncle and aunt.

WASP America and AGD

Nellie's explicitly immigrant ethnic identity contrasts with Samantha's elite background, but Mike O'Malley's recklessness, treacherousness, and heavy drinking invokes the worst stereotypes of the behavior of the unskilled male Irish immigrant that became prominent with the influx of poor Irish Catholic refugees from the 1845–52 famine. Mike is dismissed by his "lace curtain" (aspirational) fellow Irish American, Miss Brennan, as a "hooligan,"[12] an ethnic slur by derivation since the term is reputed to have originated in an 1890s music-hall song about a rowdy Irish family of that name. By contrast, rigid standards of grooming and attire are enforced upon Samantha by her grandmother, whose afternoon tea rituals, icy formality, and self-consciously queenly deportment suggest the aping of upper-class British mores that was almost universal among members of the American elite in that period.[13] Mike and Samantha represent the extreme ends of the spectrum of whiteness that pertained into the period of the Samantha/Nellie stories' setting, which ran from "off-white" ethnic of low status, to unconditionally white and "unethnicized" American of implicitly Anglo origin. That model had deep roots in America and was cemented by one of the nation's most renowned nineteenth-century writers, Ralph Waldo Emerson, in *English Traits*.[14] An America flooded by an influx of poor Catholic immigrants from Ireland shapes Emerson's volume, in which he influentially represents the "Saxon race" as the origin from which "superior" American whites descended. To understand the British history that Emerson uses to lend heft to his hierarchy of European "whitenesses" in America, a potted history is first necessary. It should be understood that although the effects of the invasions to be delineated may have been more social, linguistic, and cultural than genetic, the notion of distinctly different invader and native "blood" was useful to an elite America that attempted to "sort" various European ethnic groups into categories of preferred/"incontestably white" (Protestant northern European of Scandinavian and British origin) and less desirable/"conditionally white" (Italian, Jewish, and Irish immigrants).[15] To begin: The Angles, Saxons, Jutes, and Frisians, "Germanic" (or "Teutonic") peoples of northern Europe began settling England in the fifth century, and their collective "Anglo-Saxon" culture came to dominate. Vikings of Danish and Norwegian origin—yet more invaders of northern European origin and speakers of Germanic offshoot Old Norse—began raiding and settling in

England in the eighth and ninth century. The seventeenth- and eighteenth-century rise of a political paradigm that imagined the roots of England's parliamentary system in Saxon culture led to the kind of nineteenth-century theories of preferred northern European whiteness (and its foundational civility and love of order) that underlie Emerson's influential work.[16]

Emerson praised the Saxons who made England, and by extension, those of Saxon/deep Scandinavian heritage in the New World, great.[17] *English Traits* linked physical characteristics associated with northern European ancestry to moral, cultural, and political superiority:

> On the English face are combined decision and nerve with the fair complexion, blue eyes and open and florid aspect. Hence the love of truth, hence the sensibility, the fine perception and poetic construction. The fair Saxon man, with open front and honest meaning, domestic, affectionate, is not the wood out of which cannibal or inquisitor, or assassin is made, but he is moulded for law, lawful trade, civility, marriage, the nurture of children, for colleges, churches, charities and colonies.[18]

The openness of the white Saxon Protestant face contrasts with the implied treachery of what is coded as the non-Christian ("cannibal"), the Catholic ("inquisitor"), and the Oriental ("assassin") visage, effortless references that carry the weight of centuries of Protestant northern European stereotypes of domestic and colonial Others. Emerson's views on a Nordic/Saxon racial continuum and its positive influence on those of such descent in America dominated white America's fantasy of its origins and destiny for generations: although the acronym "WASP" was not popularized until 1964, it was long understood in establishment "old money" America that those to whom the coinage referred—White Anglo-Saxon Protestants—were the most racially "pure" and socially polished Americans.[19]

Meet Samantha implies that Nellie's slightness is the result of laboring in an unhealthy factory and an inadequate diet in early childhood, but in 1904, this slightness would have been considered evidence of racial inferiority in certain contexts: the "racial fitness" rhetoric that fueled both the eugenics and physical culture movements of the period of the *Samantha* books' setting, movements traceable to Emersonian taxonomies of race and ethnicity, is one of the most subtle ways in which Samantha's "whiteness" emerges, as she is taller and healthier than Nellie, despite the fact that they are the same age.[20]

Considering America's early hierarchy of whitenesses, it is illuminating to return to the original dolls created by Pleasant Rowland, founder of the American Girl corporation in 1986, since they represent a foundational assessment of who and what qualified as "American."[21] Rowland, a former teacher and textbook author who founded Pleasant Company in 1985, originally developed three "historical" dolls, Kirsten, Samantha, and Molly. The WASP credentials of all three foundational dolls/characters imply a normative northern European Protestant whiteness from which many subsequent dolls/characters of ethnic, "off-white," Native, or Black identity "deviate." Thus, although contemporary AGD catalogs offer an "ethnically diverse picture of the country and its girls," it is telling to pay attention to the foundational characters since their identities map precisely onto established American notions of "preferred" white immigrant Americanness and nonethnicized Anglo-Americanness.[22]

The three foundational dolls/characters are as follows: Kirsten Larson is an 1854 Swedish immigrant character, Samantha's English surname, Parkinson, represents an unethnicized (WASP) ancestry, while Molly McIntire, a character living in 1944, is given a Scottish surname. The unconditional whiteness signaled by the dolls' surnames is reinforced by Kirsten's coloring, in particular. Kirsten has blue eyes and the blond braids that F. Scott Fitzgerald (himself uneasily Irish American) once mockingly described as a "Saxon princess" hallmark.[23] Carolina Acosta-Alzuru and Peggy Kreshel's reading of the Mexican Josefina's narrative against that of Kirsten implies that the latter is the "WASPiest" AGD, when judged by her combination of ancestry and coloring;[24] young white AGD owners interviewed by Acosta-Alzuru and Kreshel used the words "American" and "White" interchangeably to describe blonde dolls such as Kirsten in the catalog, while the so-called "Hispanic" Josefina was "perceived to be a foreigner."[25]

Red Hair/Redleg

A further and deeper layer of Nellie's racial meaning is that the Nellie doll's red hair and freckles invoke the earliest moment of Irish presence and stereotype in the seventeenth-century Americas. In 2015, a photograph surfaced of Betty Fenty, the great-aunt of Black Barbadian pop singer and entrepreneur Rihanna. Betty appeared to be of white European ancestry,[26] but the *Irish America* magazine article concerned labelled Betty a "Redleg," and discussed the fact that she and many contemporary "Redlegs" on the Caribbean island of Barbados, a former and very early British colony, identify as Irish. As described in the *New York Times* in 1973, Redlegs are strikingly—even excessively—pale, yet are not considered to be white: "Today the 'Redlegs'—usually identified by complexions which seem almost bleached of all color, straw-like hair and pale blue eyes—are pariahs, a subculture unto themselves, aloof from the environment and era. Though their roots in the Caribbean now go back 300 years, they have never assimilated."[27] The southern United States was only the northernmost outpost of a plantation system for the large-scale cultivation of staple crops that encompassed many Caribbean colonies too. In the seventeenth and eighteenth centuries, huge cash crop plantations in the Caribbean islands under French and English control were worked by enslaved Africans, but a heterogeneous white underclass also worked on the English-controlled islands at first. In the wake of a 1649 English invasion of Ireland, some thirty-four thousand Irish men had been shipped abroad, and by 1660 "there were at least twelve thousand Irish workers in the West Indies, and nine year later, eight thousand in Barbados alone."[28]

The initial demand for labor "was largely color-blind," and the basis of the seventeenth-century work force in the southern two thirds of the English mainland colonies were indentured laborers.[29] In eighteenth-century America, servant ranks were swelled by Irish emigrants and by English convicts transported in lieu of prison terms or death. Prior to the 1680s, after which mainland colonies underwent a massive shift from indentured to slave labor, and in the absence of the "racial contrast" that went on to become central to the "we-they" dichotomy between master and "those who might legitimately be enslaved," attributes "such as religion and nationality" could serve as differentiation.[30] Thus, in the specific case of the Irish in the Caribbean, not just Catholicism but the kind of extreme paleness that caused skin to redden after outdoor labor in the hot climate emerged as a marker of difference. Long after the pale-skinned were no longer subject to chattel status, their pallor—and that of any equally-pale descendants—still served as a reminder of former degradation. For Barbadian historian Hilary Beckles, the deeply impoverished contemporary Barbadian "Redleg" descendants of indentured whites are "living empirical evidence that in slave society, a white skin did not necessarily symbolize wealth, power, and status."[31] In short, in the Caribbean context, when "white" did not connote such attributes, it became "red."

The association of the Irish female menial worker with red or reddened skin is a commonplace in earlier American representations of the Irish,[32] but it also is significant that stereotyped "Irish" coloring (red hair and freckles) is also deployed to denote poverty in other AG narratives. For example, in *Mia*, the white title character contrasts her implicitly "Celtic" coloring with that of other figure skaters, which she appears to feel reflects her low social status: "Vanessa Knowles ... has long dark hair, bright blue eyes, and flawless skin. I, on the other hand, have freckles that I once tried to rub out with my eraser without any luck. And when I was small, my coppery red hair and green eyes made me stand out from the other kids. ... Not only was Vanessa born beautiful, but she can afford the best of everything."[33] A further indication that pale coloring was a racial marker that links Nellie to the wider Americas is that she was the first non-Latina American Girl doll to use the mold originated for the 1997 Josefina, who is represented in the accompanying book as living on a Mexican rancho in the 1820s.[34] This mold used a more pronounced philtrum, fuller lips, and a wider nose than that of the so-called "classic" mold used for the white character dolls, a "face mold [that] most closely resembles a European/white background and has never been used on a dark-skinned doll."[35] In light of a history of Jewish "off-whiteness" in American culture that is shared with Irish America, it is notable that this patently "ethnic" mold was also used for the 2009 Rebecca Rubin, the first Jewish doll/historical character in the line's representations.[36]

Nellie and "Bridget": The Irish Servant Stereotype

If the Irish immigrant woman was often represented as a servant girl with "defective" white coloring (red hair and freckled or pale skin), then just as invariably that character was named "Bridget." As already noted, one of Nellie's sisters carries this very name and it is one that is particularly insensitive in terms of the history of Irish America: "Bridget," the name of Ireland's female patron saint, was the stereotyped moniker for the slatternly Irish maid of nineteenth-century American lampoon in print and cartoon.[37] Margaret Lynch-Brennan's survey of the lives of such immigrants in the private homes of the northeast explicitly connects the quasi-racist jokes representing "Bridget" as stupid or lacking basic domestic skills to wider nativist anti-Irish bigotry.[38] Moreover, the stereotype's fixed title of "Bridget" conveyed the dehumanizing interchangeability of one Irish maid with the next. The Mike O'Malley storyline reiterates stereotypes of the irredeemable and rough Irish male immigrant unequivocally, but other tropes of Irish bad behavior that circulated in America are also present—if repudiated—in the *Samantha* books' action. To wit: in *Samantha and the Missing Pearls*, set in 1904, Nellie is suspected of stealing her employer's jewelry. Although the Irish servant child eventually proves her innocence,[39] this storyline relies upon the well-established stereotypes that "Bridget" was prone to dressing "above her station," and, more damningly still, that this finery had sometimes been purloined from the "lady of the house."[40]

How the Irish (Doll) Became White

Near the conclusion of *Nellie's Promise*, when he has failed to extract money from Samantha's kind-hearted uncle in exchange for agreeing to sign papers that would allow for the O'Malley girls' formal adoption, dastardly Uncle Mike storms off and swears that he never wants to see Nellie again. His relieved niece "agreed . . . wholeheartedly" with the sentiment.[41] Nellie's repudiation of the irredeemable Mike O'Malley and all he represents prior to her adoption into the extended Parkington family decisively severs the girl from her "off-white" past. The parting of ways of niece and uncle enact the way that spurning "shanty" mores (or those who embody them) ultimately facilitates assimilation into mainstream Anglo-America.

The arc of the Nellie narrative maps onto a broader Irish American discourse of eventual and even inevitable assimilation to unconditional whiteness through the abandonment of low status ethnic markers and behaviors (as personified by the boorish and brutish Mike in the *Samantha* books). Nellie's movement from socially marginalized Irish servant to Anglo-American child of privilege is truer to that cultural narrative than to strict historical accuracy, despite Nielsen's praise of the *Samantha* books in this regard. Indeed, the "Looking Back" appendix of *Nellie's Promise* recognizes as much: "Adoption between nonrelatives was rare in the early 1900s. Most families who were well-off enough to give poor children good homes would not have considered adopting a child 'beneath their class.'"[42]

Zaslow's analysis of representations of Kirsten, Josefina, and Rebecca finds that readers are encouraged to apolitically celebrate social rise through the embracing of American industriousness.[43] The Nellie stories preserve traces of earlier Irish American "off-whiteness," but her suffering and eventual triumph does the work that decades of narratives of the Irish American past of varying registers also perform, which is to audit everything that the community has happily *left behind*.[44]

Priced at $82 on its introduction in 1986, the American Girl doll and book package cost about $223 in today's money.[45] As Nielsen has noted, "The irony is that most of the girls in the American Girl books could not afford (nor could their families afford) such expensive toys."[46] The Irish arrived at full assimilation and marked prosperity after World War II,[47] and in contemporary America Irish names now generally code "white."[48] Maryellen Larkin, a strawberry blonde 1950s character/2015 AGD who is unethnicized despite a name that codes "Irish," reflects this pivot.[49] This ethnoracial and economic turn is further marked by the fact that AGD could release a "Just Like You" Irish dance costume (and accompanying red wig) in 2007, accessories that suggest that those who currently identify as *or with* Irish America are now a target market for what Zaslow calls a "toy for the elite."[50] The family of a real-life Nellie in 1904 would never have been able to afford a fancy doll, as a central plotline of *Meet Samanatha* stresses, but her descendant in twenty-first-century America almost certainly would be able to do so.[51]

Notes

1. This title plays upon Noel Ignatiev's foundational account of the gradual transformation of post-Famine Catholic Irish Americans from "off-whiteness" to mainstream whiteness within an American racial symbolic in which the powerful invariably code "white." For Ignatiev, the unskilled Irish in post-Civil War America failed to make common cause with African Americans because they competed with them for jobs or wished to differentiate themselves from fellow workers who were people of color by "becoming" white. Noel Ignatiev, *How the Irish Became White* (New York: Routledge, 1995).

2. "Nellie O'Malley," American Girl Wiki, accessed January 14, 2024, https://americangirl.fandom.com/wiki/Nellie_O%27Malley_(doll).

3. Fred Nielsen, "American History through the Eyes of the American Girls," *Journal of American and Comparative Cultures* 25 (2002): 85–93.

4. Nielsen, 85.

5. Toni Fitzgerald, "American Girl by the Numbers," *Doll Reader* 8, no. 38 (November 2010): 8.

6. Emilie Zaslow, *Playing with America's Doll: A Cultural Analysis of the American Girl Collection* (New York: Palgrave Macmillan, 2017), 139.

7. Susan Adler, *Meet Samantha: An American Girl* (Middleton, WI: American Girl, 1988), 24.

8. Valerie Tripp, *Samantha's Winter Party* (Middleton, WI: American Girl, 1999). This short stand-alone book was originally published as a story in the *American Girl* magazine November/December 1995 issue under the title "Nellie's Gift"; Valerie Tripp, *Samantha Learns a Lesson* (Middleton, WI: American Girl, 1988), 30.

9. Valerie Tripp, *Changes for Samantha, A Winter Story* (Middleton, WI: American Girl, 1988).

10. "Looking Back: Adoption in 1906," appendix to Valerie Tripp's *Nellie's Promise*, (Middleton, WI: American Girl, 2004), 75.

11. Tripp, *Nellie's Promise*, 4–5.

12. Tripp, *Nellie's Promise*, 51.

13. Adler, *Meet Samantha*, 11, 14. See Edward Digby Baltzell, *The Protestant Establishment: Aristocracy and Caste in America* (New Haven, CT: Yale University Press, 1987).

14. Ralph Waldo Emerson, *English Traits*, (Boston: Philips and Samson, 1856).

15. See Jennifer Guglielmo and Salvatore Salerno, *Are Italians White? How Race Is Made in America* (New York: Routledge, 2003).

16. Jonathan Swift, "An Abstract of the History of England," *Prose Works* (London: Bell, 1900), xi, 225.

17. Emerson, *English Traits*, 176, 48.

18. Emerson, 72.

19. See E. Digby Baltzell in *The Protestant Establishment: Aristocracy and Caste in America* (1964). Nordic/Saxonist terminology and its cognates only receded from the mainstream after World War II, when it had become tainted by the revelation of the catastrophic consequences of Nazi theories of Aryan superiority for Jewish people and other minorities.

20. Adler, *Meet Samantha*, 22. On the notion of racial fitness see Shannon L. Walsh, *Eugenics and Physical Culture Performance in the Progressive Era: Watch Whiteness Workout* (Cham, Switzerland: Palgrave Macmillan, 2020).

21. Rowland claimed in an interview that she had planned to have a nonwhite doll in the original lineup but decided against it for commercial reasons. Megan Rosenfeld, "Wholesome Babes in Toyland," *Washington Post*, May 24, 1993, https://www.washington post.com/archive/lifestyle/1993/05/24/wholesome-babes-in-toyland/b4ed92ca-1571 -4ec9-9290-4dfb4dedob7b/.

22. Carolina Acosta-Alzuru and Peggy J. Kreshel, "'I'm an American Girl . . . Whatever *That* Means': Girls Consuming Pleasant Company's American Girl Identity," *Journal of Communication* 52, no. 1 (January 2002): 150, https://doi.org/10.1111/j.1460-2466.2002. tb02536.x.

23. F. Scott Fitzgerald, "Bernice Bobs Her Hair," *Flappers and Philosophers* (New York: Scribner, 1921), 190.

24. Acosta-Alzuru and Kreshel, 147–48.

25. Acosta-Alzuru and Kreshel, 153, 152. Acosta-Alzuru and Kreshel take issue with AGD's inaccurate and anachronistic marketing of Josefina as "Hispanic": "Although Josefina's books, outfits, and accessories may be historically accurate for Mexican girls of her period, *Hispanic*, a word of relatively recent usage, is commonly associated with people of Latin American origin" (147). Nevertheless, they suggest that this inaccuracy allows us to read Josefina as enmeshed with current white American (mis)understanding of Hispanic (Latin American) culture and origins in contemporary America (147).

26. Sheena Jolley, "The Irish of Barbados," *Irish America*, October/November 2015, https://irishamerica.com/2015/10/the-irish-of-barbados-photos/.

27. Lindsay Haines, "Poor, Backward and White," *New York Times*, February 25, 1973, 5.

28. Peter Linebaugh and Marcus Rediker, *The Many-Headed Hydra* (Boston: Beacon, 2000), 123. An important caveat: this acknowledgement of the brutal nature of the earliest Irish presence in the Americas does not endorse the inaccurate but popular pseudohistory—readily available online—that the Irish were "white slaves." Librarian and independent historian Liam Hogan notes that this narrative has become "a favoured derailment tactic" for those wishing to shut down conversations about race, reparation, and slavery. Without minimizing the suffering and premature deaths of many Irish transportees to the Caribbean, it is vital to acknowledge that "Irish slavery" rhetoric creates a false equivalence between an indentured servitude that was, in its worst iterations, what Peter Kolchin calls "temporary slavery," and the much more systemic and sustained debasement of people of African origin and their descendants as chattels *in perpetuity* in the Americas. Liam Hogan, "The Unfree Irish in the Caribbean Were Indentured Servants, Not Slaves," *The Journal*, October 6, 2015, https://www.thejournal.ie/readme/irish-slaves-myth-2369653-Oct2015/; Peter Kolchin, *American Slavery: 1619–1877* (New York: Hill and Wang, 2003), 8.

29. Kolchin, *American Slavery: 1619–1877*, 7, 8.

30. Kolchin, *American Slavery: 1619–1877*, 5.

31. Hilary Beckles, *White Servitude and Black Slavery in Barbados, 1627–1715* (Knoxville: University of Tennessee Press, 1989), 175.

32. In Fanny Fern's feminist novel *Ruth Hall* (1855), a boarding house is judged to be "vulgar" by a mealy-mouthed visitor because of the presence of a "red-faced Irish girl" around whom wafts the "odor of cabbage," a vegetable popular among the Irish poor. Similarly, Henry James's memories of his New York childhood include a "stout red-faced" female instructor who "must have been Irish." In Sarah Orne Jewett's "The Luck of the Bogans," the "stout" Biddy Bogan is "red-faced and bustling." In all cases it is not entirely clear as to whether the skin tone is as the result of exertion over a hot stove or being overweight, but the association of red/reddened skin and unrefined Irishness is clearly made in all three narratives. Fanny Fern, *Ruth Hall: A Domestic Tale of the Present Time* (New York: Mason Brothers, 1855), 155; Henry James, *A Small Boy and Others* (New York: Scribner, 1913), 17; Sarah Orne Jewett, "The Luck of the Bogans," *Scribner's Magazine* 5, no. 1 (January–June 1889): 105.

33. Laurence Yep. *Mia* (Middleton, WI: American Girl, 2008), 2–23. First ellipsis original.

34. "Josefina Mold," American Girl Wiki, accessed January 14, 2024, https://americangirl.fandom.com/wiki/Josefina_Mold.

35. "Classic Mold," American Girl Wiki, accessed January 14, 2024, https://americangirl.fandom.com/wiki/Classic_Mold.

36. On the relationship between Jewish and Irish racial identity, see M. Alison Kibler, *Censoring Racial Ridicule: Irish, Jewish, and African American Struggles over Race and Representation, 1890–1930* (Chapel Hill: University of North Carolina Press, 2015). The Rebecca narrative has been criticized for presenting an idealized, tolerant America into which Jewish identity "fits comfortably." Lisa Marcus, "Dolling Up History: Fictions of Jewish American Girlhood," in *Dolls Studies: The Many Meanings of Girls' Toys and Play*, ed. Miriam Forman-Brunell and Jennifer Dawn Whitney (New York: Peter Lang, 2015), 16–17.

37. The Editors of Encyclopedia Britannica, "St. Brigid of Ireland," Encyclopedia Britannica, updated October 10, 2024, https://www.britannica.com/biography/Saint-Brigit-of-Ireland.

38. Margaret Lynch-Brennan, *The Irish Bridget: Irish Immigrant Women in Domestic Service in America, 1840–1930* (Syracuse, NY: Syracuse University Press, 2009), 66.

39. Valerie Tripp, *Samantha and the Missing Pearls* (Middleton, WI: American Girl, 2001), 8, 20. (The front matter notes the story first appeared in *American Girl* magazine, but does not provide a date.)

40. Lynch-Brennan, *The Irish Bridget*, 77. For instance, in an 1881 best-seller by William Faulkner's paternal great-grandfather, an unnamed Irish maid's "inappropriately" refined clothing is ultimately revealed to have been stolen from her employer. William Clark Falkner, *The White Rose of Memphis* (Chicago; New York: Donohue, 1909), 518.

41. Tripp, *Nellie's Promise*, 69.

42. "Looking Back: Adoption in 1906," 74.

43. Zaslow, 137–68.

44. The arc of inevitable Irish assimilation fuels popular historiographies such as Stephen Birmingham's *Real Irish Lace: America's Irish Rich* (1973) and memoirs such as Frank McCourt's *Angela's Ashes* (1996).

45. Dollar Times, accessed September 25, 2023, https://www.dollartimes.com/inflation /inflation.php?amount=82&year=1986.

46. Nielsen, "American History through the Eyes of the American Girls," 86.

47. In time for St. Patrick's Day 2018, conservative business newspaper the *Wall Stret Journal* celebrated Irish America's trajectory from marginalized to establishment: "The 19th-century immigrants from Europe usually started at the bottom, both socially and economically, and the Irish epitomized this trend. . . . According to the Census Bureau, today's Irish-Americans boast poverty rates far below the national average and median incomes far exceeding it. The rates at which they graduate from high school, complete college, work in skilled professions, and own homes are also better than average." Jason L. Riley, "Lessons from the Rise of America's Irish," *Wall Street Journal*, March 13, 2018, https://www.wsj.com /articles/lessons-from-the-rise-of-americas-irish-1520982717.

48. In a study that demonstrated that all else being equal, American employers selected candidates with "White" names for callbacks 50 percent more often than candidates with "Black" names, eight out of nine surnames chosen to represent the former category were of Irish origin. Marianne Bertrand and Sendhil Mullainathan, "Are Emily and Greg More Employable than Lakisha and Jamal? A Field Experiment on Labor Market Discrimination," (National Bureau of Economic Research Working Paper 9873, July 2003), 7, footnote 19, https://www.nber.org/papers/w9873.

49. "Maryellen Larkin (Doll)," American Girl Wiki, https://americangirl.fandom.com /wiki/Maryellen_Larkin_(doll). Although AG did not market Maryellen as Irish, some fans nonetheless ascribed this identity to her: "I am thinking that if she has red hair she likely has blue/green eyes. The last name of Larkin tells me she is of Irish descent." Jeannie B. in TX, May 24, 2015, comment on "Are You Getting Maryellen, the New 50's Doll from American Girl?" at *I Dream of Jeanne Marie* (blog), https://idreamofjeannemarie.com/2015/05/are-you -getting-maryellen-the-new-50s-doll-from-american-girl/. A further hint of Maryellen's implicit ancestry is her sympathy for the Italian Angela when classmates express anti-Italian sentiments; as noted in the main text, the Irish and the Italians were both "off-white" in an earlier America. Valerie Tripp, *The One and Only: A Maryellen Classic*, vol. 1 (Middleton, WI: American Girl, 2015), 112–14.

50. "Irish Dance Costume," American Girl Wiki, accessed January 14, 2024, https://american girl.fandom.com/wiki/Irish_Dance_Costume; Zaslow, 1.

51. Adler, *Meet Samantha*, 14, 34, 49–51.

Belonging and Indigeneity in the American Girl Universe

Sheena Roetman-Wynn

Sometimes just the way the fading sunlight hits a blade of grass in the dry autumn dusk is enough to take me home. The way my skin smells after being in the sun. Hanging on corral fences during powwows, smelling the dirt that rises up from the dancers' feet hitting the earth and comes to rest in my thick, dark hair that is still the texture of a child's. The smell of sweetgrass mixed with gasoline.

Just last night, as I was pumping gas, it happened again. It was after dark, damp and hot like it is during July in Georgia after the rain. The bright gas station lights stung my eyes in a familiar way, the June bugs humming along with the distant highway. Suddenly I was nine years old, getting out of the minivan to go pee while we filled up the tank, excited for the long night ahead when my ate and I were the only two awake as we sped across prairies and rivers and mountains.[1] Both of us were too anxious to get there to bother with slowing down, stopping, sleeping. I would be curled up in the front seat, relentlessly asking about the bridges, rail yards, and combines we passed, all the while practicing my braiding on my American Girl doll who was dressed in buckskin moccasins, just like me.

By the time Thanksgiving came around in 1993, I was set to run away like Claudia Kincaid from *From the Mixed-Up Files of Mrs. Basil E. Frankweiler* if I didn't get an American Girl doll for Christmas. At the time, those of us

Photograph of Kaya'aton'my doll by Sheena Roetman-Wynn, New York City, February 2023.

inclined to obsess over Pleasant Company catalogs could select from Felicity, Kirsten, Samantha, and Molly. Who identified most with which doll?

There was just one problem: the dolls were all white. No Black girls. No Latina girls. No Asian dolls.

There certainly wasn't an *Indigenous* doll. At the time, we probably would have said *Indian*. There wasn't a Native American doll either, or a First Nations doll. Aboriginal. Indigenous. She didn't exist.

And there absolutely was not—and likely will never be—a *Lakota* doll. But I was Lakota, so what about me?

There was one character in the early nineties American Girl universe that I could potentially identify with: Kirsten Larsen's (stereotypically) mysterious Native friend, Singing Bird.

Singing Bird is, canonically, Dakota—a member nation of the Oceti Šakowiŋ, or Seven Council Fires, along with the Lakota and Nakota. You might know the Oceti Šakowiŋ better as the *Sioux*, a derogatory slang term adopted by French traders ("Sioux" comes from a term meaning "snake").

It gives me goosebumps, now, to think that there existed a relatively well-written (for the time!) Dakota character in these wildly popular books. But Singing Bird fell under everyone's radar, mine included.

Janet Shaw, the author of the original *Kirsten* books, does a good job of world-building for her targeted demographic when writing about the settlers' feelings toward the Indigenous people. But Singing Bird's character was, unsurprisingly, written with layers of racism, seemingly inherent to the nature of the story being told.

Singing Bird is Kirsten Larson's *new* best friend, introduced to readers in *Kirsten Learns a Lesson* (the second book in the *Kirsten* series). Kirsten's old best friend died of cholera on the boat from Chicago to the Minnesota territory. Marta is Swedish, like Kirsten. Singing Bird is Dakota, and her friendship with Kirsten is kept a secret.

This "secret" is notably one sided. Singing Bird brings Kirsten to her village to introduce her to the community, and Kirsten is specifically told she is welcome in Singing Bird's village and home.

But Kirsten knows better than to tell her family that she's been hanging out with Natives:

"Are the Indians really savage?" Kirsten asked.

"Some people say the Indians are kind," Lisbeth said as she gave her doll a second cake. "They say the Indians gave them deer meat and corn when they needed food. But other people say the Indians are cruel and bloodthirsty."

"An Indian came to our door once, when Mama was roasting pork," Anna said. "Mama gave him a piece of meat and he went away."

"He didn't hurt us, but he didn't say 'thank you,' either," Lisbeth said.

"He looked savage," Anna said. "He had red paint on his cheeks and eagle feathers in his hair. He didn't wear trousers. And we didn't hear him coming. We looked up and suddenly he was in the doorway." Anna's eyes were wide. "That's Indian magic."

Lisbeth laughed. "That's not magic, Anna. They wear soft shoes, that's all."

"They wear long knives, too," Anna said. She shivered and hugged her doll. "And they live in tents."

"Papa worries about the Indians," Lisbeth said. "He says that if we plant crops on their hunting land the wild animals will go away. He says the Indians won't have enough to eat then, and they'll surely be angry. I don't know . . ." Her voice trailed off and she looked at Kirsten with her gray eyes. "Papa says we need the land, too."[2]

Belonging and Indigeneity in the American Girl Universe

From this conversation with her cousins, and others undoubtedly happening around her, Kirsten begins to learn the *actual* lesson at play: America isn't a "land of promise" for everyone. Kirsten learns that the settlers—people like her family—mistrust the Native people who were already living there.

> Kirsten strung the two beads on the leather thong. She kept them wrapped in her hankie with the feather and the tiny basket. **These were her secret treasures, and the Indian girl was her secret friend.** At school, when Kirsten was tired of writing and numbers, of trying to learn her poem and trying to please Miss Winston, she daydreamed of running off across the prairie with the Indian girl. They wouldn't need to talk. They'd run faster than the wind.[3]

On the popular podcast *Dolls of Our Lives*, hosts Allison Horrocks and Mary Mahoney make an interesting observation about the "Family and Friends" illustrations at the beginning of the original books.

"Marta [Kirsten's deceased 'first' best friend] is in the rearview, for all intents and purposes, and her sort of opposite, on the previous page, is Singing Bird, who is very much alive despite her family's near-starvation status because of settler colonialism. Singing Bird is labeled the 'secret friend' and Marta gets to be the 'best friend,'" Horrocks remarks.

Mahoney responds: "This is her [Singing Bird's] bio: 'Kirsten's secret Indian friend who calls her Yellow Hair.' So, her *entire* biography is defined by the secrecy required of their relationship. By whom? Who can say! And also, by what she calls Kirsten."

Kirsten also keeps Singing Bird a secret for a second, less (obviously) racist reason: she romanticizes Singing Bird and her life. Kirsten sees Singing Bird as a plaything, something to add to her collection, her life as background research for when she wants to *play Indian*:

> Oh, how Kirsten wished she could live here in this warm tent with Singing Bird. She would wear soft moccasins like Singing Bird's. She would wear a deerskin dress and leggings. She would sleep under warm buffalo hides and play with a little buckskin doll of her own. All day she and Singing Bird would play in the fields and woods. **Instead of Kirsten Larson, who couldn't memorize her poem, she would be Yellow Hair, Singing Bird's sister.**[4]

So, what's the harm in Playing Indian? Philip J. Deloria, in his landmark text of the same name, pinpoints America's obsession with pretending to be

Native as one of identities emerging from fundamentally rotten foundations: "Indianness was the bedrock for creative American identities, but it was also one of the foundations (slavery and gender relations being two others) for imagining and performing domination and power in America."[5] From this, he argues, it is "'not just that white Americans have had a love-hate fascination with Indians.' . . . 'It's that they dress up and act out their ideas, making them material and real, and shape new identities in the process. And they do it over and over again, in every time period in U.S. history. And this practice is historically, psychologically, and socially complicated.'"[6]

Playing Indian reduces thousands of cultures down to a two-faced monolith: the merciless Indian savage or the noble, crying Indian. It caricatures human beings into funny little cartoon characters without dimension or agency.

This sort of novelization of an Indigenous character dehumanizes Indigenous people by othering Indigenous characters, and this sort of language undoes a lot of goodwill when it comes to Indigenous representation in the American Girl canon.

Singing Bird's story was decently written *for the time*. It's quite clear that Shaw pulled genuinely researched material into her writing from the tribes that were in the Minnesota territory at the time: namely the Dakota and Ojibwe. Perhaps due to the initial ambiguity of Singing Bird's specific tribal identity, her character development in terms of culture is accurate—if not a little vague. The Dakota *did* live in teepees and wear buckskin. There would have been eagle feathers and bear claws, yes. And even horses, and dogs, and a "leather pouch which held a knife, a bone needle, and a length of sinew for sewing."[7] And yes, they *did* have to move west due to (intentional) starvation.

Singing Bird's tribe isn't specifically identified until *Kirsten on the Trail*, also written by Shaw and published in 1992, six years after *Kirsten Learns a Lesson*. This is also when Kirsten and Singing Bird are outed by her younger brother, who then goes missing. Kirsten and Singing Bird embark together on a rescue mission, culminating in Singing Bird being welcomed by Kirsten's parents into their home (now that she has proven herself to be of use to them).

Nothing is *wrong* with Singing Bird's portrayal, but it is very one dimensional. It's hard not to see her lack of character development as a microaggression.

The shallow nature of her characterization means that we are forced as readers to ask: ultimately, does Singing Bird matter? While Kirsten *should* have learned a lesson about colonialism, the book insisted that the *real*

Belonging and Indigeneity in the American Girl Universe

lesson was that Kirsten should be grateful for her home (on stolen land). Singing Bird was a plot device, not a character children could identify with. She was benign and boring by design.

In 2002, American Girl released their first Native doll: Kaya'aton'my. Kaya'aton'my, shortened to Kaya, is Nimíipuu (also known as the Nez Perce) and from the mid-1700s, precontact (meaning Kaya's stories are set before the Nez Perce were aware of European settlers—and of the problems they would cause).

In 2002, I was already in high school and way more interested in local punk rock shows than I was American Girl dolls. And I certainly didn't want to think about Indigenous representation in toys. I wanted to think about getting my driver's license and kissing cute drummers.

Ahead of Kaya's debut, Ann McCormack, cultural arts coordinator for the Nez Perce tribe at the time, told *USA Today* reporter Michelle Healy, "Kaya's stories take place before the Nez Percé had contact with white people, in part to acquaint readers with the Nez Percé at the height of their culture, when it was intact and flourishing."[8]

Ultimately, McCormack is to thank for bringing American Girl to the Nez Perce, as she was responsible for bringing the concept of a Native AG doll to the tribe's executive committee. She also served on the eight-member advisory board put in place to ensure accuracy and cultural sensitivity in Kaya's character development, physical appearance, and even product development. The committee worked closely with Janet Shaw (the same Janet Shaw who authored Kirsten's books) on Kaya's manuscripts.

"Where the other characters' books follow a common template built around such milestones as birthdays, school and holidays, Kaya's do not. In 1764, the Nimíipuu had none of those patterns," Shaw says. "Their culture had its own rhythms and that influenced the pattern for Kaya's book series— and her line of accessories. There is no desk, writing table or school bench among Kaya's accessories (a popular add-on for American Girl dolls)."[9]

And, of course, there was one other problem: Kaya needed a new face. *Literally.*

To produce an accurate Nimíipuu doll, Mattel was informed they would need to produce a new face mold, because the Nimíipuu did not show their teeth while smiling. All the other dolls at the time did, but Kaya would not.

Kaya is researched. Kaya is tribal-council approved. Kaya has agency, personality, and context. Kaya is a well-developed, fully human character and yet some conversations continue to essentialize her down to and center her tribal identity.

Ultimately both Singing Bird and Kaya's characterizations were approved and filtered through (and for) a white, mainstream American lens. But based on how Kaya's stories were researched and developed, the company is clearly *capable* of cultural accuracy and able to acknowledge its importance.

As for any responsibility American Girl may have to Indigenous people, explaining Indigenous identity and the concept of blood quantum to nine-year-olds is probably too tall an order, especially considering most adults can't comprehend it.

For many US-based federally recognized tribes, blood quantum refers to the amount of "Indian" blood one may or may not possess and serves as a highly controversial marker for enrollment (or "official" status, so to speak). Strict restrictions on blood quantum will inevitably lead to "official" extinction; on the other hand, many people claim Indigenous identities without any real connection in order to access spaces that could better be served by an actual Indigenous person.

However, both Pleasant Company and Mattel were (literally) founded and operate on Indigenous land. In taking on the role of teaching history to children via play, and in self-proclaiming that history's specific focus as "America," the argument could be made that both companies know-ingly took on the responsibility of accurate storytelling when it comes to *all* American history, including the ugly bits.

So, if Kaya is still—after all that, after doing everything right—going to get swept up in a dehumanizing argument, does it even matter? Does she even matter?

After five years of research and development, Kaya debuted in Lapwai, Idaho, on the Nez Perce reservation on August 15, 2002. Fifteen years later, Mattel sponsored an anniversary celebration for Kaya.

In an interview with the *Lewiston Tribune* reporter Mary Stone, former Nez Perce National Historic Park interpreter and a member of Kaya's advisory board Diane Mallickan said, "My main focus was in the storyline, the accuracy of things. I feel like the storyline was very, very important—and it's actually part of our healing."[10]

Kaya certainly matters to the Nez Perce, because the Nez Perce value the power of storytelling.

Belonging and Indigeneity in the American Girl Universe

And so now that Indigenous girls have an American Girl doll, I've asked myself a few times: How do I feel about Kaya? Could I have potentially identified with her, if I hadn't been sixteen? Does Kaya matter *to me*?

Kaya and I have nothing in common—we are not from the same tribe. There is nothing tying me to Kaya except a shared experience of colonialism, because while Kaya's stories are set precontact, it's difficult for me to consider Kaya without seeing the looming darkness ahead. Kaya absolutely experienced colonialism. And for that, I hold on to her for dear life sometimes.

When I was part of American Girl's target age demographic, my only ties to my culture were *Little House on the Prairie* books and whatever I could poach from the library. My grandmother didn't talk a lot about it, although sometimes she whispered into my ear when we washed the dishes together at the kitchen sink. The light was yellow from the log walls of her cabin and the windows were inky black, no stars because the Georgia pines blocked our view. *Repeat after me: waŋží, núŋpa, yámni, tópa. . . . Can you say* See-chan-goo? *Can you say* Rob-i-doe?

Lakota tradition had been squashed into memories decades before. After my grandmother died, we stopped talking about it altogether. It just disappeared. No Lakota words anymore. No numbers, no songs. No Lakota anything. Nothing that reminds us. No grandmas anymore.

When I was a child trying to find her place in the world and make sense of it all, I wanted it all to fit nicely. I wanted to tick off boxes, like in the quizzes of my older cousins' copies of *Seventeen* magazine. Or like the demographic surveys at the beginning of our standardized exams: my teachers always made me erase the pencil marking next to "American Indian, Native Hawaiian or Alaska Eskimo." "You're white," they would say. "But my grandma says I am Lakota Sioux." "You don't look Indian. You're white."

What did it mean to *look* Indian? I didn't grow up around other Indigenous people, not really. I didn't grow up on the reservation, and even after my family started moving back to Wyoming and South Dakota, they had been isolated from those communities for so long that they didn't bother trying to reconnect. I don't know if it even occurred to them to try. I had studied books from the library and any middle grade novel having to do with Indians I could find. I knew exactly what *looking Indian* meant, and I knew I didn't fit the mold. I didn't fit in that box nicely at all.

This is my experience with colonialism. In a little over two hundred years, between the time when Kaya was nine years old and the time when I was nine years old, Indigeneity was literally being erased before my eyes.

So, with Kaya being released after my time, and Singing Bird being a mere blip on my Indian radar, in 1993 I was still without a doll (and her corresponding book character) who looked like me.

So, I settled on Sammy.

Samantha Parkington, nine years old in 1904, was an orphan who lived with her rich grandmother in upstate New York. Samantha was curious, loyal, and fair and she hated wearing wool stockings. Samantha made sense to me.

No one ever asked why I liked Samantha best. Samantha was rabidly popular during the nineties, so presumably people just thought I was following the trend.

As a society, we were utterly obsessed with anything turn-of-the-century, and *especially* rich orphans. *A Little Princess* was released in 1995, based on a rich orphan in 1905. *Newsies*, released in 1992, is based on the Newsboys Strike of 1899 and single-handedly introduced me to the concept of a bad boy being a good man. And while Mary Lenox's story unfolded at the turn of the twentieth century rather than the twenty-first, it was immortalized in the 1992 film adaptation of *The Secret Garden*. And never, ever forget: *Titanic* and the collective sexual awakening of 1997 were just a few short years away.

But on top of all that, Samantha was a light-skinned girl with long, dark brown hair and bangs. That's all I could have hoped for at the time. And in many ways, I liked adapting Sam to my own identity.

Before I even knew Samantha would soon be mine, my grandmother had made traditional outfits and beaded jewelry for her (along with replicas of other American Girl ensembles). To this day, Samantha stays in her trunk wearing her moccasins, beadwork, and fringed tunic with her hair braided. She is wrapped in the little seal skin coat I wore as a child, handed down to me from my father.

She was there every night, reading with me in bed with a hot pink flashlight I kept hidden under my pillow. She was there, even though I lived out in the country and didn't have any neighbors to play with. Together we read *The Boxcar Children* and then pretended to be orphans on the run from an evil uncle, forced to survive off the berries and acorns the forest provided.

George Strait is on the radio because we are good Indian women. We are coming over the bridge into Wheatland during a rare rainstorm. I'm playing with a cheap souvenir puzzle I bought in Omaha with my allowance. I am seven years old and I have fallen in love for the first and only time. I am in love with this land, with the mountains in the distance, with the way the rain clouds look on the horizon, with the way the dusty air smells and tastes when I jump from the car, barefooted, and leap into my unci's arms.

By playing with a doll, can you impose your identity upon it? Is it possible to "make" a doll Indigenous, simply by a Native child (and that part's important!) playing with the doll *as if it were* Indigenous?

Again, what makes, or breaks, Indigeneity? What does it mean to be Indian? What does it mean if I don't look Indian? What does it mean if I do? Indigenous identity is not simply a matter of racial markers or blood quantum, it's community connection. It's someone claiming you. It's someone saying, *You belong to me.*

I am my father's daughter. Our black hair, strange eyes, freckles from Dutch ancestors sprinkled on top of red Indian skin. Our restlessness, our wildness; the way our hands constantly shake. Our anger.

He would take me out on the four-wheeler, showing me eagles and hawks, soap seeds, tipi rings. He taught me the names of flowers and clouds. We saw Ghost Dance circles from ninety years ago, still visible there on the high prairie. The old ones, they are still there.

One time he found a pile of scrap paper in the back of the minivan. I had scribbled poems on each piece, just little bits of feeling. About tall brown grasses, glass beads lost in the ant piles, an attic full of old records, the little house we stayed in that was painted John Deere green-and-yellow.

There are countless studies on the importance of visibility, representation, and exposure to diversity, and their intersection with play and imagination. In more ways than one, and for long after I grew out of playing with dolls, American Girl gave me the confidence I needed to be myself, a self that was inherently different from all the other kids around me. Because I always had Samantha, I always had someone in my corner.

And that's why, in 1993, I received the best Christmas present of my life (second only to my dog in 2019, of course): Samantha Parkington, orphaned rich girl *but also* a Lakota girl running through the prairie with the wind in her hair *but also* just a normal nine-year-old girl who likes to play school and capture butterflies and sneak away to secret rooms. Samantha is all of me, and that's the beauty of dollhood: not only can our dolls be characters from someone else's imagination, they can be characters in our internal lives as well.

Notes

1. "Ate," pronounced "ah-tay," is Lakota for "father." The term "unci," pronounced "un-chi," means "grandmother."

2. Janet Shaw, *Kirsten Learns a Lesson* (Middleton, WI: American Girl, 1986), 17–18.

3. Shaw, *Kirsten Learns a Lesson*, 25. Emphasis added.

4. Shaw, *Kirsten Learns a Lesson*, 43–44. Emphasis added.

5. Philip J. Deloria, *Playing Indian* (New Haven, CT: Yale University Press, 1998), 185–86.

6. Deloria, 98.

7. Shaw, *Kirsten Learns a Lesson*, 43.

8. Michelle Healy, "Meet Kaya, the Authentic Nez Percé doll," *USA TODAY*, Aug. 11, 2002, https://web.archive.org/web/20121128215350/http:/usatoday30.usatoday.com/life/2002-08-11-kaya_x.htm.

9. Healy, "Meet Kaya."

10. Mary Stone, "Kaya Returns Home to Tell Her Story," *Lewiston (ID) Tribune*, September 9, 2017, https://www.lmtribune.com/northwest/kaya-returns-home-to-tell-her-story/article_02256246-99ba-546d-a5a1-d1573b5bcf0a.html.

Ivy Ling, Corinne Tan, and Chinese American Misrepresentation in American Girl

Mackenzie Kwok

In 2022, American Girl released Corinne Tan, "the first American Girl of Chinese heritage." Corinne is undeniably modern, even cool: her parents are divorced, she has dyed blue hair, and she lives in a mountain town in Colorado. She learns to stay balanced, both on the slopes as a skier and in her personal life—even as she is forced to learn to call out racism when a boy at the local skating rink accuses her of having coronavirus.[1]

> "Don't touch that door," one said. "She just touched it." She was me.
> "What are you talking about?" said the other boy.
> "Her!" The boy with jagged bangs pointed at me. "She has coronavirus. Kung flu!"[2]

At first, Corinne walks away feeling bothered, but presses down her feelings. She doesn't always know if or when the appropriate time and place is to tell her mom and stepdad about the boy at the skating rink who made a racist remark, but she musters up the courage to call him out later on: "I forced myself to look straight at the boy. 'Why do you keep saying that?' I asked him. 'It's really mean, and it's not clever at all.' I took a deep breath. 'It's racist, if you want to know the truth.'"

I see elements of myself in Corinne: I, too, have dyed hair, and family in a Colorado mountain town. I call out injustice when I see it, even if I feel pressured to stay quiet at first. It feels like I am precisely the audience for Corinne Tan, and that I ought to be satisfied that an Asian American doll was finally offered center stage as Girl of the Year. Instead, I wonder why Corinne Tan is the first when Chinese Americans have made innumerable contributions to the fabric of American life. The Girl of the Year line endeavors to feature one doll per year with a unique skill from the past or present, who faces challenges and issues similar to those facing girls today. It seems fitting that following the COVID-19 pandemic and the anti-Asian racism that arose in response, American Girl would respond with a Chinese American doll that calls out racism. But this rings hollow for many reasons. Why did it take until 2022 for American Girl to reckon with anti-Asian racism, even though there have been numerous other Asian dolls in other collections? Why is this siloed as Corinne's struggle, tied only to the 2020 novel coronavirus?

In 2007, American Girl debuted Ivy Ling, the "best friend" character and doll in the Julie Albright series. Ivy is a Chinese American girl who lives in San Francisco's Chinatown, the oldest in North America. Her series begins in 1974, at the height of political activism and counterculture movements in the United States. Julie, the main (white) character, moves to the Haight Ashbury neighborhood, home of the 1960s Summer of Love movement, and learns tools for civic engagement. She learns about Title IX and gathers petition signatures with Ivy to convince her school's basketball coach to let her play on the team with the boys.[3] Julie learns about wildlife preservation and, with Ivy, spreads the word about habitat destruction to save indigenous eagles from property developers.[4] Ivy joins Julie in her pursuits of justice, but she does not always share Julie's drive to change the world. Instead, Ivy's passion is gymnastics. Her family owns a restaurant called the Happy Panda. Her mother is studying to become a lawyer. Her brother idolizes Bruce Lee and is dedicated to martial arts.[5]

Ivy was the only Best Friend doll to be released concurrently alongside her "primary" doll (previous dolls featuring "best friends" saw the release of the secondary character months—if not years—after the debut of the primary, as in the case of Samantha and her friend Nellie). Julie was released with an entire six-book series, complete with historical context chapters at the end of each book. Ivy, as a Best Friend doll, was released with only one book, *Good Luck, Ivy*, which has no historical context chapter at the end. Ivy was discontinued in 2014.[6]

I wish we had more of Ivy Ling. I related to her, too, as a multiracial Chinese girl who grew up in San Francisco. Like Ivy, I celebrated the Lunar New Year there with my family, and called my grandparents *Gung Gung* and *Po Po*. It's hard not to see the discontinuation of Ivy, as well as the lack of depth in her story, as representative of American Girl's shortcomings in Asian American representation. To see an Asian American doll only reemerge as a result of rising anti-Asian racism is bittersweet at best.

In recent work, folklorist Juwen Zhang speaks to the absence of Asian American perspectives in his discipline.[7] Zhang draws on the concept of "implied nowhere," the unspoken assumptions or elements that are absent in American folklore studies, arguing that Asian Americans occupy this category.[8] For instance, a 1947 essay titled "Cantonese Riddles in San Francisco" does not name an author or translator. Instead, the author thanks a man named "Mr. Chen" for "his witty translations." Mr. Chen was not recognized as an author or translator, or even a collaborator. The Asian author, in this case, is "implied nowhere." Despite Asian Americans' presence in folklore studies over decades if not centuries, their omission from folklore studies works perpetuates the notion that they are simply absent.

To me—a Chinese American folklorist from San Francisco—Ivy represents the "implied nowhere" of Asian Americans in the American Girl world. When Julie's books take place in the 1970s, the Bay Area and Asian America at large were experiencing pivotal social and political shifts. In 1974, the term "Asian American" itself was new. Asian Americans, especially in San Francisco and the Bay Area, were part of progressive politics that drew heavily on the civil rights movement and Black Power movement. They were present in counterculture. They were mobilizing in labor and tenant rights movements. Asian American historian Catherine Ceniza Choy writes in *Asian American Histories of the United States* that Asian American history has no singular origin, but multiple, "like a galaxy of stars . . . most meaningful when collectively visible as a constellation, revealing intricate connections that present new ways of seeing, understanding, and moving forward."[9] Ceniza Choy emphasizes the importance of recognizing the multiple histories, lest we overlook and erase Asian American involvement in social movements.

Ivy represents a missed opportunity not only to show the power struggles Ivy's community engages with; she also is a missed opportunity to highlight the political presence of Asian Americans, namely Chinese Americans, in the same social movements and political moments in which Julie exists in the 1970s. By only addressing anti-Asian racism with Corinne, American Girl missed the opportunity to show that Asian Americans were present and driving forces in counterculture and progressive politics.

This essay imagines what Ivy Ling's experience could be if her story were regarded as a pivotal Asian American historical moment, like Corinne's. This piece interrogates what we could learn from Ivy were she written into the same civic engagement and social movements featured in her best friend Julie's narratives. Through examining the Asian American and Yellow Power movements of the late 1960s through the 1970s, Asian Americans' participation in counterculture, and a close reading into the flatness of Chinese representation of Ivy and her proximity to whiteness, it is clear that Ivy Ling represents the absence of Asian Americans while examining American history. Ivy represents a missed opportunity for interrogating progressive politics, while maintaining a white-centric status quo, while Corinne underscores the harm of using COVID-19 as a reminder to engage with Asian American girls.

1974 San Francisco

In *Playing with America's Doll: A Cultural Analysis of the American Girl Collection*, Emilie Zaslow interrogates the meaning of whose story gets to be told and why: "The very decision of whose American stories get told, by whom, and in what way is political and loaded with meaning," she writes, noting that the absence of whose story is told is just as loaded.[10]

"Why, for example, do we have Molly's story on the WWII home front but not one of an interned Japanese American girl? Why does Maryellen's friend Angela, the Italian American girl who is discriminated against based on her country's role in the Axis powers in World War II, play a secondary role? Why is Samantha the star and her orphan friend Nellie the understudy? Where is the anti-Native sentiment in Kaya's story?"[11]

Like Angela and Nellie, Ivy plays a secondary role in Julie's story. Through Julie, readers learn basic facts about Chinese culture in San Francisco in the 1970s: Ivy's family speaks Cantonese, reflecting the immigration patterns of the time, and cuts her hair before Lunar New Year.[12] But the story is still primarily Julie's. Ivy's story is secondary; it provides readers with a slightly different perspective but ultimately supports Julie's arc.

The Julie books begin in 1974, when she moves to the Haight Ashbury neighborhood of San Francisco after her parents' divorce. She meets her new neighbors and schoolmates. She sends around a petition so she can play basketball with the boys at school. Ivy, whom Julie sees on the weekends, helps Julie out but is not quite on the same page about wanting to change the world. Ivy's focus is on gymnastics and her family. Ivy tags along with Julie as she learns to create petitions for causes like allowing girls to play basketball with boys, or to save eagles from habitat destruction. Ivy is a bit confused as to why her friend is so dedicated to saving the world. This is a case of "implied nowhere"—Ivy and Chinatown are removed from the civic engagement associated with Julie and the Haight Ashbury when, in reality, Chinatown and the Chinese community were experiencing large political shifts and took active roles in resisting systemic racism.

In 1974, Chinatown was undergoing tumultuous changes. Recent gang activity was publicized in local newspapers, and Chinatown residents fought against its reputation as a dangerous place. In 1977, the *Washington Post* published an article covering a Chinese gang shooting at a cornerstone restaurant, the Golden Dragon. In addition to gang-related violence, the article, "The Ugly Realities of Chinatown,'" revealed the systemic housing and education inequity issues that fueled population density and violence in 1970s San Francisco. Journalist Lou Cannon wrote:

> "The newspapers treat Chinatown like it's a mysterious, exotic place," says Gordon J. Lau, who next week will become the second Chinese-American in San Francisco's history to be named a county supervisor.... Chinatown has the highest population density of any California community, largely caused by past patterns of housing discrimination. It also has in extreme form the problems of physical and mental illness, suicide and unemployment some-times associated with overcrowding.... Not until the Supreme Court struck down restrictive housing covenants was it possible for Chinese to find homes outside Chinatown.[13]

Cannon describes the factors leading to Chinatown's high density, unemploy-ment, and illness—namely, housing discrimination that prevented Chinese Americans from living anywhere but one neighborhood. Cannon's coverage of

Chinatown in 1977 addresses the ways non-Chinese people regard Chinatown as a perpetually foreign, "exotic" place, while the realities of discrimination and racism run rampant. Cannon continues to contextualize the anti-Asian racism that led to Chinatown's disarray: "Anti-Oriental prejudice, referred to by California historians as 'the bloody shirt,' has been prevalent in San Francisco since Chinese were imported in great numbers a century ago for use in the building of the transcontinental railroad."[14] Many Chinese Americans responded to discrimination by becoming what Lau calls "overachievers." The value of education was stressed, and many Chinese Americans went into white-collar professions, especially engineering and accounting.

While Chinatown remained a tourist hub for non-Asians in San Francisco, its population density that resulted from labor and housing discrimination gave way to housing inequity, unemployment, and violence. The article even touches on what we now know as the "model minority myth"—the valorized image of Asian Americans as "upwardly mobile and politically docile" people, particularly in comparison with Black power and civil rights activists.[15] Chinese communities, especially in the 1960s and '70s, were regarded as highly successful because of their pursuits of education and white-collar jobs, which perpetuates the impression that "Chinatown had no real crime problem," along with its people. Cannon covers the simultaneous treatment of Chinatown as a gilded, exotic attraction for white Americans and its reality as an underresourced neighborhood. Cannon's coverage of this instance of Chinatown gang violence brings to light the "implied nowhere" of Chinese Americans in social justice movements and politics.

Just before the events in Ivy and Julie's stories, in 1968, activists and UC Berkeley students Yuji Ichioka and Emma Gee coined the term "Asian Americans."[16] Previously, people of Asian descent referred to themselves as their specific ethnic or national groups. "Asian American" was part of a pan-Asian movement that sought to unify Asian peoples against racism and imperialism, while resisting the pejorative term "Oriental."[17] Drawing heavily on the Black Power movement, the Asian American movement was a pivotal time for Asian American communities for political mobilization. The Bay Area was even home to the Red Guards, a revolutionary organization modeled after the Black Panthers.[18] Red Guard members were involved in labor organizing, registering voters, and advocating for affordable properties, Asian American–led social services, arts organizations, and Ethnic Studies programs in universities and schools nationwide.[19]

People involved in the Asian American movement employed many of the same tactics Julie learns about. They canvased, traveled door to door to collect petition signatures, and organized protests. Why, then, is the narrative of civic engagement removed from Chinatown in these books? In the Julie series, the Haight is the setting for Julie's education about social engagement. Chinatown is where Ivy and her siblings take gymnastics and kung fu lessons, or where Ivy goes to Chinese school. Chinatown is a stand-in for teaching Julie and (presumably white) readers about the basics of Chinese culture.

Joy Takako Taylor describes how American Girl books about Kanani, a Japanese Hawaiian girl, represents multicultural ideology while "doing little to dislodge racism."[20] Similarly, Ivy provides a lens into multicultural ideology—through Julie's eyes. While Julie treats Ivy with respect, Ivy and her Chinatown community are portrayed as typical immigrants who are expected to work hard to achieve the American Dream. In *Good Luck, Ivy*, Ivy's mother studies to become a lawyer as Ivy and her brother Andrew take turns caring for their baby sister. While Ivy's story reflects many real, lived experiences of Chinese Americans in the 1970s, this portrayal of her life should not be the only image of Chinese Americans. The themes of social change woven into Julie's storyline could have been extended to Ivy as well, to represent an Asian American character who is just as engaged in social justice work as her white counterpart.

On Luck, White Proximity, and Chinese American Misrepresentation

Ivy's Chinese culture is primarily presented as being steeped in "luck"— a trope commonly employed to explain Chinese culture to non-Chinese people. This kind of representation is flattening, and does little more than perpetuate stereotypes. In *Happy New Year, Julie*, Julie learns to take her shoes off when she enters Ivy's home—"a tradition at Ivy's house"—and learns that red is a lucky color.[21] At Ivy's family's restaurant, The Happy Panda, both of Julie's parents join for dinner for the first time since their divorce for Lunar New Year (which the author, Megan McDonald, calls "Chinese New Year," though many other Asian cultures celebrate this too). "Chinese New Year was all about good fortune and family togetherness,"

McDonald writes, "Right now [Julie's] family didn't have much of either."[22] These portrayals of Chinese culture and history are educational on a very superficial level. The historical background chapter included at the end of *Happy New Year, Julie* covers ping-pong diplomacy, the origin myths of Lunar New Year practices, and traditions of New Year celebrations versus 1970s Christmas celebrations.[23] While the chapter does attempt to educate readers about US-China relations of the era (along with some perfunctory background information on the Lunar New Year), little else describes lived day-to-day life in Chinatown outside the New Year season, repeating the themes of "lucky" we see in the book's plot: "During Chinese New Year, the color red is considered good luck. People wear new outfits that often have a little red—or a lot—in the design. . . . Red envelopes are supposed to bring good fortune to the giver as well as the receiver."[24] Furthermore, the chapter explains New Year practices while referencing Ivy's family, but ultimately supports Julie's narrative:

> Chinese New Year celebrates togetherness and new beginnings. It is a time when families reflect on the past and look forward to making a fresh start in the new year. For Julie, the Chinese New Year celebration was a perfect opportunity to think deeply about how things had changed in her family—and how she could help make her family relationships as good as possible in the coming year.[25]

In *Good Luck, Ivy*, these background tropes assigned to Ivy take center stage. "Ivy feels unlucky," says the first line of the text.[26] Why? Well, her best friend has moved away, her mom is studying to become a lawyer and the family has been eating takeout from The Happy Panda while she craves American food her white peers enjoy. Ivy must balance her loyalty to her Chinese family and her dedication to her gymnastics team. Ivy's grandmother tells her a story about how dragons make their own luck. Later, when Ivy is struggling on a balance beam in gymnastics, she remembers, "Dragons make their own luck," and completes her routine.[27] The story ends with Ivy beaming at her family reunion after her gymnastics competition, saying, "I had no idea how lucky I was."[28]

Good Luck, Ivy has no historical context chapter at the end like the other books in Julie's series have. A reader of *Good Luck, Ivy* is left with a surface level understanding of tropes typical to depictions of Chinese Americans:

a preoccupation with "luck," a narrative of a typical immigrant girl who learns to balance her family with her own identity, and an ultimate desire to assimilate into whiteness.

Ivy's doll mold and accessories similarly underscore an aspirational proximity to whiteness while simultaneously racializing her features. Emilie Zaslow's "Racial Logics and African American Identity in American Girl" details the physical attributes of each American Girl doll mold that suggest racial or ethnic distinction.[29] The first mold is the Classic mold, used on over sixty dolls. The Classic mold has "a thin upturned nose, thin lips, and a rounded chin."[30] Ivy's doll is made with the Jess mold, named after 2006's Girl of the Year. Jess was notable for being the first biracial American Girl, with an Irish father and a Japanese mother. According to Zaslow,

> The Jess mold, used for seven dolls including two biracial dolls, each with one Asian American parent, has a less pointy and less upturned nose and a shorter, slightly rounder face than the Classic mold. For Ivy, and again in 2015 for a Truly Me doll, this mold was altered slightly with a small detail on the outer edge of the eyelid to suggest an epicanthic fold.[31]

Interestingly, American Girl already had an "Asian" mold. Zaslow again: "The Asian mold with eye sockets that tilt slightly upward at the outer edge, and a wider nose than the Classic mold, was first released in 1995 for a Just Like You Doll, and used only once and then taken out of production in 2011."[32] Ivy does not have the Asian face mold (which has never been used for a historical character), but instead has an altered version of the "Jess" mold. Her ethnic distinction is suggested in her eye shape. Consumers have criticized American Girl for whitewashing Asian American dolls with "biracial" characteristics in the name of inclusion, erasing more identifiably "Asian" features with identifiably white features. Until Ivy Ling's release, the Just Like You Asian doll was the only available Asian doll that was designed to be visibly as such. "By the time Julie's friend, Chinese American Ivy Ling, was added to the collection in 2007," writes Zaslow, "the Just Like You doll was no longer identified as Asian and her skin tone had been changed to fair."[33] The Asian Just Like You Doll no longer appeared Asian, leaving Asian American consumers without a doll to represent their own stories.

Moreover, Ivy's wardrobe is not distinctly Chinese. She wears a patterned cowl neck shirt, green pants, and tan boots. The cover of *Good Luck, Ivy,* which the doll comes with, pictures Ivy in a cheongsam or qipao, a traditional silk dress. In *Happy New Year, Julie,* this dress even plays a central role in the story. Ivy and Julie both covet these new dresses in a store window in Chinatown. Ivy's mom surprises them both with the new dresses—so why was this dress not included in Ivy's outfit? Perhaps American Girl did not want to only picture Ivy in what could be considered stereotypical Chinese clothing, but still, Ivy's representation remains stereotypical in the stories. Ivy's doll holds proximity to whiteness through its face shape and outfit, but the books perpetuate stereotypical tropes of "luck" and "good fortune," representing multicultural ideology in the most cursory sense.[34]

Conclusion

Simply put: Ivy Ling deserved better. As a young girl in a pivotal moment in Asian American history, her story is important beyond her love of gymnastics. She deserved to be present in the social movements readers learn about through Julie because Asian Americans were. Ivy deserves to have a distinct narrative not shaped by stereotypes of "lucky" and "unlucky."

Asian American girls, too, deserved better—and continue to be entitled to understand their place across many eras of American history. Our history should be accessible, tangible, and celebrated across all eras. We deserve to know about Chinatowns and social movements, to see ourselves outside of shallow stereotypes. We deserve to learn antiracist Asian American history that begins long before COVID-19 created a wave of violence toward our communities.

While Corinne Tan's story is valuable, hers should not be the first to acknowledge anti-Asian racism, especially since American Girl characters are typically known for their independence and ability to speak up against injustice. Perhaps Corinne came about because Asian consumers expressed anger after American Girl discontinued Ivy Ling.[35] To me, introducing the first Chinese American Girl of the Year as a response to both the COVID-19 pandemic and the anger Asian American consumers felt when Ivy Ling was no longer available, falls far short of fair representation.

Ceniza Choy, again, describes many distinctive origins of Asian American history, but "sadly, these origins have been erased, obscured, and forgotten in the traditional histories of the United States."[36] She writes that the histories are most meaningful when collectively visible, like a constellation. Corinne's story arriving during a rise in anti-Asian hate is a step in the right direction, but should not be the only—or even first—story where an Asian American girl confronts injustice in her community. Centering Corinne's story only as a response to anti-Asian racism still fails to show the many other instances of Chinese American girls taking active roles in social justice community work, further "implying nowhere" the real, lived histories of Chinese American presence in such movements. We cannot have Corinne's story without a fully fledged narrative about Ivy, whose story seems to be forgotten in one of the United States' "traditional histories."[37]

Corinne and Ivy's stories are just two stars in the galaxy of stars of the Asian American experience. American Girl is giving light to more, slowly, with Kavi as the first South Asian Girl of the Year. I am looking forward to more stories—not just from other Chinese girls, but from Hmong, Sri Lankan, Filipino, Korean American girls and more. I am looking forward to the day when American Girl's Asian American dolls make up a fuller constellation of stories that reflect our complexity and presence across forgotten points of history.

Notes

1. Rachel Treisman, "American Girl's 1st Chinese American 'Girl of the Year' Doll Aims to Fight AAPI Hate," *NPR*, January 5, 2022, https://www.npr.org/2022/01/05/1070616965/chinese -american-girl-doll-corinne-tan-aapi-racism#:~:text=Hourly%20News-,American%20Girl's %20first%20Chinese%20American%20doll%20of%20the%20year%20aims,amplify%20 young%20voices%20like%20Corinne's.%22.

2. Wendy Wan-Long Shang, *Corinne* (Middleton, WI: American Girl, 2022).

3. Megan McDonald, *Meet Julie: An American Girl* (Middleton, WI: American Girl, 2007), 24–55.

4. McDonald, *Julie and the Eagles* (Middleton, WI: American Girl, 2007), 14–70.

5. McDonald, *Happy New Year, Julie* (Middleton, WI: American Girl, 2007), 12–52.

6. "American Girl Discontinues Its Only Asian-American Doll," *NBC News*, June 16, 2014, accessed January 14, 2024, https://www.nbcnews.com/news/asian-america/american-girl -discontinues-its-only-asian-american-doll-n132266.

7. Juwen Zhang, "Where Were/Are Asian American Folklorists?" *Journal of American Folklore* 136, no. 540 (Spring 2023): 199–211.

8. Shelley Ingram and Todd Richardson, *Implied Nowhere: Absence in Folklore Studies* (Oxford, MS: University Press of Mississippi, 2019).

9. Catherine Ceniza Choy, *Asian American Histories of the United States* (Boston, MA: Beacon, 2022), 1.

10. Emilie Zaslow, *Playing with America's Dolls: A Cultural Analysis of the American Girl Collection* (London: Palgrave Macmillan, 2017).

11. Zaslow, "This is My Home," in *Playing with America's Dolls*, 139.

12. McDonald, *Happy New Year, Julie*, 14–33.

13. Lou Cannon, "The Ugly Realities of Chinatown," *Washington Post*, September 11, 1977, https://www.washingtonpost.com/archive/politics/1977/09/11/the-ugly-realities-of-chinatown/5512f584-d118-43f0-9176-7371e2930c2/.

14. Cannon, "The Ugly Realities of Chinatown."

15. Ellen D. Wu, "Asian Americans and the 'Model Minority' Myth," *Los Angeles Times*, January 23, 2014, https://www.latimes.com/opinion/op-ed/la-oe-0123-wu-chua-model-minority-chinese-20140123-story.html.

16. Wallace, "Yellow Power: The Origins of Asian America," Densho, May 8, 2017, https://densho.org/catalyst/asian-american-movement/.

17. Wallace "Yellow Power."

18. Hing, "Movement."

19. Ceniza Choy, *Asian American Histories of the United States*, 3.

20. Takako Taylor, "Adorable Aloha: Tracing the Tourist Gaze in the American Girl Books," in *Growing Up Asian American in Young Adult Fiction*, ed. Ymitri Mathison (Oxford, MS: University Press of Mississippi, 2018), 207–24.

21. McDonald, *Happy New Year, Julie*, 24–50.

22. McDonald, *Happy New Year, Julie*, 49.

23. Ping pong diplomacy was a period in the early 1970s in which Chinese and American table tennis players competed in public matches, easing some tensions between the two nations after the Cold War.

24. McDonald, *Happy New Year, Julie*.

25. McDonald, *Happy New Year, Julie*.

26. Lisa Yee, *Good Luck, Ivy* (Middleton, WI: American Girl, 2008).

27. Yee, *Good Luck, Ivy*.

28. Yee, *Good Luck, Ivy*.

29. Zaslow, "From 'This Where Freedom Supposed to Be At' to 'She Knew She Would Never Stop Speaking Out for What Was Right': Racial Logics and African American Identity in American Girl," in *Playing with America's Doll*, 105–35.

30. Zaslow, "From 'This Where Freedom Supposed to Be At.'"

31. Zaslow, "From 'This Where Freedom Supposed to Be At.'"

32. Zaslow, "From 'This Where Freedom Supposed to Be At.'"

33. Zaslow, "From 'This Where Freedom Supposed to Be At.'"

34. Taylor, "Adorable Aloha."

35. "American Girl Discontinues Its Only Asian-American Doll," *NBC News*.

36. Ceniza Choy, *Asian American Histories of the United States*, 1.

37. Ceniza Choy, 1.

Caught Between "Jewish" and "American"
Rebecca Rubin and the Americanization of the Jewish Immigrant Experience

Samantha Pickette

In 2001, American Girl introduced a new line centered on a "Girl of the Year"—an annually released, limited edition character meant to reflect the everyday experiences of ordinary girls, filtered through the lens of contemporary social issues and a story arc driven by the character's hobbies, their family/school life, and the challenges they face over the course of a year in their lives. Lindsey Bergman, the inaugural Girl of the Year, was also the American Girl Company's first Jewish character/doll, a choice that reflected the company's ongoing commitment to increasing the diversity of the (mostly white, all Christian) American Girl doll collection, but that ultimately failed in its execution. Lindsey, a clumsy, loud, meddling preteen passionate about animals but unable to harness her energy productively, spends the year leading up to her brother Ethan's bar mitzvah getting into trouble at school, navigating her dysfunctional family, and playing matchmaker for her teachers, relatives, and friends. Throughout *Lindsey*, Chryssa Atkinson's book that accompanied the Lindsey doll, the extent of Lindsey's Jewish identity manifests itself in two ways: first, through the negative stereotypes of Jewish femininity that Lindsey embodies, in her inability to contain her "too muchness," which renders her unable to relate to other, more "normal" (i.e., non-Jewish) children in her grade, her self-deprecating attitude and insecurities, and her busybody tendencies that mark her as a younger version of the traditional *yenta* (Yiddish: busybody, gossip); and secondly, through the descriptions of the plans for Ethan's bar mitzvah, a watered-down ceremony of "becoming a man" that deemphasizes any of the religious and cultural significance of the ritual and instead focuses on Ethan's dislike of studying Hebrew, and the invitations, food, and music featured at the party following the ceremony. The image of American Jewishness reinforced by *Lindsey* is as much of a "slippery . . . blob of mush" as the matzo balls that Lindsey so eloquently mocks during her brother's bar mitzvah party.[1] In other words, Lindsey's Jewishness lacks substance, and she as a character does nothing to challenge the role that Jewish identity often plays in American popular culture—paradoxically as a marker of behavioral/social difference and as an amorphous ethnoreligion with minimal cultural distinction from middle-class whiteness.

With Lindsey's retirement in 2002—and the redesign of the Girl of the Year line due to the Lindsey doll's poor sales—no Jewish characters appeared in any of American Girl's named character lines until the 2009 release of American Girl's first Jewish historical character, Rebecca Rubin, an aspiring actress, budding labor activist, and daughter of Russian Jewish immigrants living on the Lower East Side circa 1914.[2] Upon Rebecca's debut, including the six-book series written by author Jacqueline Dembar Greene as well as the accompanying doll and accessories, many Jewish activists, including then-president of the Anti-Defamation League (ADL) Abraham Foxman, praised the "sensitivity" with which Rebecca's narrative—a sweeping, multigenerational tale featuring a variety of Jewish characters at different stages of the immigration process, centered on Rebecca's perspective as an "American" girl whose Americanness is indelibly shaped by her Jewishness (and vice versa)—is crafted.[3] Much of the nuance found in Rebecca's story stems from both Greene herself, who infused Rebecca's Lower East Side adventures with stories taken from her own parents and grandparents, and from the years-long research process that occurs during the development of any new American Girl historical character, which in Rebecca's case, involved informational trips to the Lower East Side Tenement Museum, Ellis Island, Coney Island, and other New York landmarks that figured prominently in stories of Russian Jewish immigration to the US.[4]

As a character, Rebecca reflects the Russian Jewish immigrant experience with a level of complexity and authenticity not usually found in American popular culture (especially aimed at children). The version of Rebecca seen in Greene's books—spunky, intelligent, creative, deeply tied to her family yet engrossed in her dreams of becoming a famous actress—reflects the challenges of the Jewish immigrant experience. She struggles throughout her stories with conflicting feelings of shame and pride, confident in her own American identity, yet forced to confront at various points throughout her story the tenuousness of the immigrant community in which she lives. Rebecca's books ultimately paint a version of the Jewish immigrant experience that captures the ambivalence of the era—about holding dual identities, about the relationship between tradition and modernity, about the overlap between religious and secular Jewish cultures—while also making a more general argument both for the legitimacy of immigrants as "real" Americans and for the importance of feminism to young girls who, as Rebecca discovers after giving a speech at a labor rally and helping her uncle find a new job outside the sweatshop where he was working, can "do just about anything."[5] As such, this chapter explores the ways in which Rebecca Rubin—as a character, as a doll, and as a representation of Jewish femininity filtered through the lenses of middle-grade fiction, the educational consumerism promoted by the American Girl company, and the popular culture tropes that dictate Jewish identity for American audiences—reflects a larger conversation about what it means to be both Jewish and American, the place that Jews have within American popular culture, and the dichotomy between Jewish cultural specificity and American universality in Jewish American storytelling.

Meet Rebecca: Jewish Identity and Jewish Immigrant Girlhood in the Rebecca Rubin Series

From 1881 until 1924, roughly 2.5 million Eastern European Jews arrived in the US, escaping the pogroms, oppression, and poverty that had defined their lives in the Russian Pale of Settlement and looking to establish themselves in what many Yiddish-speaking immigrants referred to as *di goldene medina* (the golden land).[6] This wave of immigration indelibly changed the landscape of American Jewry in terms of ethnic/cultural makeup, religiosity, language, political leanings, and culture, with newly arriving immigrants creating shtetl-like enclaves in major American cities and, through public education, access to new social/leisure activities, and an embrace of American popular culture, subsequently undergoing the dual processes of assimilation and Americanization. In her study of gender and Jewish immigration, Paula Hyman posits that Jewish immigrant women were in a particularly primed position to absorb the cultural norms of their new American homes:

> America was "the promised land" for Jewish immigrants irrespective of gender, but women appear to have been particularly attuned to the possibilities of renegotiating the norms that governed their access to education as well as their behavior in the public realms of work, leisure-time activities, and politics. America permitted the continual rethinking of the boundaries between the domestic and the public spheres.[7]

It makes sense, then, that Rebecca Rubin acts as American Girl's representative of this period in Jewish-American history. Rebecca, as the American-born daughter of Russian Jewish immigrants, lives between two worlds—the Russian Jewish world of her parents and grandparents and the American world of her birth and upbringing—and her stories see her navigating, negotiating, and ultimately finding balance between the two spheres of her identity, embracing the changes and challenges that she and her family experience as members of a minority culture and harnessing her power as a young woman to help her family continue their upward path.

Feminist literary scholar Lisa Marcus argues that part of the commercial popularity of Rebecca's stories stem from the fact that "the version of American history for sale in the Rebecca doll and the books that accompany her presents an idealized America in which anti-Semitism and anxieties about Jewish American identity are minimized and glossed over."[8] Marcus goes on to say that the timing of the story—1914, after the 1911 Triangle Shirtwaist Factory Fire and before the Leo Frank lynching in 1915, the US's entry into WWI in 1917, and the introduction of strict anti-immigration policies meant to curb Russian Jewish entry into the US in 1921 and 1924—further reinforces "patterns of ideological desire that resonate more broadly throughout the Jewish American imagination: the desire for fictions of a tolerant and welcoming America, and of a Jewish American identity that fits comfortably within it."[9] In some ways, Marcus's assertions ring true in the sense that Rebecca's problems are, for the most part, easily solved, and the trajectory of her narrative leaves readers with a decidedly positive impression of the place that American Jews held in early twentieth-century American society, steadily climbing toward an American Dream that is not only attainable but accessible to anyone with a bit of luck and a willingness to work hard.

However, Marcus's cynicism overlooks both the intentionality and the depth with which author Jacqueline Dembar Greene crafts Rebecca's story, both as an immigration story and as a multigenerational family narrative. According to Greene, placing Rebecca's story in 1914 reflected her desire to showcase the various stages of the immigration process and the ways in which, after only a few decades in the US, the Russian Jewish population had already made an impact on American culture (and vice versa): "I wanted to show the dynamics of how societies change, and how immigrants make our country more interesting and stronger, and open up opportunities because of their bringing in ideas that no one had noticed or thought about as possibility."[10] The Rubin household spans three generations, each of which have their own approach to Americanization: Bubbie and Grandpa, the least assimilated and least open to the idea of integrating American and Jewish traditions; Rebecca's parents, born in Russia and still immersed in the culture of their homeland, but more willing to embrace change; and Rebecca and her siblings, American-born and therefore tasked with "teaching" their parents and grandparents what it means to be American.[11]

Intergenerational conflict thus marks Rebecca's story, even as Greene depicts the Rubin family as loving and warm. Bubbie, for example, criticizes her son-in-law for opening his shoe store on Saturdays (a compromise that he sees as a financial necessity), objects to Rebecca singing secular Christmas music at home, and sees the family's trip to Coney Island as *meshuggah* (Yiddish: crazy); Rebecca's parents dream of Rebecca becoming a teacher (a hallmark of upward mobility and successful assimilation, as well as a "respectable" profession for an unmarried woman), while her grandmother helps her arrange a trousseau of handmade linens to bring to her future husband; Rebecca bristles against her parents' and grandparents' expectations, dreaming of becoming an actress and selling her trousseau in order to buy her own set of Shabbat candlesticks when her parents will not allow her to light the family's candles on Friday nights (a financial venture she eventually comes clean about, instead using the money to help her father fund her uncle, aunt, and cousins' passage to America). Each generation of the Rubin family thus provides a different perspective of the immigration process, and how various factors—age, gender, occupation, etc.—impact the ways in which Americanization takes hold. In this way, the Rubin family dynamic paints a decidedly realistic picture of family life during the immigration era; as Sydney Stahl Weinberg argues, immigrant-era families were often divided between daughters with "longings alien to their parents, whose main concern was basic survival."[12]

It is no mistake, then, that Greene chose acting, and specifically movie acting, as Rebecca's dream career. Through Rebecca's interactions with her cousin, Max Shepard (née Moyshe Shereshevsky), and famous actress Lily Armstrong (née Lillian Aronovich), the Rebecca books demonstrate yet another facet of Russian Jewish immigrant culture: the building of Hollywood as an American Dream factory, powered by the ideas and creative energy of Russian Jewish immigrants and children of immigrants who, in Jewish cultural scholar Donald Weber's words, "appropriated the existing popular media to address the emotional concerns of their audiences; in the process they helped shaped—indeed invented—a vision of the country designed to help negotiate the often bewildering, *alien* landscape (external and internal) in which the immigrants found themselves."[13] With their Americanized names, their immersion in the creative arts, and their desire to contribute to American popular culture, Max and Lily represent a different pattern of Americanization than either Rebecca's more traditional parents or grandparents. Moving to California by series' end to help build Hollywood, Max and Lily are "Jewish pioneers," shaping American culture even as they snack on matzo during a film shoot that falls on Passover.[14] Rebecca's desire to become an actress—a profession considered both impractical and "unladylike"—thus violates the boundaries of her parents' and grandparents' understanding of propriety and, more importantly, emblematizes the trope of "progress" that characterizes immigrant narratives in American popular culture. Just like Jack Robin/Jakie Rabinowitz in the 1927 Warner Brothers classic *The Jazz Singer*, Rebecca's narrative places her between her dream of contributing to the canon of a decidedly American artform (in her case, movies; in Jack's, jazz) and the dated expectations of parents/grandparents that do not see the value in the American culture that Rebecca finds so enthralling.

However, even as Rebecca embraces her Americanness, her sense of herself as an American is challenged throughout her stories. This destabilization of her self-perception illustrates the tenuousness of holding dual American and Jewish identities, and adds a layer of complexity to the series' positive representation of the immigrant experience. The second book in the series, *Rebecca and Ana*, in which Rebecca's uncle, aunt, and cousins arrive from Russia and move in with the Rubins, provides one of the series' most nuanced story arcs, as Rebecca finds herself increasingly embarrassed by the "greenhorn" behavior of her newly arrived cousin Ana. At first excited about Ana's arrival, Rebecca sees herself as her cousin's mentor, taking on a maternal role as she teaches Ana how to be American—influencing the way Ana dresses, helping Ana practice English, and touring Ana around the Lower East Side.

The irony at the heart of *Rebecca and Ana*, of course, lies in the fact that while Rebecca sees herself as fully American, her Jewishness marks her as "other" in the eyes of non-Jews. Rebecca herself is oblivious to this fact, as is obvious in the scene where she takes Ana to Orchard Street, the location of "dark," "cheap" tenements and pushcart peddlers where, as Rebecca explains to Ana, her family originally lived when they arrived in America, before they were able to move "blocks away in their row house, with large windows facing the front and the back" and "fresh air" even on "the hottest days."[15] The tour both establishes Rebecca's pride in her own family's upward mobility (and, by extension, her unconscious feelings of superiority over Ana) and Rebecca's lack of self-awareness that, despite her family's ascent into a more stable socioeconomic position, she is still immersed in a largely insular immigrant community. Ana's reaction to the sights, sounds, and smells of Orchard Street—"Listen! I hear Yiddish!"—is reminiscent of the scene from Joan Micklin Silver's 1975 Jewish immigrant saga *Hester Street* wherein Gitl, a newly arrived Russian immigrant remarks to her more assimilated husband, Jake, "I go with Mrs. Kavarsky, Rivington Street, Delancey Street, everywhere Jews. The Gentiles keep in another place, huh?"[16] Rebecca's America is a Jewish enclave that affirms her limited understanding of what American culture is and of how non-Jewish Americans at the time perceived Jews. It is only when Rebecca realizes that Ana's foreignness reflects negatively on her own claims to Americanness—as a result of bullying from both classmates and from her non-Jewish teacher, who forces Rebecca to teach Ana the lyrics to "You're a Grand Old Flag" and then denigrates both girls for Ana's accented rendition of the song—that Rebecca experiences a sense of shame and self-hatred for her Jewish difference, which she then begins to project onto Ana for "humiliating" her.[17]

School proves to be an unaffirming space that forces Rebecca to reconsider the boundaries of her Jewish and American identities. As Historian Sydney Stahl Weinberg suggests, "the public schools facilitated this transformation of young immigrants into Americans. To be a 'real American' seemed to require giving up the external signs of being Jewish."[18] Rebecca's shame at Ana's "greenness," as well as the trepidation she feels in *Candlelight for Rebecca*, when the same non-Jewish teacher forces the Jewish students to create Christmas decorations for their families under the guise of Christmas being an American holiday (an experience Greene drew from her own upbringing), provides readers insight into the small-scale impact of anti-Jewish discrimination and internalized antisemitism. These challenges to Rebecca's sense of self are temporary and resolved through identity-affirming moments—e.g., Rebecca apologizes to Ana and the two successfully perform "You're a Grand Old Flag" at a school assembly, and Rebecca's Bubbie, a bastion of Jewish tradition, praises Rebecca's Christmas decoration and answers Rebecca's concerns about whether the Rubins are American enough by telling her that "some Americans celebrate Christmas, and some don't"—but their presence in Rebecca's narrative sheds light on the ambivalence that characterized the Jewish immigrant experience and complicates the conception of who or what can classify as "American."[19]

The world that Greene builds around Rebecca introduces young readers to the trials and triumphs faced by Jewish immigrants and American-born Jews during the immigration era; throughout Rebecca's six books, Greene introduces readers to labor unions, anti-immigrant policies at Ellis Island, Jewish rituals related to kashrut, holidays, and celebrations both within the home and the synagogue, American Jewish cultural landmarks, and core Jewish values such as *tikkun olam* (repairing the world) and *tzedakah* (charity). Perhaps even more importantly, however, through her characterization of Rebecca as a determined, opinionated, creative, and proud Jewish girl, Greene's books challenge stereotypes of young Jewish femininity embedded in American popular culture. Rebecca provides a clear antidote to the selfish, materialistic, superficial Jewish American Princess—a pervasive stereotype coined in the mid-twentieth century but whose characteristics are rooted in negative representations of Jewish women dating back to the films, literature, and theater of the immigration era—in her thoughtfulness (e.g., hand-crocheting a yarmulke for her grandfather as a Chanukah present), her passion for justice (e.g., speaking at a labor rally in defense of garment workers' rights), and her selflessness and sense of adventure (e.g., rescuing Ana from a broken Ferris wheel during a trip to Coney Island). At the same time, however, Rebecca is still "big-mouthed" and unwilling to compromise her dreams—characteristics that usually have negative connotations in depictions of Jewish femininity but that Greene spins as positive indications of Rebecca's independence and individuality. Even as she missteps and learns from her mistakes, Rebecca evokes sympathy. Her books frame the familial and social issues she encounters through her perspective; as the hero of her story, Rebecca is empowered and provided with the interiority necessary to elicit empathy and understanding. As such, Rebecca draws inspiration from similarly complex Jewish female representations that have come before her; she is at once a younger version of Fanny Brice, the funny, attention-grabbing, and supremely talented stage performer and subject of *Funny Girl*, and a companion to the bevy of intelligent, strong-willed, and often conflicted young Jewish women featured in the short stories and novels of Polish Jewish immigrant author Anzia Yezierska. In this sense, Rebecca Rubin's importance to the American Girl canon cannot be overstated—not only does she carve space for Jewish stories within the American Girl Company's tapestry of female-oriented American historical narratives, but she asserts a sensitive, more nuanced version of young Jewish femininity that encourages readers to identify with rather than against American Jewish women.

All Dolled Up? Accessorizing (and Whitewashing) Rebecca's Story

While the Rebecca books include a wide array of experiences, traditions, and cultural markers that help to firmly situate her story in the hybrid immigrant-American world from which she comes, the history and development of the Rebecca doll/accessories (as well as the evolution of the American Girl Historical Character Collection in general since 2009) both whitewash and water down Rebecca's Jewishness and the realities of her first-generation Americanness that unfold throughout her stories, even as the doll's creation aimed to ensure a physical authenticity to accompany the historical authenticity of Greene's stories. Rebecca's research and development process focused on both the physical appearance of the doll itself and the accuracy of the objects and accessories that accompany the doll in the American Girl mail-order catalog. As Megan Boswell, American Girl's then-Director of Design and Development, explains, Rebecca's hair color proved to be particularly challenging, as designers wanted to avoid shades of brown that were either "too typical" (and therefore too stereotypical, promoting the idea of a monolithic Jewish "look") or that were too similar to already existing dolls, including Samantha, the brunette circa-1904 historical doll whose time period falls closest to Rebecca's; the end result of "a new mid-tone brown hair color with russet highlights" reflects the extent to which the American Girl company considers the optics of its choices, especially as it relates to ethnic dolls.[20]

Yet, at the same time, Rebecca's face—taken from the same mold used for the Josefina doll, the first nonwhite character featured in American Girl's Historical Collection—speaks to a certain level of ethnic interchangeability between the historical dolls whose backgrounds, cultures, and traditions are interpreted and marketed to be appealing to wider audiences. As media scholar Emilie Zaslow suggests, the variety of the hair textures, skin colors, eye colors, and facial features that American Girl offers "lead[s] to a nonessentialist and diverse production of racial identity markers . . . that avoid using stereotypical facial markers that would essentialize or potentially create caricatures of the token Eastern European Jewish, Mexican American, and Irish American characters."[21] While Zaslow's point is true—she rightly argues that the fact that Rebecca Rubin and Lindsey Bergman share no facial features in common speaks to American Girl's conscious effort to avoid claims that there is a singular way of "looking Jewish"—the interchangeability of Rebecca and Josefina as two "ethnic" dolls who share the same face suggests a flattening of the cultural pluralism inherent in American Girl's mission and a visual insistence on the "sameness" of each character, even as their differences are celebrated within the context of their stories.

Rebecca's accessories further exemplify this "cultural flattening," especially since American Girl rebranded its original Historical line as the BeForever line in 2014, and the products sold alongside the Rebecca doll were redesigned with much less detail and much less connection to the Jewish immigrant world Greene paints in her books. Rebecca's rebranded "Sabbath Set"—originally sold with a brass samovar, two Shabbat candlesticks (given to Rebecca by her Italian neighbor Mr. Rossi at the end of *Candlelight for Rebecca*), challah, and tea accessories—now only includes the samovar, tea accessories, and challah. The Shabbat candlesticks—an integral part of Rebecca's story, and a sign both of her coming-of-age as a young Jewish woman and of her maturation as she learns to overcome her prejudices and bonds with Mr. Rossi—are now sold just as "candlesticks" alongside "Rebecca's Parlor Table," and are reimagined as part of a group of generalized accessories (including a vase of flowers and a lace table runner) to decorate the table; this lack of specificity is particularly ironic given the candlesticks' role in Rebecca's story, both as a material object that brings Mr. Rossi and Rebecca together as members of parallel immigrant groups and, since Mr. Rossi mistakes Shabbat candlesticks for a Chanukah menorah, as a sign of the often misunderstood cultural differences that separate Rebecca from both immigrant and American-born non-Jews despite her desire to melt seamlessly into the "pot" of American identity. The only other explicitly Jewish accessory available for purchase is Rebecca's Chanukah set (including an ornate brass menorah, a dreidel, and coins), despite the fact that Passover figures prominently in *Rebecca at the Movies*, the fourth book in her series. Rebecca's Phonograph Set similarly flattens the circumstances of Rebecca's world; in *Rebecca at the Movies*, Rebecca and her school friend Rose loiter in a neighborhood candy shop so they can listen to music on the shop owner's phonograph, while the product sold implies that the phonograph belongs to Rebecca herself. This detail is small, but it conveys a different kind of existence than what Rebecca actually experiences: one that is more economically stable, less immersed in her immigrant neighborhood, and further removed from the historical reality she is meant to represent.

Likewise, Rebecca's clothing embodies a disconnect from the reality of her stories and the era from which she comes. While the original Rebecca doll came in a modest burgundy tweed dress with a shawl and a cameo pin featuring an image from a Russian folk tale shared by Bubbie in *Meet Rebecca*, Rebecca's BeForever clothing—made of satin, fur, and velvet— overlooks her family's immigrant origins and the fact that the Rubin family, while financially comfortable compared to more newly arrived families, struggles to save money. Rebecca, as the youngest child in that family, wears hand-me-downs and spends *Candlelight for Rebecca* self-conscious about the fact that she has to wear a dress she has outgrown to her family's Chanukah celebration; the lace and satin dress that American Girl sells as "Rebecca's Chanukah Outfit" does not convey this significant piece of Rebecca's identity, and, in fact, emphasizes the position that the American

Girl company holds as a marketer of a specific brand of what Michelle S. Bae refers to as "postfeminist girl power" that centers on aesthetics, consumerism, and commodification.[22]

The BeForever rebranding further problematized the disconnect between Rebecca's clothing/accessories and her character because of the changes made to the original book series. While the pre–BeForever Historical Collection included six books, all themed around a various challenge/event that exemplified the character's capacity for growth and change (for Rebecca, the arrival of her immigrant cousin, the opportunity to work as an extra on a film set, a labor strike that threatens her uncle's ability to support his family, etc.), the BeForever books condense the six stories into three narratives, omitting the "Looking Back" section (which provided historical detail about the events described in the story), the "Family and Friends" section (which provided an outline of the supporting characters that make up the protagonist's world), and the illustrations that help to bring to life each story's historical and cultural references. The covers also "glamorize" the protagonist in a way that undermines the authenticity of the narrative: on the cover of *Meet Rebecca* (volume one of the original series), Rebecca stands in front of her block of row houses, arms crossed and smiling, with a modest dress and her hair in an era-appropriate style; the cover of *The Sound of Applause* (volume one of the BeForever rebrand, which combines *Meet Rebecca* with *Rebecca and Ana*), on the other hand, features a slimmer, more mature-looking Rebecca with a decidedly modern blowout and makeup, posing on her front stoop wearing a purple tweed and velvet dress with a matching necklace. If American Girl provides, as former AG Public Relations Manager Stephanie Spanos says, "a window and a mirror" that reaches girls interested in dolls but old enough to be "aware of the larger world around them and . . . able to understand the stories' historical, cultural, and familial themes," the BeForever rebrand signals a decided turn away from that ethos.[23] The end result is a watering down of the impact of Rebecca Rubin as a Jewish female character who not only encourages young female readers to speak for themselves, assert their own power, and find pride in their identities, but who also challenges Jewish stereotypes, normalizes Jewish cultural and familial traditions, and illuminates the complexity of the relationship between Jewishness and Americanness in an accessible and nuanced manner.

Conclusion: Rebecca Rubin, American Girl

A major facet of the American Girl mission is to take "big historical themes and bring them down to girls' size"; in many ways, this mission both encourages young female readers to see themselves as active agents at the center of heroic narratives and fosters a sense of cross-cultural identification with characters from a variety of ethnic, religious, and racial backgrounds.[24] As American Girl's major Jewish representative, confident, opinionated, and outgoing Rebecca Rubin thus acts as a universal feminist touchstone and as a translator of Jewish history and ritual for American Girl readers (and, to a lesser extent, shoppers). Jacqueline Dembar Greene wrote Rebecca as an inspirational character, one whose spunk and self-assurance empowered Greene herself as much as she hopes Rebecca empowers younger readers: "[Rebecca] is somebody I would have liked to have been more like, but I wasn't. Interestingly, writing these books gave me self-confidence, and changed me a lot."[25] Greene goes on to describe the universal appeal of Rebecca's story, describing a fan letter she received from a Catholic third grader who knew nothing about Judaism until reading the Rebecca series:

> After [the student] read the book, she realized how Jewish values and Catholic values were so similar. And she saw so many connections between what she learned in school and at church, compared to what she was reading about in the Jewish family. And it was an eye opener for her. And she wrote that to me in her letter, how much it woke her up to something she didn't know about.[26]

The blend between the universal and the culturally specific is a hallmark of American Jewish storytelling, and part of the power of Rebecca Rubin's presence in the Historical Doll Collection is the implicit assertion that the daughter of Yiddish-speaking Russian Jewish immigrants is just as much an American Girl as a Revolutionary War–era Virginian (Felicity), an Edwardian-era New York socialite (Samantha), or a Midwesterner living on the home front during WWII (Molly). Rebecca's Americanness—and the work that her stories do in merging her Jewishness and her Americanness (through her visit to the film set and the subsequent connection made between Jewish artists and American storytelling, through her bartering for the sheet music to "You're a Grand Old Flag" with a pushcart peddler on Orchard Street, through her confidence in her ability to mentor Ana through the assimilation process as someone who understands herself as both an American and a Jew)—expands the scope of what American identity looks like, not because Greene's books simplify or romanticize the Jewish assimilation story, but rather because they present a version of that story where, despite outward pressures to Americanize, despite ignorant authority figures who impose Christian values as "American" values, and despite struggles with poverty and stability, Jewish immigrants and first-generation Jewish Americans still find a balance between tradition and modernity that embraces Eastern European cultural traditions even as it makes room for new, hyphenated Jewish-American ones.

As Emily Schneider points out, Rebecca Rubin's impact is best embodied by the moment from *Candlelight for Rebecca* where Rebecca talks to her grandfather about Chanukah after being told by her teacher that Christmas is the only winter holiday celebrated by "real" Americans:

> He folds his paper and gives her his full attention as he explains the meaning of the Maccabees' revolt, pointing out that immigrants need to learn new ways, but that "we can't forget who we are, even if it means being a little different." As a generic message of pride and loyalty to traditions, the grandfather's conclusion may appeal to any reader. For Jewish readers it has a specific resonance, as unique to Jews as Rebecca's candles.[27]

This moment in the text accomplishes two goals that are inherent in Rebecca's story: first, celebrating the strength and vitality of Jewish culture; and second, and perhaps more importantly, expressing that Jewish culture in ways that both Jewish and non-Jewish audiences can relate to and recognize. Non-Jewish audiences understand Rebecca's grandfather's advice through a universal lens of "being true to one's identity," while Jewish readers understand the double-coded message within his words: that the balance between Jewish "difference" and American assimilation is a persistent aspect of the Jewish-American experience, and that the "othering" that Rebecca and her family/friends face throughout the narrative forms the major paradox of an American society that both benefited from the contributions of Russian Jewish immigrants and demanded the total assimilation of those immigrants, even as it rejected the legitimacy of their adopted American identities. Rebecca's status as an "American Girl" thus undermines the systemic othering of Jews, both from an historical perspective and from the perspective of the tropes and patterns that dictate Jewish representation in contemporary American popular culture. Rebecca herself functions as a wish-fulfillment fantasy—a first-generation immigrant, upwardly mobile and infused with Jewish pride, American ingenuity, and a modern feminist spirit who succeeds without compromising her sense of self—but she also embodies something much deeper in her presence as a Jew within a canon of children's literature and educational toys aimed at teaching young girls what it means to be an American.

Notes

1. Chryssa Atkinson, *Lindsey* (Middleton, WI: Pleasant Company, 2001), 1.

2. While American Girl's "Girl of the Year" series is designed around each doll being "retired" at the end of their respective year, information about the Lindsey Bergman doll/character is still widely available on various AG fandom/hobby sites put together by collectors and fans of the American Girl company. See, for example, Paige Davanzo, "A Collector's Guide to the American Girl 'Girl of the Year' Dolls," Hobby Lark, December 22, 2022, https://hobbylark.com/collecting/A-Collectors-Guide-to-the-American-Girl-Girl-of-the-Year-Dolls; "Lindsey," AG Playthings, http://agplaythings.com/ledolls/lindsey/lindsey.html; and "Lindsey Bergman," American Girl Wiki, https://americangirl.fandom.com/wiki/Lindsey_Bergman.

3. Allen Salkin, "American Girl's Journey to the Lower East Side," *New York Times*, May 22, 2009. https://www.nytimes.com/2009/05/24/fashion/24Doll.html.

4. Jacqueline Dembar Greene, interview by Samantha Pickette, April 7, 2023. For more information about the research process that goes into the creation of each of the historical characters (as well as their dolls/accessories), see Meilan Solly, "The Enduring Nostalgia of American Girl Dolls," *Smithsonian Magazine*, June 3, 2021, https://www.smithsonianmag.com/history/evolution-american-girl-dolls-180977822/.

5. Jacqueline Dembar Greene, *Changes for Rebecca* (Middleton, WI: American Girl, 2009), 70.

6. Here, "Pale of Settlement" refers to the roughly 386,000-square-mile area of Czarist Russia—from the Baltic to the Black Sea, comprising much of present-day Belarus, Ukraine, Poland, Lithuania, Moldova, and parts of western Russia—in which Eastern European Jews living under the yoke of Czarist Russia were permitted to live. Established by Catherine the Great in 1791, the Pale had a Jewish population of 4,900,000 Jews (94 percent of the total Jewish population of Russia, and about 12 percent of the population of the region) by 1897. The Pale of Settlement was abolished with the Russian Revolution in 1917. For a description of Jewish life in the Pale—including the renaissance of *Yiddishkeit*, or Yiddish culture, the birth of Zionism, the Bund, and other Jewish nationalistic movements, and the poverty, anti-semitism, and oppression that characterized daily life for Russian Jews—see Irving Howe, *World of Our Fathers: The Journey of East European Jews to America and the Life They Found and Made*, 30th anniversary ed. (New York: NYU Press, 2005). With the assassination of the relatively "benevolent" Czar Alexander II in 1881, life for the Jews of the Pale became increasingly precarious, leading to the mass immigration of Russian Jews to the US. While not all Eastern European/Russian Jews immigrating to the US at this time came from the Pale, the

vast majority did. Rebecca's family would have been part of this immigrant population, and the escape from the Pale of Settlement is the cultural and historical context that forms the foundation of her family's story.

7. Paula Hyman, *Gender and Assimilation in Modern Jewish History: The Roles and Representation of Women* (Seattle: University of Washington Press, 1995), 93.

8. Lisa Marcus, "Dolling Up History: Fictions of Jewish American Girlhood," *Girlhood Studies* 5, no. 1 (Summer 2012): 16.

9. Marcus, 16.

10. Greene, interview.

11. According to Greene, the choice to mismatch the names of Rebecca's grandparents—i.e., calling her grandmother "Bubbie" (Yiddish: grandmother) and her grandfather "Grandpa" rather than the Yiddish "Zeyde"—reflects the "fine line" between "keeping things authentically Jewish, and . . . straddling the wider culture" that characterizes American Girl's approach to depicting history through an ethnic lens. More importantly, Greene goes on to explain that this specific choice provides yet another indication of the assimilation process that each generation of the Rubin family undergoes throughout the Rebecca series:

> Remember that the backdrop of immigration and assimilation was at the top of the list of significant goals. So when it came to choosing the best titles for the grandparents I considered that the grandchildren are all American-born. They would be most likely to choose American words. Also, the grandfather works daily in the shoe store, so he is exposed to more of the public and more local culture. Each generation assimilated a little more completely, and yet each tried to keep traditions. So I thought that the grandchildren would be most likely to call their grandmother "Bubbie" at her choice. She is the most traditional of all the family members. And it's an easy Yiddish word to introduce to readers. It could be possible that the grandchildren, or even their parents, might have chosen to call their grandfather with a more Americanized version. And it's likely he would have been fine with that. Without explaining through the story line, it shows how immigrant families were [acculturated], and how they adapted. Greene, interview.

12. Sydney Stahl Weinberg, *The World of Our Mothers: The Lives of Jewish Immigrant Women* (Chapel Hill: University of North Carolina Press, 1988), 117.

13. Donald Weber, *Haunted in the New World: Jewish American Culture from Cahan to The Goldbergs* (Bloomington: Indiana University Press, 2005), 50.

14. Jacqueline Dembar Greene, *Rebecca and the Movies* (Middleton, WI: American Girl, 2009), 55–56.

15. Jacqueline Dembar Greene, *Rebecca and Ana* (Middleton, WI: American Girl, 2009), 36–37.

16. Greene, *Rebecca and Ana*, 37; *Hester Street*, directed by Joan Micklin Silver, Midwest Films, 1975.

17. Greene, *Rebecca and Ana*, 51.

18. Weinberg, 112.

19. Jaqueline Dembar Greene, *Candlelight for Rebecca* (Middleton, WI: American Girl, 2009), 54–55.

20. Salkin, "American Girl's Journey to the Lower East Side."

21. Emilie Zaslow, *Playing with America's Doll: A Cultural Analysis of the American Girl Collection* (New York: Palgrave Macmillan, 2017), 116.

22. Michelle S. Bae, "Interrogating Girl Power: Girlhood, Popular Media, and Postfeminism," *Visual Arts Research* 37, no. 2 (Winter 2011): 29.

23. Quoted in Michelle Wildgen, "The Rise of American Girl Rebecca Rubin," *The Forward*, January 2, 2013, https://forward.com/culture/168334/the-rise-of-american-girl -rebecca-rubin/.

24. Wildgen, "The Rise of American Girl Rebecca Rubin."

25. Greene, interview.

26. Greene, interview.

27. Emily Schneider, "I Re-Read American Girl's Rebecca Rubin Books, and They Hold Up," Jewish Book Council, December 3, 2018. https://www.jewishbookcouncil.org /pb-daily/i-re-read-the-american-girl-rebecca-rubin-books.

PART 3

AMERICAN GIRL TEACHES A LESSON

"Nothing but Each Other and Hope"
Addy and the Black Feminist Tradition

Cary Tide

In 1993, Addy Walker became the first American Girl of color: an expensive doll, and the protagonist of six associated historical novels routinely stocked in children's libraries. Critics objected to the setting of her narrative: Addy's story begins in 1864, while she and her family are enslaved. The associate manager of public relations for Pleasant Company, which published and produced American Girl, framed this setting as imperative: they were advised that Addy's story "*must* start in slavery—that anything else would be an abdication of our responsibility to tell not just the real history of African Americans, but the real story of *America itself*."[1] Company founder, Pleasant Rowland, explicitly cited the Black scholars hired to advise the series: they "recommended unanimously and in no uncertain terms that we must deal with the issue of slavery."[2] Neither commented on the book's depiction of Addy's self-emancipation, or upon the relationships that underpin her freedom.

Meet Addy introduced me to the historical reality of enslavement when I was about Addy's age. I knew it was fiction, but it felt true; so did the books following her escape to Philadelphia, in which Addy experiences partial freedom, material deprivation, family reunion, and community care. By providing clues about how the world around me came into being, *Addy* shaped my intellectual development. By portraying the strategies that helped Addy survive after her escape, the series supported my survival in a differently violent environment. *Addy* let me, as a nonblack child of color, form an empathic relationship with a fictional Black girl rather than with her oppressors. This essay turns the accusation that such stories are radically subversive against its repressive purpose.[3]

The problems with the Addy doll are nothing new: white desire for possessing Black people (or—sublimated—their images) is fundamental to racial capitalism. Pleasant Company merely capitalized upon the 1990s multicultural moment to frame their doll as a contribution to social justice. The doll made Pleasant Company far more money than the books and, although it was also marketed to Black families, the doll appears to have been primarily produced for white consumption. Company founder Pleasant Rowland told a reporter, "If I got hit by a car tomorrow, I could die knowing that we made toy history. We made a black doll the object of status and desire for white children."[4]

Addy's author, Connie Rose Porter, observed that although an earlier character's family were enslavers, "no one ever challenged *that* story." Pleasant Company "had an opportunity to talk in the Felicity books about the issue before Addy came out and they didn't take it."[5] Carrying out this deferred responsibility affects everything Addy can do. Race is as foregrounded for Addy as it is backgrounded for white characters; her girlhood itself is seldom referenced.[6] Although the back-cover series synopsis meant to help a reader find the American Girl who's right for them calls Addy "brave," her circumstances are too dangerous for her to perform feminist interventions with the safely adorable courage allotted white protagonists. Preceding American Girl stories were pluralistic only insofar as they presented both a comforting return to times of yore *and* girls' participation in US history. Portraying a Black girl in 1864 complicated this plot. This is appropriate to Addy's setting: Black women's struggles have frequently troubled "American" narratives by making the limits of those terms explicit.

Addy's direct creators were primarily concerned with caring for Black readers. In the context of its genre, this care was a radical political act—and it was founded in the Black feminist tradition.[7] For instance, in her extensive scholarship on Black feminist approaches to children's literacy, series advisor Violet J. Harris has argued that, when "curricula materials, educational philosophies, and pedagogical techniques combine to inculcate an ideology that denigrates a group, omits or misrepresents the history and status of a group, or limits access to knowledge that would enable the individual or

"Nothing but Each Other and Hope": Addy and the Black Feminist Tradition   117

group to participate in all cultural institutions," literacy alone is insufficient.[8] With coauthor Arlette Ingram Willis, Harris later advocated for children's "individual and collective right to learn literacy in a socially and culturally supportive, responsible, and respectful democratic classroom" and suggested educators move towards this goal by employing radical critiques such as critical race theory.[9] The legitimization of some forms of knowledge via material published in accordance with market demands has cast out others at every point. Only contestation made *Addy* what it is.

For instance, Melodye Rosales had to fight Pleasant Company to properly illustrate the first three *Addy* books. In one instance, Rosales drew newly freed people looking tired and sad as they arrived in Philadelphia; she says that Rowland wanted them to smile, and told Rosales when she objected, "I'm not paying you to be a historian, I'm paying you to be a pair of hands."[10] Pleasant Company disputes this, and Rosales's belief that she was fired from the project over such conflicts. But Zaslow describes another, more complicated conflict:

> Rosales wanted to illustrate Addy's teacher and her wealthy, free born classmate, Harriet, with lighter skin in order to depict colorism within the African American community. The author and editor, however, wanted to make the differences among the characters be based on social class rather than based on color because racism within the black community is so divisive and they did not want to exploit these tensions, nor address issues that might be too complex for young readers.[11]

During the era of *Addy*'s publication, Black women's historian Elsa Barkley Brown argued that segregated history elides crucial dialogue between *and within* racialized communities of women. Merely formal historical inclusion, lacking the context of such textured exchange, is insufficient: that is, if historians would like to support readers in understanding the past or engaging in the present. If *Addy* merely diversified and thus morally safeguarded a product line primarily consumed by white, wealthy girls, the series would have figured as such shallow inclusion. Because series creators chose to respectfully negotiate their differences, they were able to complicate that simple story. Harris supported Rosales in the debate, and Porter ultimately chose to describe skin tone in the text as well.[12] The story bears the marks of their efforts in more than image or description: it provides readers a way to, as Brown puts it, "recognize not only differences but also the relational nature of those differences."[13]

Recognition of difference in pursuit of shared struggle is a primary tenet of Black feminism. From jail, Angela Davis observed that the Black women who lived the reality *Addy* figures were assigned, "by virtue of the brutal force of circumstances . . . the mission of promoting the consciousness and practice of resistance."[14] In the era of *Addy*'s publication, Patricia Hill Collins depicted the Black mothering tradition as care shown by all sorts of Black people towards children to whom they were not necessarily related by blood. Around the same time, bell hooks was writing about how she came to theory young, "desperate, wanting to comprehend—to grasp what was happening around and in me."[15] Porter defined herself as a "black female writer"—and made her choices plain when she added, "Racism and sexism are what can pigeonhole you. They can limit, even stop you. Not describing myself as a black woman will not prevent that from happening."[16] Coercive circumstances do not preclude choice; and it is the *choices* of series creators to build solidarity through caring respect for difference that most locates *Addy* within the Black feminist tradition.

This tradition provided *Addy* a power that ensured its popularity—and, ironically, its profitability. Yet because of the persistently exploitative generic, corporate, and social context in which series creators worked, their effort to portray and complicate Addy sometimes required metatextual work.[17] Pleasant Company encouraged authors to describe multiple outfits for their protagonists so the company could sell more doll accessories; Porter, however, knew that an impoverished Black child in this era would lack many clothes—especially the kinds of dresses that a 1990s child might beg a parent to purchase. She found a creative way to meet the demand without undermining the story's historical plausibility.[18] In *Addy's Surprise*, a white customer returns a too-small dress, unfairly blaming Addy's mother's sewing. Her contingently supportive white employer and landlord, Mrs. Ford, unexpectedly defends Momma's work; she gives the customer a refund but keeps the dress, resizing it to fit Addy as a Christmas present. With Mrs. Ford's permission, Addy makes her mother a scarf from the leftover fabric.[19] Like Addy, Porter crafted significance from scraps.

Making *Addy* required negotiating the terrible fact that many children's real experiences are not appropriate reading for children. While the creators chose to elide many experiences common to enslaved girls, *Meet Addy*—and

"Nothing but Each Other and Hope": Addy and the Black Feminist Tradition

the series generally—remains a distressing read. Black feminist scholar and series advisor Janet Sims-Wood recalls that the advisors' own emotional needs drove one of the series' most powerful interventions.[20] To successfully escape enslavement, Addy and her mother must leave baby Esther behind: in the care of Aunt Lula and Uncle Solomon, enslaved elders who are part of the Walkers' chosen family. The advisory committee could not bear to leave Esther there. At their request, Porter depicted the Walkers joining the real, massive family reunion effort freedmen undertook after the Civil War in *Addy Saves the Day*.

Porter also depicted Addy's loving parents sharing coping strategies. When Addy's father tells her he is going to go back to the plantation to look for Esther, Addy shivers with immediate fear, remembering what she escaped and thinking of the dangers he will face. But:

> Addy looked deep into Poppa's dark eyes. They looked calm and peaceful. "Is there anything I can do, Poppa?" she asked. "I'll do anything to help."
>
> "Keep on working in the garden," Poppa said. "Don't let the weeds grow back. And something else, too." He held Addy close in his arms. "Try not to trouble your heart with worry."[21]

This is also an act of care on Porter's part: she told an interviewer, "I wanted Addy to be an active child, but not a martyr. Her mother and father are not about to let her save the world."[22] The shelter Porter created for her audience resembles what bell hooks calls "homeplace": where one can renew one's sense of self in caring relation with others. For hooks, such work is "a radically subversive political gesture."[23] In intervening against reductive tropes of its publication era—Emancipation as a white gift and Black families as inherently pathological—*Addy* also does the sort of work hooks imagined from this framing: "when black women renew our political commitment to homeplace, we can address the needs and concerns of young black women who are groping for structures of meaning that will further their growth, young women who are struggling for self-definition."[24]

Her own parents, hooks remembers, were often too tired from their daily struggle to answer her questions or comfort her.[25] She found homeplace at her grandmother's house; like a fairytale character, hooks had to journey through a threatening environment to reach it. She remembers "white faces on the porches staring us down with hate. . . . Such a contrast, that feeling of arrival, of homecoming, the sweetness and the bitterness of that journey, that constant reminder of white power and control."[26]

Addy can act as a fictive refuge for children in similar situations—if they survive the journey between refuge and violence: in the library, at school, in the world. Although porches are more commonly depicted as spaces of entrance into belonging, hooks's childhood memory of porch surveillance inversely reflects, as Hortense Spillers puts it, the "vestibular" location of Black people in the United States. This location is reinforced not only by the police and social workers who routinely invade Black homes kept "in a state of breach" but by how physical and mythic barricades guard against the entrance of all people of color into US belonging.[27]

The *premise* of Addy's welcome within the premises of American girlhood and US history—lucrative exploitation presenting as liberal inclusion—strengthens these fortifications. But while the series' direct creators may have been hired only to provide an authenticating gloss, they chose otherwise. It is by virtue of their skill, care, and political commitments that *Addy* exceeded such generic inclusions/enclosures. In bequeathing a portion of the Black feminist tradition's accumulated knowledge to their readers, *Addy*'s direct creators rose to an obligation that, albeit inherited, can only be taken up by choice.[28] Emilie Zaslow has generously observed:

> American Girl is not *just* capitalizing on difference. It is dealing with some difficult questions: How does a company represent race or ethnicity without reducing it to semiotic markers? Must stories that feature girls of color address racial oppression? How does a company represent race at a time when it is now common for "proponents of colorblindness" to consider racial categories, race awareness, and the suggestion that "race matters in human interaction" to be distasteful and itself racist?[29]

Addy and the doll that the series accompanied suggest questions with rather different subjects. How and to whom do Black lives *matter* in US society? Is normative girlhood something to be reclaimed, refigured, or escaped? Is belonging, in the context of exclusion that has altered forms but not ended, a desirable goal? These stakes have long been present in Black children's relationships to dolls.[30] No corporation seems likely to meet them adequately.[31] Black children have had meaningful, significant relationships to the Addy doll. However, it is not necessary to know Addy's story or to have a personal relationship to the reality upon which it depends to own an Addy doll; to restyle its hair, to give it a new name; to keep the doll in the box and on display; to benefit from its accumulating market value. In setting up nonblack children to treat a representation of an enslaved girl as a commodity, Pleasant Company prioritized profit over Addy's story of self-emancipation and the wellbeing of their child consumers.[32]

The dynamic Pleasant Company created resembles what American studies scholar Shana Redmond has termed "the refuge of whiteness": "that separate and special place that allows white people to find safety in their power and possessions."[33] This refuge could perhaps be understood as an antithesis to homeplace in its opposite effect upon social relationships. The refuge of whiteness reinforces structural differences by disappearing "particular negotiations and struggles," thus preventing its inhabitants from forming the empathy and respect for difference basic to real solidarity. Engagements with Black suffering and struggle from this place are instead based in a relationship of *possessive identification*. Redmond argues further that, in only protesting spectacular antiblack violence, white liberals simultaneously "exorcise and exercise" their privilege—and erase racism's *everyday* nature.[34] When critics called Addy a "slave doll," this is part of what they were critiquing: white consumers exercising their ability to buy a figure of an enslaved girl; ridding themselves of any guilt for present Black plight; safe in the feeling that purchasing such an object constituted an antiracist act.[35]

Zaslow contends that Pleasant Company's Black dolls are "meant to be loved and cared for, they are meant to be protected as one would protect a friend or sibling."[36] However, market motivations do not require racist intention to have exploitative effects. Everyday play with possessions can build possessiveness; empathy *with* can be rationalized into *belonging to* until the latter seems like the only relation available.[37] It was this very sort of Clinton-era refiguration of racialized commodity relationships that made the doll a profitable endeavor, in terms of money and image, for Pleasant Company. Zaslow summarizes Rowland's stated motivations: "She had envisioned Addy from the brand's inception and . . . was no longer listening to market analysts who told her that an African American doll at this price point would not sell. The rise of the black middle class and the company's strong record had given her the leverage to take what the market considered to be a risk."[38] Some white parents explain their reasons for demanding the excision of Black history from libraries and curricula as a defense of their own children from exposure to racist violence, however vicarious. This is a recent development: in the 1800s, Zaslow observes, "white children were encouraged to play with black dolls by positioning them in acts of servitude as well as beating, throwing, and hanging them."[39] White parents sometimes brought their children to see lynchings, viewing them as educational opportunities. In the early 1900s, white children stoned Black people during a racist massacre. White parents told their children to violently harass Black student integrators in the 1950s. White children participated in 1960s riots against housing integration.[40] Few white parents today seem concerned with defending children of color.

Helping children recognize the fundamental entanglement of all peoples' interests requires taking greater risks than markets provide.[41] One danger of telling Black girls' stories is that readers may form the basis of a desire to intervene against the ongoing reenactment of their suffering. *Addy* shares with all its readers some of the tools Black people have used to survive profound pain. The *Addy* novels provide a path away from both the refuge of whiteness and the miserable tale of its depredations: toward the respect for difference and chosen care essential to real struggle and solidarity.

Like many real Black girls' stories, *Addy* broke a restrictive mold. Several other early American Girl series transmit progressive politics, or contain radical moments that resituate US historical girlhood. The brand's overall style and content, however, reflect a nostalgic pioneer aesthetic, an uncontroversial Americana easily supported by segregated historiography. *Addy* made room for an uneven but general shift in American Girls stories toward greater historical accuracy and more heterogenous protagonists, thereby facilitating a past narrative for many more readers.[42] Writers and educators who center Black children's individuality and specificity may likewise generate empathy with real Black children: the sort that respects their differences rather than referring to tired tropes. This work requires the commitment to and knowledge of the Black feminist tradition that supported *Addy*'s complication of the plot.

In the series' conclusion, Aunt Lula returns Esther to the Walker family; she tells them that her husband died on the way to Philadelphia, happy to have briefly experienced freedom. Aunt Lula soon dies too. On New Year's Eve, the whole family is preparing for their church's Emancipation Celebration—but although Addy has an important job to do there, her mother finds her sitting in the dark. Addy tells her mother, "I don't think

"Nothing but Each Other and Hope": Addy and the Black Feminist Tradition   123

I can stand up in front of all them folks and read those words in the Emancipation Proclamation about freedom. . . . Uncle Solomon's dead, Auntie Lula's dead. My dream of having our whole family together in freedom can *never* come true now." [43] Her eyes are full of tears.

It is December 1865: time for the Walker family to dissolve into American narrative. Aunt Lula and Uncle Solomon have become an impediment to the plot. Addy understands this transition, made via their sacrifice, as a profound loss. Baby Esther tries to comfort her with a doll—but Addy mourns, "Oh, Momma. Look at Esther. We never got to see her first steps or hear her first words. We can't ever get back the time we missed with her." Her mother touches the cowrie shell Addy inherited from an ancestor who survived the Middle Passage, and does not deny the depth of this loss. Instead, she reminds Addy of their history. "You remember when I give you this? We were running away from slavery. We had nothing but each other and hope. . . . This shell was to remind you that we are linked to the people in our past forever. They live in our hearts. Their lives, and their strength and courage, are part of us even though they gone."[44]

Addy's creators provided this token of survival to assist their readers with Addy's prescribed and partial passage into formal belonging—and with its lingering implications. Their devotion to real Black children may have helped with this act of care; Rosales, for instance, modeled Addy after her own daughter.[45] Her illustration of Addy and her mother handing Esther to Aunt Lula and Uncle Solomon conveys heartbreak, but also portrays their trust in a form of family often excised from US belonging.[46] *Addy* was published amidst punitive welfare reforms designed to enforce nuclear families; some of the series' readers were likely isolated from such networks of interdependent care. Hill Collins describes this isolation as an outcome of formal desegregation without accompanying material equality: a partial freedom that "tested" the Black mothering tradition.[47] *Addy* not only validates the loss readers may feel: it provides reassurance that chosen families have existed—and can thus be created again.

Addy makes place a problem: Addy escapes Southern slavery to meet Northern racism in the city of brotherly love. Time is tricky: *Addy* is brought into the world at the end of the Civil War—but here, too, the text intervenes against its prescribed reading. Amidst a crowd celebrating the end of hostilities, Addy reflects: "This was the day she had been waiting for. It was not perfect. If it were, her brother and sister would be right there with her, but this was the best day she could imagine without them. She turned to Momma and Poppa. 'I want today to be my birthday,' Addy said."[48] Addy's entrance into American history and formal humanity is not glossed as progress: it prohibits resolution and thus portends the incompleteness of future victories in Black struggle. Her birthday was unknown because of a real, intimate theft: many enslaved mothers prohibited from literacy could not tell their children exactly when they were born. Addy's day is not perfect: but in the Black feminist tradition, she chooses to take it up.

Notes

1. Susan Jevens, quoted in Emilie Zaslow, *Playing with America's Doll: A Cultural Analysis of the American Girl Collection* (London: Palgrave MacMillan, 2017), 106; emphasis in original.

2. Zaslow, *Playing with America's Doll*, 106, citing Barbara Brotman, "The Multicultural Playroom: Today's Dolls Have Ethnicity That's More Than Skin Deep," *Chicago Tribune*, 1993. This essay would not be possible without Emilie Zaslow's comprehensive research. It was developed in extensive conversation with Bryttani Wooten and is indebted to feedback from Kimberly Stern and Aaron Pattillo-Lunt. For all of these, my gratitude. Unless otherwise specified, "Addy" refers to the character; "*Addy*," italicized, refers to the six primary novels of the *Addy: An American Girl* series.

3. See Isabella Zou's commentary, "Black Studies is Under Attack by Conservatives, but the Teaching Is for Everyone," May 31, 2023, *Teen Vogue*, https://www.teenvogue.com/story /black-studies-under-attack-schools.

4. Elizabeth Mehren, "Playing with History," *Los Angeles Times*, November 28, 1994, 139; 143 (E1; E5): 143.

5. Zaslow, 107, citing a personal communication with Porter.

6. This absence also reflects the foundation of normative gender in antiblack violence: see Hortense Spillers, "Mama's Baby, Papa's Maybe: An American Grammar Book," *Diacritics* 17, no. 2 (Summer 1987): 64–81.

7. This language acknowledges Cedric Robinson's formulation of the Black radical tradition: "the continuing development of a collective consciousness informed by the historical struggles for liberation and motivated by the shared sense of obligation to preserve the collective being, the ontological totality." *Black Marxism*, 3rd ed. (Durham: University of North Carolina Press, 2021), 170–71. While *Black Marxism* markedly neglects Black women, front-matter in this edition testifies to Robinson's commitment to *practicing* Black feminism.

8. Violet J. Harris, "African-American Conceptions of Literacy: A Historical Perspective," *Theory into Practice* 31, no 4 (Autumn 1992): 277.

9. Violet J. Harris and Arlette Ingram Willis, "Political Acts: Literacy and Teaching," *Reading Research Quarterly* 35, no. 1 (2000): 75–78.

10. Aisha Harris, "The Making of an American Girl," *Slate*, September 21, 2016, https:// slate.com/culture/2016/09/the-making-of-addy-walker-american-girls-first-black-doll.html.

11. Zaslow, 109–10, citing a conversation with Porter.

12. Harris, "The Making of an American Girl."

13. Elsa Barkley Brown, "'What Has Happened Here': The Politics of Difference in Women's History and Feminist Politics," *Feminist Studies* 18, no. 2 (Summer 1992): 298.

14. Angela Davis, "Reflections on the Black Woman's Role in the Community of Slaves," in *The Intersection of Work and Family Life*, ed. Nancy F. Cott (Berlin: De Gruyter, 1992), 45–57, 47.

15. hooks, "Theory as Liberatory Practice," *Yale Journal of Law and Feminism* 4, no. 1 (1991): 1–12.

16. "Connie Rose Porter," *Gale Literature: Contemporary Authors*, Gale Literature Resource Center, 2007, https://www.gale.com/c/literature-resource-center.

17. bell hooks argues that institutional Black exclusion in the 1970s and 1980s meant many Black feminists moved into fictional and literary spaces, and others into writing Black women's history without publicly identifying as feminists. See "Feminist Scholarship" in *Teaching to Transgress* (New York: Routledge, 1994).

18. Porter interviewed by Jennifer L. Stevenson, "Porter's Addy Touches Today's Girls," *Tampa Bay Times*, November 6, 1996, https://www.tampabay.com/archive/1996/11/06/porter-s -addy-touches-today-s-girls/.

19. Connie Rose Porter, *Addy's Surprise: A Christmas Story* (Middleton, WI: Pleasant Company, 1994), 41–49.

20. Janet Sims-Wood and interviewer Denise Gines, "Janet L. Sims-Wood Recalls Developing an American Girl Doll," tape A2007.159, April 24, 2007, session 1 (4, 6), *The HistoryMakers Digital Archive*, https://da.thehistorymakers.org/story/628815;q=janet%20 sims-wood.

21. Connie Rose Porter, *Addy Saves the Day: A Summer Story* (Middleton, WI: Pleasant Company, 1993), 33.

22. Elizabeth Mehren, "Writer Brings Painful Part of Past to Life," November 28, 1994, *Los Angeles Times*, 143 (E5).

23. hooks, "Homeplace," 43. As if replying to Davis, hooks adds about Black women who make homeplace: "It does not matter that sexism assigned them this role. It is more important that they took this conventional role and expanded it to include caring for one another, for children, for black men, in ways that elevated our spirits, that kept us from despair, that taught some of us to be revolutionaries able to struggle for freedom" (44).

24. hooks, "Homeplace," 48. This section is especially indebted to Bryttani Wooten, who in our conversations described the Black feminist project as *building the house of care*— and *Addy* as a fictive house of care. See also Elizabeth Alexander, *The Black Interior* (New York: Graywolf, 2004), and Barbara Smith's introduction to *Home Girls: A Black Feminist Anthology* (Latham, NY: Kitchen Table Women of Color Press, 1983).

25. See hooks, "Theory: A Liberatory Practice."

26. hooks, "Homeplace," 41.

27. Spillers: "In the context of the United States, we could not say that the enslaved off-spring was 'orphaned,' but the child does become, under the press of a patronymic, patrifo-cal, patrilineal, and patriarchal order, the man/woman on the boundary, whose human and familial status . . . had yet to be defined. I would call this enforced state of breach another instance of vestibular cultural formation where 'kinship' loses meaning, *since it can be invaded at any given and arbitrary moment by the property relations*." "Mama's Baby, Papa's Maybe," 73; emphasis original. While her argument is specific to Black descendants of enslaved people, strategies developed to subject Black people are frequently and flexibly deployed against other people of color.

28. Terrion Williamson suggests that rising to such obligations "is the very enabling condition of black social life." While representations "*necessarily* fail to account for the reality of black lived experience," care given by choice by "our grandmothers, mothers, and othermothers help[s] us to reckon with what it means to live wholly and completely, *in spite of.*" *Scandalize My Name: Black Feminist Practice and the Making of Black Social Life* (New York: Fordham Press, 2016), 138, 16, 9; emphasis original. For historical intervention through such a lens, see Badia Ahad-Legardy, *Afro-Nostalgia: Feeling Good in Contemporary Black Culture* (Urbana: University of Illinois Press, 2021).

29. Zaslow, 113.

30. See Nazera Sadiq Wright, "Black Girls and Representative Citizenship," in *From Bourgeois to Boojie: Black Middle-Class Performances*, ed. Bridget Harris Tsemo and Vershawn Ashanti Young (Detroit: Wayne University Press, 2011): 91–109; and the "doll tests" undertaken by Kenneth and Mamie Clark and inadequately taken up by the 1954 *Brown v. Board of Education* Supreme Court ruling.

31. See, for instance, another historically inspired doll: Mattel's 2022 "Ida B. Wells Barbie Inspiring Women Doll," https://shop.mattel.com/products/ida-b-wells-barbie-inspiring-women-doll-hcb81. The doll's accessories include a copy of the *Memphis Free Speech*: the paper in which Wells castigated the lynch mob that, in 1892, murdered her friends for opening a grocery store. Wells responded by using the paper to organize a Black boycott of public transit; to support a mass Black exodus from Memphis; and to debunk a common lynching pretext (that Black men assaulted white women). In retaliation, white Memphis residents destroyed the *Free Speech*'s press. Neither this context, nor how these events inspired Wells's intellectual, material, and lifelong fight against lynching, are included with the Barbie doll made in her image. Ida B. Wells and Michelle Duster, eds., *Crusade for Justice: The Autobiography of Ida B. Wells*, 2nd ed. (Chicago: University of Chicago Press, 2020), 42–58.

32. These remarks are indebted to Jan Susina's "American Girls Collection: Barbies with a Sense of History," *Children's Literature Association Quarterly* 24, no. 3 (1999): 130–35.

33. Redmond, 26–27.

34. Redmond, 20–21. See also Sharon P. Holland, "The Last Word on Racism: New Directions for a Critical Race Theory," *South Atlantic Quarterly* 104, no. 3 (2005): 403–23.

35. See Aisha Harris's and Zaslow's discussions of these critiques.

36. Zaslow, 131.

37. Following Jennifer Morgan's arguments in *Reckoning with Slavery: Gender, Kinship, and Capitalism in the Early Black Atlantic* (Durham: Duke University Press, 2021).

38. Zaslow, 105, citing the *New York Times*, "Rejecting Barbie, Doll Maker Gains," September 1, 1993.

39. Zaslow, 122, drawing from Robin Bernstein's *Racial Innocence*.

40. Such accounts are widespread; I am specifically thinking of incidents described in Ida B. Wells, *The Light of Truth*, ed. Henry Louis Gates (New York: Penguin Books, 2014); Mary E. Jones Parrish, *The Nation Must Awake: My Witness to the Tulsa Race Massacre of 1921* (San Antonio: Trinity University Press, 1998); Melba Pattillo Beals, *Warriors Don't Cry* (New York: Simon & Schuster, 1994); and Arnold Hirsch, *Making the Second Ghetto: Race & Housing in Chicago, 1940–1960* (Chicago: University of Chicago Press, 1983).

41. Reflecting on his experiences as a school integration lawyer, critical race theorist Derrick Bell suggests that Black representation in historically white spaces tends to diffuse racism rather than end it—at least when such representation remains unaccompanied by

significant material change. "Serving Two Masters: Integration Ideals and Client Interest in School Desegregation Litigation," *Yale Law Journal* 85, no. 4 (1976): 470–516.

42. However, American Girl's treatment of *Black* girls after *Addy* has been uneven; see Zaslow, 125–30.

43. Connie Rose Porter, *Changes for Addy: A Winter's Story* (Middleton, WI: Pleasant Company, 1994), 47.

44. Porter, *Changes for Addy*, 48. Series advisor Cheryl Chisholm stated that the cowrie shell was included to convey resilience: Zaslow, 108.

45. Melodye Rosales, "TBT The muse I used to model the original Addy . . ." @artnsoulful, Instagram, July 1, 2021. Her daughter is now herself a professional artist; see harmoniarosales.com.

46. Connie Rose Porter, *Meet Addy: An American Girl* (Middleton, WI: Pleasant Company, 1993), 35.

47. Hill Collins, 181.

48. Connie Rose Porter, *Happy Birthday, Addy! A Springtime Story* (Middleton, WI: Pleasant Company, 1994), 50.

Teaching Girl(')s History
American Girls, Curricular Standards, and Historians

Tara Strauch

In 2016, Colonial Williamsburg published an extraordinary photo: twenty-five female employees and junior interpreters posing with their American Girl dolls. The photo was part of a blog post entitled "We are the 'Felicity Generation,'" which argued that the American Girl franchise had shaped these women and their careers. The term "Felicity Generation" generated quite a buzz on social media and on academic blogs as women claimed the term and thought about its scholarly implications. Professional historians, historic site interpreters, archivists, and librarians rooted their professional interests and career choices in a collection of dolls and stories from the late twentieth century and found meaning in viewing these choices not as individual but as a collective part of a cohort of women.[1]

All of this came before the rise of American Girl memes and social media accounts that used the dolls to challenge social norms and create a virtual community around the American Girl franchise. In other words, before Twitter (now X) accounts like @KlitKlittredge and @hellicity_m used the dolls to create subversive and humorous memes, there was a generation of (mostly) women who used American Girl stories to understand their world. For many of these women, that understanding was a private and passive experience, but a subset of these women went on to become professional historians whose relationship to the past as fostered by Pleasant Company was more external.

This essay argues that the "Felicity Generation" is a cohort of scholars and other adults who learned to think with and through American Girl stories. This cohort absorbed social history through the American Girl stories as well as K–12 curriculum that began to reflect social historians' research by the 1990s. American Girl books drove a surge in juvenile historical fiction offerings that, in turn, redefined the way publishing companies understood the genre as it became more focused on female readers. Because Pleasant Company and other children's literature publishers used scholars and scholarly research to develop their book series, young readers were also influenced by contemporary historiography. These girls drove the future of historical research as a generation of female historians who were raised on American Girl stories asked new historical questions. In other words, American Girl books shifted American historical teaching, and even the historical profession itself, towards narrative-driven content and standards.

Who Is the "Felicity Generation"?

When the first American Girl dolls were released in 1986, women made up just over 30 percent of history doctorates granted per year.[2] The field was dominated by men. Even in the field of public history, which was more open to women because it was less likely to require a terminal degree, men still held a strong majority of degrees granted. By 2007, however, both academic and public history had started to shift with women earning over 40 percent of history doctorates and holding a majority of public history positions.[3] By 2012, women almost achieved parity with 49.6 percent of doctorates granted—a number that has since decreased. While there are many factors that led to this increase in women historians, many women-identifying historians themselves named the American Girl franchise as crucial toward giving them an early push into the field.

This cohort of historians also had scholarly interests that differed from previous generations. The American Historical Association has observed a seven-fold increase in women's history and other fields in which the lives of women, children, and other underrepresented groups is taken seriously.[4] In a recent study of historical subfields and specialties, researchers argued that women historians are slightly more likely than their male counterparts to examine the history of the body, the family, consumption and consumerism, and education.[5] While these thematic specialties could have developed out of their graduate student training or might be a product of women's research choices being siloed into specific subfields deemed appropriate for women, many individuals from this generation report that these interests developed much earlier.

I am one of those women.[6] As a (very) junior academic in 2014, I was interviewed in a regular blog series for the American Historical Association to answer a few questions about who I was and how I became a historian. One of the questions was, "When did you first develop an interest in history?" I answered, "That is a tough question! It's a toss-up; either American Girl books or the genealogy 4-H project I did when I was 10. I was simultaneously enthralled by the choices Felicity's parents made and by the newfound knowledge that my great-grandmother hoarded sugar under her bed in the years following the Great Depression."[7]

In the weeks after the blog post appeared, many older academics teased me about this comment, expressing shock that a historian would openly admit that historical fiction drew them to the profession. But I wasn't really the first professional historian to share the role American Girl played in my career path and I certainly wouldn't be the last. In their recent article in the *Public Historian*, historians and podcasters Allison Horrocks and Mary Mahoney further elaborate on the American Girl fan to historian pipeline. "There is strong evidence," they note, "that early American Girl devotees are well-represented among professionals working in careers related to history, museums, or the study of material culture."[8] And they really are: Rebekkah Rubin is a public historian with a well-known AG Instagram account (@iamexcessivelydollverted); the mostly anonymous @apeekintothepantry is also a public historian whose blog combines the American Girl dolls with historical recipes. I couldn't make an exhaustive list of historians inspired by American Girl if I tried; the list is simply too long.[9]

Professional historians weren't just admitting that the American Girl stories led them to history. They also claimed that the stories had helped to drive their historical questions and methodology. Following a panel at the 2021 (virtual) annual conference for the Society for Historians of the Early American Republic (SHEAR), historians openly discussed the role

American Girl dolls played in shaping modern historians on Twitter and other virtual platforms. One of the scholars involved in the discussion, Rebecca Brenner, argued that the conversation should demand attention from the scholarly community. The discussion proved two things, she says: "First, the rise of American Girl dolls in professional history communities is worth taking seriously. . . . And finally, both strengths and weaknesses of what these dolls represent have likely influenced broader historical understanding."[10] At the same time that women were (briefly) achieving parity with men in the number of doctoral degrees granted, many of these women were also stating that they had been influenced by American Girl's stories and focus on material culture. These scholars themselves see a link between their childhood interests and their present fields of study.

American Girl and the Classroom

Pleasant Rowland's experience in educational publishing was fundamental in preparing her for the creation of the American Girl products and Pleasant Company as a whole. Starting in the late 1970s, Rowland worked with the Addison-Wesley Publishing Company to create reading curriculum for elementary students. Her most important contribution was the *Superkids* syllabus: a phonics-based reading program that emphasizes the importance of introducing early elementary students to engaging literature.[11] *Superkids* continues to be a successful reading curriculum and Rowland and other curriculum experts wrote small readers designed to accompany the textbooks. This emphasis on fiction that dovetailed with curricular needs anticipated how American Girl books would fit into the world of elementary education.

In the 1980s, leaders in education were increasingly concerned that textbooks were a poor way of educating students about history and the newer field of social studies. In their 1982 report "Making History Come Alive" for the Council for Basic Education, James Howard and Thomas Mendenhall noted that "the interest of children can be tapped and turned to history as early as they will listen to stories. . . . It is important to avoid the pap that grownups too often have judged right for children simply because it is both sweet and bland."[12] In other words, Howard, Mendenhall, and many other pedagogical experts wanted to move elementary history teaching away from simplistic stories and toward more nuanced content. One education scholar said this about textbooks in the 1980s: "Very often, in the classroom, mere facts become a body of information that seems irrelevant and dull to students. . . . When students cannot grasp the idea of historical figures as real people, then history becomes more mythology than reality. Paradoxically, historical fiction is an excellent tool to upset this mythology."[13] As a successful textbook creator, Rowland intended the American Girl Doll books to support the nation's curricular standards and she recognized that there was a gap in existing children's literature. In the history standards commissions of the 1980s, few true historical fiction novels appear on recommended reading lists because of concerns over accuracy.[14] Rowland's American Girl products were designed to fill this gap by providing stories for girls filled with historical accuracy and social-emotional learning.

Rowland has repeatedly stated that the dolls and books were intended to provide girls access to interesting and relatable history akin to the male-centered books that dominated the juvenile history book market in the 1970s and 1980s. Books like *Johnny Tremain* and *My Brother Sam is Dead* were seen as engaging and historically accurate unlike much historical fiction.[15] Other popular juvenile historical fiction books that featured girl protagonists instead of boys include Elizabeth George Speare's *The Witch of Blackbird Pond* (1958), Carol Ryrie Brink's *Caddie Woodlawn* (1935), Scott O'Dell's *Island of the Blue Dolphins* (1960), and Patricia MacLachlan's *Sarah Plain and Tall* (1986). None of these books, however, had content accurate enough for teaching history. And all of these books were aimed at a "middle grade" and older audience, i.e., approximately nine- to thirteen-year-olds.

Pleasant Rowland imagined something different for her new company. Rowland aimed to make stories and dolls that were historically accurate and appealing to girls. In particular, Rowland thought that girls deserved to see American history through the eyes of other girls—and she was convinced that uniting stories written for the juvenile age category (seven to eleven) with accompanying dolls to encourage imaginary play would help these girls see themselves as full participants in American politics and culture. These books would also dovetail with pedagogical interventions that were changing the shape of educational publishing. As one researcher noted, "What we initially need to do, then, is to show young children that their lives are part of history, and they are connected to people who came before them and who will come after them. The latter is very important because it allows children to see that they can be history makers."[16] By connecting students

Teaching Girl(')s History: American Girls, Curricular Standards, Historians   133

learning about history with their future ability to be "history makers," many teachers and curriculum specialists in the 1980s and 1990s sought to connect past and future. Rowland felt similarly; how better to show children that they are connected to the past and can be change makers than to give them historical stories that could be played with?

Most of the work on history education in the 1980s stressed three main themes: history should not be taught as a subject of rote memorization; all grade levels could meet historical standards, even early elementary school students; and history should not be taught as having a single narrative but should involve contingency, nuance, and competing interpretations.[17] Politicians were also interested in revising curricular standards, and so it was clear that changes would come to the educational publishing field. When Pleasant Company released its first characters in 1986, these stories already met the needs of a changing educational landscape as Rowland had an insider's understanding of how the field was changing. American Girl company historian Mark Spelz notes, "The structure [of the book series] allowed girls to compare and contrast, to consider the past, and to think about how things have or have not changed in the time since."[18] This structure was very like the recommendations from pedagogical experts to connect children to the past and to embolden them to make changes in the future. In other words, the books allowed children to make observations and opinions about historical narratives while also putting themselves into the stories.

For example, in *Meet Samantha*, Samantha and her friend Nellie go in search of the Black seamstress, Jessie, whom Grandmary, Samantha's guardian, has fired. Samantha is shocked by the neighborhood Jessie lives in. When Nellie explains that this is the Black neighborhood Samantha exclaims, "'You mean Jessie *has* to live here?' . . . Nellie looked at her. Samantha was smart about so many things that Nellie was always surprised at what her friend didn't know. 'Yes, of course,' Nellie said."[19] This section of *Meet Samantha* introduces readers to class differences, racial discrimination, and the fact that these systems can operate without historical actors, in this case Samantha, recognizing how these systems function. The reader here is free to consider why racial segregation is happening and can compare this way of creating neighborhoods with the present.

We can compare this passage with a textbook for seventh graders published in 1983. *American Adventures* has this to say about segregation: "Even before the Civil War, some Northern towns and cities had kept black Americans separate from whites. Blacks could not stay at the same hotels. They could not occupy the same sections in theaters. These practices were known as segregation. After Reconstruction, segregation spread to the South."[20] The textbook discussion of segregation makes it seem as though this is an action that only happens in certain times and in certain places. *Meet Samantha*, on the other hand, shows readers the daily experience of segregation and the complexity of the system. The sense of segregation as structural racism is evident in this passage in a way that is less clear in the textbook.

While American Girl books may have been some of the first on the market to provide accurate, serialized historical fiction for early readers, they would not be the only. Pleasant Company's creation of the original dolls and books spurred a flurry of other younger reader historical fiction books including *The Magic Treehouse* series and eventually the *Dear America* series.[21] These series were overwhelmingly driven by the publishing companies as K–12 curricular changes demanded more access to standard-aligned works of fiction. Scholastic Publishing Company, for example, expanded its educational and book fair arms in the early 1990s in response to new trends in grade-school pedagogy and new curricular standards. Their responsiveness to the success of books like the American Girl series was noted by financial writers of the times.[22] The proliferation of juvenile historical fiction was important; children who were predisposed to an interest in history found ready material in a wide variety of age categories. These books were narrative-driven, exciting, and featured children as the main character, which centered the role of children in history. In other words, these books told a very different kind of history than the textbooks of the 1980s and 1990s.

American Girls, Social History, and Changing Classroom Experiences

In 1989, newly elected president George H. W. Bush called for a dramatic overhaul of the nation's educational standards with the America: 2000 strategy. History was one of the disciplines particularly marked out for improvement with a set of "New World Standards" and a number of commissions and organizations formed to facilitate this new curricular attention.[23] One of these organizations was the National History Standards Project based at UCLA and begun in 1992. Led by renowned historian Gary Nash and esteemed education scholar Charlotte Crabtree, the project was intended not only to overhaul how history was taught in America but to "build a bridge between history educators in the schools and those in colleges and universities, something akin to building a bridge across the Grand Canyon."[24] Before this project, many history standards for K–12 students emphasized content over analysis. The expectation was that analytical skills would come in college education once the content had been covered. The National History Standards Project approached the study of history differently. They emphasized that even young learners in kindergarten through grade four should learn that history was narrative-based and not just about rote memorization.

The National History Standards Project created standards for K–12 students for both American and World history that were widely adopted by various states between 1995 and 2005.[25] Throughout the explanation of the standards, the K–4 committee noted the importance of stories, especially historical fiction, for this group. Their two "Basic Principles" for teaching K–4 history were that students should be exposed to "ordinary and extraordinary" people from the past and that this age group should learn history through "stories, myths, legends, and biographies that capture children's imaginations."[26] Thus, for those thinking about these standards, historical fiction was appropriate content for teaching children about history. This emphasis continued the pedagogical trends of the 1980s and influenced the publishing trends of juvenile fiction begun by Pleasant Company.

In fact, these two basic principles seem to describe the American Girl books completely. Think about how the original American Girl books begin: each book starts with a "family tree" of important characters centering these historical stories within family units. For example, Kirsten's family tree features two nuclear families and her teacher while Samantha's includes domestic servants. These family trees reinforce the centrality of home and family to people in the past and set up a natural comparison for the reader between their family and these historical family units. American Girl stories and dolls also emphasize material culture through clothing, foodways, furniture, toys, and other objects central to these characters' daily lives. This attention to historical detail fulfills the National History Standards Project's demand that children's historical exposures "capture children's imaginations and immerse them in times and cultures."[27] *Meet Felicity* begins with a description of the smells of a merchant's shop in colonial Williamsburg. Felicity smells coffee, chocolate, pine soap, spice tea, and apples. Only a few sentences later, the author describes Felicity's hat—which many readers could not only imagine but touch themselves on their own doll.[28] Through family units and material culture, Pleasant Company aligned their books with the nascent curricular standards developing in the late 1980s and early 1990s.

These standards did more than reinforce the centrality of stories to the study of history, however. The National History Standards Project centered on the experiences of average historical actors far more than previous history standards had done. This shift was in large part because of the kind of historians involved in curriculum reform. The majority of these historians were social historians whose academic interest in the family and daily life meshed well with the standards for elementary school students.[29] Many of these historians were also committed to the idea that underrepresented groups like women and minority groups would benefit from having historical narratives that centered people like them. For example, Standard 4B for K–4 students required students to "Analyze in their historical context the accomplishments of ordinary people in the local community now and long ago who have done something beyond the ordinary that displays particular courage or a sense of responsibility in helping the common good."[30] This standard encouraged teachers to feature lesser known stories in their classrooms that might involve minority community leaders, women, and others who wouldn't be found in major textbooks. This emphasis on ordinary people marked a change from the standards and textbooks of the 1970s and 1980s driven by social historians' emphasis on the historical importance of everyday life.

We also see the way that American Girl stories included this kind of everyday history. For example, Molly's "Lend-a-Hand" project in *Molly Learns a Lesson* details how Molly and other children in the 1940s could participate in the war effort from their hometowns. Throughout the Molly series, readers see how collecting scrap metal fits into the historical context of World War II; Molly's family has a victory garden, they raise money through the Miss Victory pageant, and her father goes off to serve in the war. The American Girl stories, by centering the actions and contributions of young girls, took their role in the world seriously in the same way that social historians were doing in academic scholarship.

The National History Standards Project Standard 5A also points at the role of social history and historians' emphasis on oppressed peoples. According to this standard, Kindergarten through fourth graders should be able to "gather data in order to describe the forced relocation of Native Americans and how their lives, rights, and territories were affected by European colonization and the expansion of the United States, including examples such as Spanish colonization in the Southwest, Tecumseh's resistance to Indian removal, Cherokee Trail of Tears, Black Hawk's War, and the movement of the Nez Perce."[31] This list of examples is fascinating because these topics all point to Indigenous people's agency as well as contingent moments when the course of American history could have changed because of Native people's resistance.

Pleasant Company was already developing Josefina's story when these standards were released. Kaya was released in 2002 and was Nez Perce—a decision that clearly reflected history standards nationwide. In *Meet Josefina*, author Valerie Tripp introduces young readers to the fact that Josefina and her family speak Spanish and the storyline ties Santa Fe to Mexico as Josefina's Abuelito leads caravans between the two cities. Kaya's story series is different than all the previous books because there is no school or birthday stories. A change from the repetition of the stories that reinforced that Kaya's pre–European contact community of Nez Perce people had different values and understandings of the world. American Girl used its readers' expectations to reinforce diversity in historical periods.

The National History Standards Project was not universally acclaimed. In fact, the "history standards controversy" became a part of the American culture wars of the 1990s. National Republican leaders Lynne Cheney and Newt Gingrich, both of whom hold doctoral degrees in history, were particularly chagrined at the standards.[32] Lynne Cheney called the standards the "end of history" while Gingrich and others suggested that the standards were anti-American. The long and drawn-out political debate over the standards obscured the reality; teachers and school districts were already embracing many of the ideas encompassed within these standards because they reflected contemporary pedagogy and the educational publishing field.

Conclusion

Because of the two federal initiatives on education, America: 2000 and the Educate America Act (1994), American students between 1990 and 2005 had a robust education in historical literacy and narrative history. Students who actively engaged with historical fiction outside of the classroom, particularly with works like the American Girl books, which blended historical accuracy into the story, were continually exposed to the history of everyday people, the inherent reality that all individuals were history makers, and the idea that history was about more than paper records of historical events. American Girl readers were also encouraged to see the importance of material culture to understanding the past with the dolls, doll clothes, and accessories that added to their learning experience.

When we look at the history profession today, we can see how this emphasis on the lived experience of regular people has shaped the current makeup of the profession. Scholars of women, gender, and cultural history have continued to increase since the 1980s. Material culture is also a burgeoning field with studies of clothing, goods, consumption, and other related topics growing in recent studies of the historical profession.[33]

The women who earned PhDs between 2005 and 2023 were influenced not only by exciting advances in scholarship but in their early formation as readers in elementary school and in their pleasure reading. As Horrocks and Mahoney observe in their essay in the *Public Historian*, "When we would share this affinity with some professionals, they would dismiss American Girl as 'childish.' . . . Play and levity are integral to how we approach this topic, and even when using our expertise as historians, our goal is not to show what pop culture gets wrong about history."[34] For Mahoney and Horrocks, history and fandom have always gone hand in hand. They recognize that a shared love of historical fiction has led a generation of women to view their world, to borrow a phrase from Gordon Wood with a "historical sense."[35] Other historians have stumbled into this recognition as they have become parents of daughters or stumbled into the fandom and its core belief in the power of a historical story in other ways.[36]

Are historians, particularly female historians, today really the "Felicity Generation"? I'm not so sure that we can untangle the American Girl stories from the K–12 standards championed in the 1990s. American Girl dolls and stories did not emerge fully formed from Pleasant Rowland's head; instead, they were a carefully calculated business decision that was in-line with the direction educators, the education support industry, and historians were already moving. Perhaps this generation of historians would have focused on women, gender, culture, and understudied groups without American Girl. But there is no doubt that American Girl stories have shaped what children learn and that for a particular generation of women, American Girl taught them to expect to find history makers across social, racial, ethnic and religious spectrums. American Girl and curricular standards combined to give these women a solid foundation in social history.

Notes

1. Here is the original blogpost that coined the phrase: Whitney Thornberry, "We Are the 'Felicity Generation,'" *Making History*, January 12, 2016, https://web.archive.org/web/2016 0115072550/http://makinghistorynow.com/2016/01/we-are-the-felicity-generation. To see some of the response to Colonial Williamsburg's posts about the "Felicity Generation" see https://www.facebook.com/ColonialWilliamsburg/posts/are-you-a-part-of-the-felicity -generation-we-have-several-dozen-women-from-all-p/10153425197579576/.

2. Robert B. Townsend, "What the Data Tells Us about Women Historians," (presented at the OAH Annual Meeting, Washington, DC, April 9, 2010), https://www.historians.org /research-and-publications/perspectives-on-history/april-2010/what-the-data-tells-us -about-women-historians.

3. Townsend, 2010.

4. The AHA regularly reports on the state of the field and job market. In their last major analysis of specializations in 2015 they noted that the number of faculty whose focus was women and gender had increased 797 percent over the previous forty years. Those studying "culture" had increased 109 percent. Robert B. Townsend, "The Rise and Decline of History Specializations Over the Past 40 Years," *Perspectives on History*, December 1, 2015, https:// www.historians.org/research-and-publications/perspectives-on-history/december-2015 /the-rise-and-decline-of-history-specializations-over-the-past-40-years.

5. Stephan Risi, et al., "Diversifying History: A Large-Scale Analysis of Changes in Researcher Demographics and Scholarly Agendas," *PLOS ONE* 17, no. 1 (January 19, 2022), fig. 2, https://doi.org/10.1371/journal.pone.0262027.

6. This anthology is full of women like me—Rebekkah Rubin, Laura Traister, Janine B. Napierkowski, and Mary M. Burke all shared with me how American Girl has shaped their scholarship.

7. Matthew Keough, "AHA Member Spotlight: Tara Thompson Strauch," *Making History,* September 24, 2014, https://www.historians.org/perspectives-article/aha-member-spotlight -tara-thompson-strauch-september-2014/.

8. Allison Horrocks and Mary Mahoney, "*American Girls*: A Podcast and a Community," *Public Historian* 43, no. 1 (February 1, 2021): 164–80, https://doi.org/10.1525/tph.2021.43.1.164.

9. Rebecca Brenner Graham talks about the importance of American Girls dolls to academic women in "The Power and Responsibility of American Girl Dolls," *U.S. Intellectual History Blog*, Society for U.S. Intellectual History, September 27, 2021, https://s-usih.org/2021/09/the-power-and-responsibility-of-american-girl/; PhD candidate Holly Genovese also discusses her childhood relationship to American Girl for *Medium*: "American Girl Dolls and Women in History," *Medium*, July 31, 2020, https://medium.com /@hollygenovese/american-girl-dolls-and-women-in-history-f8472075a06c.

10. Graham, 2021.

11. *Superkids* is still an actively used curriculum now published by Zaner-Bloser. For more information on *Superkids* see The Superkids Reading Program, Zaner-Bloser, https://www.zaner-bloser.com/reading/superkids-reading-program/index.php. *Superkids* is still seen as a very effective program; see Geoffrey D. Borman and N. Maritza Dowling. "Student and Teacher Outcomes of the Superkids Quasi-experimental Study." *Journal of Education for Students Placed at Risk* 14, no. 3 (2009): 207–25.

12. James Howard and Thomas Mendenhall, "Making History Come Alive: The Place of History in the Schools," Report of the History Commission of the Council for Basic Education (1982), 54, https://files.eric.ed.gov/fulltext/ED237384.pdf. Other experts who came to similar conclusions include: Allan R. Brandhorst, "Historical Fiction in the Classroom: Useful Tool or Entertainment?" *Southern Social Studies Quarterly* 14, no. 1 (1988): 19–30; Miriam Bat-Ami, "Revising History Learning through the Reading and Writing of Peoplestories: Using Children's Literature in the Multi-Disciplinary Classroom," *Language Arts Journal of Michigan* 7, no. 2 (January 1, 1991), https://doi.org/10.9707/2168-49X.1638; Evelyn B. Freeman and Linda Levstik, "Recreating the Past: Historical Fiction in the Social Studies Curriculum," *Elementary School Journal* 88, no. 4 (1988): 329–37.

13. Sarah K. Hertz, "Using Historical Fiction in the History Classroom," Curriculum Unit 81.ch.10 (New Haven, CT: Yale–New Haven Teacher's Institute, 1981), 5.

14. Carol A. Brown, "A Literature-Based Handbook for Teaching American History" (PhD diss.,University of Dayton, 1993).

15. *Johnny Tremain* was written by Esther Forbes who, although not a trained historian, held an honorary PhD from Clark University and wrote a Pulitzer Prize–winning biography of Paul Revere. *My Brother Sam is Dead* was written by historian Christopher "Kit" Collier and his brother James. Kit was a prolific writer of both academic history and historical fiction and brought careful attention to historical detail to his fictional works for both adults and juveniles.

16. Miriam Bat-Ami, "Revising History Learning through the Reading and Writing of Peoplestories: Using Children's Literature in the Multi-Disciplinary Classroom," *Language Arts Journal of Michigan* 7, no. 2 (January 1, 1991), 6, https://doi.org/10.9707/2168-49X.1638.

17. For examples of these calls for new methods of historical teaching see: Linda W. Rosenzweig and Thomas P. Weinland, "New Directions for the History Curriculum: A Challenge for the 1980s," *History Teacher* 19, no. 2 (1986): 263–77, https://doi.org/10.2307/493801; John J. Patrick, "The Bradley Commission in the Context of 1980s Curriculum Reform in the Social Studies," *History Teacher* 23, no. 1 (1989): 37–48, https://doi.org/10.2307/494599.

18. Mark Speltz, "No Ordinary American Girl," *Public Historian* 43, no. 1 (February 1, 2021): 3, https://doi.org/10.1525/tph.2021.43.1.123.

19. Susan S. Adler, *Meet Samantha, an American Girl* (Middleton, WI: Pleasant Company, 1986), 41.

20. Ira Peck, *American Adventures* (Austin, TX: Steck-Vaughn, 1983), 342, http://archive.org/details/americanadventuro0000peck,

21. Penguin Random House approached Mary Pope Osborne, the author of the *Magic Treehouse* books, in 1991 and asked her to write a series for younger readers.

22. See Stephen Kindel, "When Girls Put Down Their Barbies: Hit Products, Great Demographics and Education Reform Make Staid Scholastic a Hot Publisher," *Financial World*, April 13, 1993, 52.

23. The "New World Standards" were an attempt to show America as a leader in history education and to provide a framework for other countries to follow. These commissions include the National Council on Education Standards, the Nation Council on History Education, and the National Forum for History Standards.

24. "In Memoriam: Charlotte A. Crabtree, Professor of Education Emeritus, UC Los Angeles, 1927–2006," University of California, https://senate.universityofcalifornia.edu/_files/inmemoriam/html/charlottecrabtree.html.

25. This *Education Week* article from 1997 shows how textbook companies began to use the National History Standards in new editions of their textbooks: Kathleen Kennedy Manzo, "Glimmer of History Standards Shows Up in Latest Textbooks," https://www.edweek.org/teaching-learning/glimmer-of-history-standards-shows-up-in-latest-textbooks/1997/10.

26. "Basic Principles," Developing Standards in Grades K–4, UCLA Public History Initiative, accessed January 14, 2024, https://phi.history.ucla.edu/nchs/standards-grades-k-4/developing-standards-grades-k-4/.

27. See both the "Basic Principles" section as well as the Historical Thinking Standards for K–4, which include students learning to read historical texts "imaginatively."

28. Valerie Tripp, *Meet Felicity: An American Girl* (Middleton, WI: Pleasant Company, 1991), 1.

29. Gary Nash was the cochair of the National History Standards Project and an acclaimed social historian. He wrote about the role of social history in modern history standards in his book on the history standards controversy: Gary B. Nash, Charlotte A. (Charlotte Antoinette) Crabtree, and Ross E. Dunn, *History on Trial: Culture Wars and the Teaching of the Past*, 1st ed. (New York: A. A. Knopf, 1997), http://catdir.loc.gov/catdir/bios/random057/97002819.html.

30. "Topic 3: The History of the United States," Standards in Grades K–4, UCLA Public History Initiative, accessed June 20, 2023, https://phi.history.ucla.edu/nchs/standards-grades-k-4/standards-k-4/topic-3/.

31. "Topic 3."

32. For more on the history standards controversy see Nash, Crabtree, and Dunn, *History on Trial.*

33. Risi, et al., "Diversifying History." Of particular interest are the connections between the study of women, gender, social history, and consumption in Figure 2.

34. Horrocks and Mahoney, "*American Girls*," 17.

35. Gordon S. Wood, *The Purpose of the Past: Reflections on the Uses of History* (New York: Penguin, 2008), 11.

36. See for example, Christopher Jones, "#VastEarlyAmerica(n) Girl Doll Books: Reflections of a Father and Historian," *The Junto* (blog), June 7, 2017, https://earlyamericanists.com/2017/06/07/vastearlyamerican-girl-doll-books-reflections-of-a-father-and-historian/.

As American (Girl) as Girl Scout Cookies

Janine B. Napierkowski

If you were a child in the United States in the 1990s, you likely encountered two iconic American brands: Girl Scouts and American Girl dolls. Girl Scouts is a household name because of their cookies, but as the Movement has fifty million alumni, it is also probable that you, a family member, teacher, or neighbor were involved.[1] Perhaps you saw Girl Scouts in their iconic uniforms volunteering in your community, or marching in a local parade. It is also possible you were exposed to American Girl dolls, whether through the dolls themselves, their accompanying books, the catalog, or the magazine. You may have even had a Girl Scout uniform for your doll! It is far less likely that you saw direct connections between the two brands as a child. In fact, Girl Scouts held the trademark for the name "The American Girl," under which it published magazines and books, from 1919 to 1979. Girl Scouts and American Girl continue to share an audience, with both marketing to girls ages seven to twelve (though Girl Scouts also has programs for girls younger and older than that range). Valerie Tripp, author of more than thirty American Girl books, including stories for Felicity, Molly, Josefina, and Samantha, was a Girl Scout as a child, and summed this connection up in an interview with me thusly: "Girl Scouts and American Girl are similar in that they both teach girls to respect themselves and they respect girls."[2] As the Project Coordinator for Cultural Assets at Girl Scouts of the United States of America (GSUSA), I manage the organization's extensive collection and archives. The role of the Cultural Assets department at GSUSA is to preserve, study, and share Girl Scout history through storytelling, inspiring people to honor the past and serve the future, while positioning the founding of Girl Scouts as a pivotal moment in American history.

Seventy-four years before the American Girl Collection was founded by Pleasant Rowland, the largest national girl-focused organization in our country, GSUSA was founded by Juliette Gordon Low. GSUSA is the national umbrella organization that governs 111 Girl Scout Councils in the United States and Girl Scouts Overseas. Mrs. Low, widely known by her nickname "Daisy," started Girl Scouts in March 1912 in her hometown of Savannah, Georgia.[3] The first troop was made up of eighteen girls who all shared a sense of curiosity and a belief that they could do anything. During a period when women in the United States could not yet vote and were expected to abide by strict social norms, encouraging girls to embrace their unique strengths and create their own opportunities was game changing. That small gathering of girls over 110 years ago ignited a Movement across America where every girl could unlock her full potential, find lifelong friends, and make the world a better place. Girl Scouts continues to emphasize inclusiveness, appreciation for the outdoors, self-reliance, and community service today. There is no record of Rowland having been a Girl Scout, but it is possible she was exposed to the Movement as she grew up in Chicago in the 1940s and 1950s when enrollment numbers were high.

Many notable similarities exist between Girl Scouts and American Girl, whether intentional or not, such as their focus on service, responsibility, and respect. Many of the doll characters' books feature storylines of them helping their community and families, just as Girl Scout troops do through earning merit badges, and both model responsibility to young readers and participants. Relatedly, the first Girl Scout handbook was titled *How Girls Can Help Their Country* (1912) and the earliest programming was modeled heavily on militaristic traditions of forming troops, and learning and drilling activities such as semaphore (signal flags). The parallels between Girl Scouts and American Girl continue with their mission statements; Pleasant Company's mission "to champion and celebrate girls" and Girl Scout's mission to "build girls of courage, confidence, and character" even contain similar alliterations.[4] Valerie Tripp told me "American Girl and Girl Scouts both teach you to take yourself seriously, learn how to do things; you're capable and you could be more capable."[5] Girl Scouts and

American Girl are intended to be brands parents can feel good about supporting. While interviewing mothers who purchased American Girl dolls for their daughters, author Emilie Zaslow found "they generally believe that they are contributing to the public good by raising daughters who can be self-determined but also learn to fight for social justice and equality, and that American Girl can help them reach this goal."[6] Relatedly, 90 percent of volunteer Girl Scout troop leaders surveyed in 2020 said they "feel they make a difference in the lives of girls" and 99 percent of parents/caregivers surveyed said "their girl feel(s) like part of a group."[7] Though feminist critiques of both brands exist, it remains true that neither brand has girls rely on sexualization for identity, in the way that fashion dolls or beauty pageants do.

Storytelling was at the heart of the American Girl brand during the Pleasant Company years. According to Rowland, "The stories of American Girls' lives, simple on the surface but rich and rewarding in their emotional truth, will stay with a girl for years to come. . . . That . . . has the power to change her and, through her, change the world."[8] The storylines in American Girl's historical books demonstrate examples of friendship, overcoming obstacles, and activism through relatable and entertaining characters. Of the six "original" (pre-Mattel) American Girl characters, Molly was the only one from a time period during which Girl Scouts existed. In fact, Girl Scouts was mentioned numerous times in Molly's books, including in the "Peek into the Past" (later "Looking Back") sections at the end of the stories where girls could see historical images and read about real events from the time period. Much like Molly did in her stories, during World War II in the 1940s, Girl Scout troops operated bicycle courier services, ran Farm Aid projects, collected scrap metal, and grew Victory Gardens, as well as sponsored Defense Institutes that taught women survival skills and techniques for comforting children during air raids like Molly did with her refugee friend, Emily.[9] Valerie Tripp recalled a personal childhood experience as a Girl Scout that influenced the plot of one of her American Girl books:

> One story specifically about Molly is that in my Girl Scout troop we were studying Hawaii. I suppose we would be accused of cultural appropriation now, but it came from adoration and respect. Hawaii and Alaska had just become states. There was a lot of excitement. And also, my friend Bobby's sis-

ter was so much older than Bobby that she was already married and moved to Hawaii. So, we were very fascinated by Hawaii. And in Girl Scouts, we learned how to make grass skirts out of a newspaper . . . at Girl Scouts, you had the equipment that you needed, literally and metaphorically. Then, I show Bobby how to make a grass skirt. And then we went trick-or-treating and this guy squirted us with a hose. And so, I put that in *Meet Molly*. What I learned in Girl Scouts, I put into the books.[10]

Other "Looking Back" and "Peek into the Past" sections, such as Kit Kittredge's, which was set in Cincinnati, Ohio, in the 1930s, also mention the activities of real-life Girl Scouts during that time period. Similar to Kit's charitable act of donating her coat to a girl in need described in *Changes for Kit*, throughout the Great Depression, Girl Scouts participated in relief efforts by collecting clothing and food for those less fortunate. Likewise, American Girl character Nanea Mitchell's stories depict her participation in war efforts, including buying war bonds, after she lives through the attacks on Pearl Harbor in Honolulu. Real-life World War II–era Girls Scouts ran a "Minute Maids" war bond campaign in Hawai'i and across the nation.[11] Another similarity between the American Girl historical character stories and actual Girl Scouts can be found in Julie Albright's stories. Julie is a young basketball player in the 1970s supporting Title IX, the federal civil rights law that was part of the Education Amendments of 1972, which required girls' sports teams in federally funded schools. Historically supportive of girls' sports, Girl Scouts troops as early as 1914 played basketball and formed their own troop teams.[12] The title of the 1960 Girl Scouts' *The American Girl* fictional collection, *Stories to Live By*, captures the essence of the stories in the American Girl historical character books.

GSUSA used their trademark of the name "The American Girl" for magazines from 1920 to 1979 with the tagline "for all girls." The magazine, which was originally named *The Rally* from 1915 to 1920, was published in monthly issues for a circulation of over five hundred thousand subscribers at its peak.[13] The bulk of the magazine's contents were not specific to Girl Scouts, though some regular features were about Girl Scout activities and badges. Most of the magazine's contents were original pieces like chapters of serialized fictional stories, as well as short stories, poems, recipes, monthly columns, national and international news, and artwork. The covers of many issues were original paintings, and later photographs, commissioned by Girl

Scouts for the magazine, and usually depicted images of girls doing various activities or with animals/in nature. The magazine contained a few advertisements in each issue for things that girls might be interested in such as nylon stockings and current movies. Girls could interact with the magazine by writing to the advice columns, which were later republished as volumes in book form. Valerie Tripp was a Girl Scout and remembers reading Girl Scouts' *American Girl* magazine with her three sisters cover-to-cover in the 1950s and 1960s when she was a Girl Scout.[14]

Pleasant Company started publishing their *American Girl* magazine in 1992, and Mattel continued publishing the title until 2019. Originally, this *American Girl* magazine promoted the company's products, but it also had many features similar to the Girl Scout magazine of the same name, including advice columns, arts and crafts projects, short stories, and interviews with real girls. Pleasant Company's *American Girl* magazine reached 750,000 girls bimonthly, and accounts from many of these girls, as described on the popular American Girl fan podcast *American Girl Women*, say the arrival of the magazine was an exciting day of the month and remember reading it cover to cover, along with the doll product catalog.[15]

Along with the fiction books published by American Girl and Girl Scouts, both brands also have nonfiction books, including Pleasant Company's 1996 *American Girls Club* handbook, which is similarly structured to the Girl Scout handbooks that have been produced since 1912. Additionally, both Girl Scouts and American Girl publish books containing advice, self-help tactics, and activities. American Girl's 1998 publication of *The Care and Keeping of You: The Body Book for Girls*, by Valorie Lee Schaefer, was not the first book for girls about puberty, but it is the one millennial American girls remember best. When compared, Girl Scouts' *The American Girl Book of Teen-Age Questions* (1963) and *The American Girl Beauty Book* (1954) could be seen as forerunners to *The Care and Keeping of You*, as all were compilations of columns published in their respective magazines. Ms. Schaefer shared that "*American Girl* magazine was flooded with letters from girls who were some combination of curious, distressed, anxious, excited and confused about the changes ahead."[16] The introduction of the Girl Scouts' *The American Girl Book of Teen-Age Questions*, which carries the tagline "With Answers by Nancy Davies, *American Girl* Magazine's 'What's on Your Mind?' columnist," reads like it could be from *The Care and Keeping of You*:

Do you occasionally come up against problems too big for you to handle? Does it seem impossible to live up to your dreams of the kind of person you'd like to be? Do your parents seem to resist every move you make toward growing up? . . . You are not alone; and you'll find the answers to these and countless other questions in this book, whose purpose is to help you on the way to becoming a responsible, happy, and well-adjusted woman.[17]

Similarly, Girl Scout's *The American Girl Beauty Book*, first published in 1954 with the subtitle "including answers to questions often asked by readers of *The American Girl* Magazine," gives the advice that a good "beauty program . . . [is] a triple-barreled plan that aims first, for sound health; second, for grooming know-how; and third, for an appealing manner" and reads like it could be a combination of *The Care and Keeping of You* with the American Girl title *Oops! The Manners Guide for Girls*.[18] The press release for *The Care and Keeping of You* describes it thusly:

This age-appropriate, head-to-toe guide gives preteen girls the facts about their bodies and sound advice to help them take care of themselves inside and out. Responding to concerns raised in hundreds of girls' letters to *American Girl* magazine, *The Care and Keeping of You* covers topics ranging from skin care to healthy eating to major changes such as breast development and periods. It does not, however, address issues regarding sexuality, letting parents decide when the time is right to talk about it. The book's friendly illustrations and straightforward explanations promote and invite conversation between girls and their parents when it's needed most.[19]

It is worth noting that GSUSA, as an organization, also does not address sexuality; the official stance since 2003 is that:

Girl Scouts of the USA does not take a position or develop materials on these (human sexuality, birth control, and abortion) issues. We feel our role is to help girls develop self-confidence and good decision-making skills that will help them make wise choices in all areas of their lives. Parents or guardians make all decisions regarding program participation that may be of a sensitive nature.[20]

Beginning in the 1996 American Girl Holiday catalog, a Junior Girl Scout doll-sized uniform was offered as part of the "Girl of Today" collection.

This partnership was an authorized license with Girl Scouts; therefore, American Girl was able to use the trefoil service mark, which is the green three-leaf clover logo used on all Girl Scout merchandise. As the dolls represent nine-year-old girls, the Junior level was chosen to correlate with this age group. This was an "official" uniform with the correct insignia, colors, and style vest of that era's girl-sized uniform. The catalog description of the outfit reads "Dress your Girl Scout for a troop meeting in her official uniform" and even refers to the Girl Scout Promise "On my honor . . ."[21] The license was considered mutually beneficial for both organizations financially. It seems this is the first and only license Pleasant Company engaged in; the license was discontinued in 1999 after the Mattel acquisition, though Mattel has made licensed Girl Scout Barbies as recently as 2014. The other doll "uniforms" shown on the same pages as the Girl Scout uniform, which were soccer and cheerleading uniforms, were for fictional teams.[22] The patches and badges featured on the doll uniform are two membership stars (indicating that the doll is a second-year Junior), the rainbow Bridge to Brownie Girl Scouts (indicating that the doll had been in Brownies before Girl Scouts and completed a bridging project), Brownie Wings (indicating that the doll completed the Brownie program), pin tab with the WAGGGS (World Association of Girl Guides and Girl Scouts) logo and Girl Scout trefoil logo, and merit badges for Ecology, Healthy Relationships, Safety Sense, Self Esteem, Dabbler, Creative Solutions, Geography Fun, Girl Scouting in the USA, World Neighbors, Aerospace, Do-It-Yourself, and Geology.[23] Girl Scouts have been making their own branded dolls since 1920 and selling them through the Girl Scout National Equipment Service catalogs and later in independent and partner department stores. Girl Scouts produced uniforms and branded outfits for 17–19" dolls (which fit American Girl dolls) from 1994–2001 including a Brownie uniform, sweater, sweatshirt, and leggings, a Junior uniform, sweatshirt, leggings, and Cadette and Senior uniforms. These Girl Scout–produced doll uniforms were different from Pleasant Company ones in that they were all one piece, whereas the licensed uniform was separate pieces. The Girl Scout–produced doll uniforms also included directions and patterns for girls to make their own accessories like beanie hats and badge sashes.[24]

A common criticism of both American Girl and Girl Scouts is that both brands can promote consumerism among children and can be exclusive because of pricing and membership fees, though this is where Girl Scouts and American Girl differ. While American Girl is a for-profit company that exists to meet a bottom line, Girl Scouts is a nonprofit organization dedicated to inclusion. Annual membership is $25, which is voted on by representatives from every council, and many councils offer scholarships to cover membership dues.[25] All the money raised through Girl Scout cookie sales stays within the troop, and the members of the troop decide how to spend it. The colorful catalogs are very enticing to children, and the American Girl historical character books describe various items as part of the character's stories, such as jewelry, that are then available for purchase in real-life for your doll, and sometimes in child sizes, too. The dolls possess resale value, with limited-edition pieces sometimes going for much higher than original price. Girl Scouts has produced many types of branded and licensed products since the beginning of the Movement, with items ranging from clothing and accessories to toys and camping equipment, not to mention Girl Scout cookies. And while the two brands do promote positivity, it must be noted that they both also cater to the consumers' market by releasing new items frequently and creating a "collect them all" feeling among their audiences.

As of the time of writing, many adult women with disposable income are collecting American Girl dolls and their accessories. There is a roaring trade for vintage Pleasant Company merchandise, magazines, and catalogs on websites like eBay and Mercari. Doll restoration how-to videos are numerous on YouTube and replacement eyes, wigs, and copy-cat outfits are easily available on websites like Etsy. There is even an American Girl Wiki that lists every product for the dolls' collections, which people can use to identify unknown items. From 1987 to 2023, The Madison Children's Museum, near the headquarters of American Girl in Madison, Wisconsin, held a benefit sale of donated back-stock, which was an opportunity for people to purchase dolls at a discount, as well as an opportunity for American Girl aficionados to gather.[26] There is an American Girl resale store named "Girl AGain" in White Plains, New York, run by the nonprofit Yes She Can, Inc. that sells donated and refurbished dolls to support their mission of "help(ing) teens and young women with autism spectrum disorders and related social and learning disabilities develop transferable job skills to enable them to join and be successful in the competitive workforce."[27] Similarly, there is a market for vintage Girl Scout items with alumni audiences' nostalgic for the simpler times of their pasts and fantasies of youthful freedom driving sales of vintage uniforms and memorabilia. There are several annual "Girl

Scout Collector's Weekends" hosted by councils, and many items can also be found in antique stores. Like the American Girl Wiki, there is a trusted source for Girl Scout collectors in the *Girl Scout Collector's Guide*. Unlike American Girl, Girl Scouts has been producing merchandise for over a hundred years and the market is flush with items like classic badges, and older style uniforms are relatively easy to find.

In addition to the promotion of consumerism, additional criticism of American Girl and Girl Scouts includes the notion that both brands acculturate girls to gender stereotypes and construct traditional gender roles. Toys can shape or prescribe gender norms, and doll play, along with certain Girl Scout badge activities, can be seen as girls' practice for motherhood, similarly to the way toy kitchens can socialize girls to become housewives, but both brands have the potential to be so much more than that. The Girl Scout program teaches entrepreneurship, financial literacy, and accountability, as well as lessons in outdoor skills, first aid, and cultural appreciation, and helps girls develop an understanding of community service. American Girl's characters model independence and activism. Both GSUSA and American Girl have always had female CEOs and/or presidents (the American Girl line has its own president under Mattel). It is easy for critics who may never have read the American Girl books, or been involved with Girl Scouts, to call out both brands for perceived failings, but when compared to other organizations that are religion-based and appropriate Indigenous practices, or dolls that have unrealistic bodies and focus mainly on fashion, it is clear that American Girl and Girl Scouts are different. While both brands can be exclusive because of pricing or locality, their popularity, as seen through Girl Scouts membership numbers and American Girl sales figures, reflects mainly positive individual experiences. The American Girl books, or Girl Scouts alone, if they are the only exposure a girl has to new and different ideas, are not enough to fully form a girl's character or ideals; they are but one small piece of the larger scaffold of learning that is part of American girlhood.

What truly is an American girl? "Katherine," a thirteen-year-old American Girl fan, said, "An American girl is a girl with the opportunity to make history, be a part of history."[28] As part of the research for this essay, a survey was conducted through social media and nearly two hundred people born between 1938 and 2010 responded. Approximately 73 percent of respondents who had dolls during the height of American Girl popularity (late

1980s to the early 2000s) were also Girl Scouts. Ninety-seven percent of people surveyed who had/have the dolls would consider buying them for children in their lives; similarly, nearly everyone surveyed who was or is a Girl Scout would consider registering a child now. The popular American Girl fan podcast *American Girl Women* always closes its interviews with the question "What lasting effects did American Girl have on your life?"[29] A similar question was asked on the survey, while also asking participants the lasting effects of Girl Scouts on their lives. Many people who responded to the survey credited American Girl and Girl Scouts with influencing their career choices, hobbies, and who they were/are friends with. One survey respondent said, "They both empowered me as a girl to realize my potential," while another respondent said, "I think both have helped me feel proud to be a girl."[30] American Girl and Girl Scouts continue to share an audience today with 2.5 million girls registered in Girl Scouts and net sales of $226.9 million for American Girl in 2022.[31]

As a millennial, American Girl doll collector, and Girl Scouts alum who pursued art education and ended up working with public history and material culture in museums, I understand that sharing history through storytelling is a compelling learning method that can inspire people to honor the past while serving the future. American Girl characters help children to connect to something larger than themselves through history, and in Molly's case, the history of the Girl Scout Movement. The parallels between Girl Scouts and American Girl, while not necessarily intentional, are apparent in more than just two organizations using identical names for a magazine and sharing an audience of girls the same ages. As Valerie Tripp, American Girl author and former Girl Scout, says, both organizations teach you to "take yourself seriously, respect yourself."[32] These related brand traits and values, along with comparable missions to serve girls, founders with similar dedication, parallel self-help books based on their magazines, and common positive consumer sentiments cement Girl Scouts and American Girl as analogous history-making brands in the minds of their enthusiasts. The American Girl doll-sized Girl Scout uniform is the ultimate representation of pride and connection for girls involved with both institutions. With thirty-six million American Girl dolls sold since 1987 and Girl Scout alums consisting of one third of the adult female American population, it is easy to see the sheer depth of influence Pleasant Rowland and Juliette Gordon Low's brands created on American girlhood.[33]

Girl Scouts' *American Girl* books and magazines, with American Girl doll Molly in the Pleasant Company Girl Scout doll uniform. From the author's collection.

Notes

1. "Facts about Girl Scouts," Girl Scouts, https://www.girlscouts.org/en/footer/faq/facts.html#:~:text=Girl%20Scout%20Mission,the%20world%20a%20better%20place. "Movement" is the term used by the Girl Scout organization to describe its history.

2. Valerie Trip, interview by Janine B. Napierkowski, June 2, 2023.

3. "Girl Scout History," Girl Scouts, https://www.girlscouts.org/en/discover/about-us/history.html.

4. Emilie Zazslow, *Playing with America's Doll: A Cultural Analysis of the American Girl Collection*. (New York, Palgrave Macmillian, 2017), 28, 31, 175.

5. Tripp, interview by Napierkowski.

6. Zazslow, *Playing with America's Doll*, 28, 31, 175.

7. Girl Scout Research Institute, *The Benefits of Being a Girl Scout Volunteer* (New York: Girl Scouts of the United States of America, 2020), https://www.girlscouts.org/content/dam/girlscouts-gsusa/forms-and-documents/about-girl-scouts/research/GSUSA_GSRI_Troop-Leader-Benefits_Summary.pdf

8. Carrie Anton, Laurie Calkhoven, and Erin Falligant, *American Girl Ultimate Visual Guide: A Celebration of the American Girl Story*, expanded ed. (New York: DK Penguin Random House, 2016), 10, 11, 33.

9. "Girl Scout History," Girl Scouts, https://www.girlscouts.org/en/discover/about-us/history.html.

10. Tripp, interview by Napierkowski.

11. "Girl Scout History."

12. "Girl Scout History."

13. "Circulation Analysis of the *American Girl Magazine*," April 1958, Girl Scout Archive Management System, https://archives.girlscouts.org/Detail/objects/6905.

14. Tripp, interview by Napierkowski.

15. Lisbeth Levine, "A Different Kind of Dollhouse Debuts," *Baltimore Sun*, December 6, 1998, https://www.baltimoresun.com/news/bs-xpm-1998-12-06-1998340163-story.html.

16. Valorie Lee Schaefer, interview by Janine B. Napierkowski, June 20, 2023.

17. Nancy Davis, *The American Girl Book of Teen-Age Questions*, (New York: Random House, 1963).

18. Glynne, *The American Girl Beauty Book*, (New York: Random House, 1954), 4.

19. American Girl, "News Release: American Girl New Body Book for Preteen Girls," September 1998.

20. "Social Issues," Girl Scouts, https://www.girlscouts.org/en/footer/faq/social-isues-faq .html.

21. American Girl catalog, Holiday 1996, Changnon Family Museum of Toys & Collectibles, accessed July 20, 2023, https://toysandcollectismuseum.org/aghd1996.

22. American Girl catalog, Holiday 1996.

23. Mary Degenhardt and Judith Kirsch, *Girl Scout Collector's Guide: A History of Uniforms, Insignia, Publications, and Memorabilia, Second Edition* (Lubbock: Texas Tech University Press, 2005), 478.

24. Degenhardt and Kirsch, 478.

25. "Become a Girl Scout," Girl Scouts, https://www.girlscouts.org/en/get-involved /become-a-girl-scout.html.

26. "American Girl Benefit Sale," Madison Children's Museum, accessed November 13, 2023, https://madisonchildrensmuseum.org/utility/american-girl-benefit-sale/.

27. "About Yes She Can," Yes She Can, https://yesshecaninc.org/about-yes-she-can-inc/.

28. Carolina Acosta-Alzuru and Peggy J. Kreshel, "'I'm an American Girl . . . Whatever That Means': Girls Consuming Pleasant Company's American Girl Identity," *Journal of Communication* 52, no.1 (1999): 139–61.

29. Lindsey Adams-Franke and Laura Tretter, interview by Janine B. Napierkowski, *American Girl Women*, podcast audio, September, 6, 2023. https://open.spotify.com /episode/3ja2VfpdqMP3gcP5Obu3km.

30. Janine B. Napierkowski, "Girl Scouts and American Girl Research Survey," 2023.

31. "Girl Scouts: Fun Facts and Figures," Girl Scouts, https://www.girlscouts.org/content /dam/girlscouts-gsusa/forms-and-documents/about-girl-scouts/facts/GSUSA_facts _English_3–19.pdf; Mattel Annual Report, 2022, https://s201.q4cdn.com/696436908/files /doc_financials/2022/ar/Mattel-2022-Annual-Report-Web-Ready.pdf.

32. Tripp, interview by Napierkowski.

33. "Our Story," American Girl, https://www.americangirl.com/pages/our-story; Girl Scout Research Institute, *The Girl Scout Alum Difference: A Lifetime of Courage, Confidence, and Character*, (New York, NY: Girl Scouts of the United States of America, 2021), https:// www.girlscouts.org/content/dam/gsusa/forms-and-documents/about/research/GSUSA _GSRI_2021_The-Girl-Scout-Alum-Difference.pdf.

The Care and Keeping of Me
A Moment, a Year, a Book, and Returning Home to Our Changing Bodies, Again and Again

Hannah Matthews

On September 1, 1998, my girlhood abruptly changed its shape. Two things happened on that blustery back-to-school morning that fell exactly a month after my eleventh birthday. I got my first period; and a colorfully illustrated paperback hit bookshelves across the nation. The book—published on this fateful day by American Girl, the company that had long furnished me with the beloved plastic dolls and accompanying literature that taught me simplistic and sanitized stories about our nation's history—was called *The Care and Keeping of You.*[1] A glossy-covered oversized paperback, *TCAKOY* was nothing like the four or five American Girl books I already owned, slim chapter books of historical fiction, each series starring a spunky heroine from a specific era and geographical region of my country. Those miniature epics followed a neat and tidy formula, in which our chosen Girl would rescue either her family or a less-fortunate member of her community from (depending on the girl): bullying, racism, poverty, war, various forms of sadness or disappointment caused by America's ills (but with the help of America's charms and strengths, of course, which the reader understands to be innate and foundational to our heroine's personality).

No, this book was an entry into American Girl's self-help collection: nonfiction, contemporary, and purely educational. Over time, from edition to edition, the aesthetic of its illustrations changed. On the cover you'll see

The Care and Keeping of Me: Returning Home to Our Changing Bodies

on shelves now, in the year 2023, three elementary-aged girls of varying heights and skin colors stand together, smiling, in bath towels. One cheerfully holds a toothbrush, her hair wrapped in a matching second towel (for me, a universal symbol of maturity and womanhood. How sophisticated I felt, the first time I figured out that turban-towel technique!). Another is, presumably, just as naked as the other two under her towel, but has still accessorized it with matching hair clips and sandals. And the one in the middle, pale skin like mine and long hair falling loose around her shoulders, is in a wonder-woman stance, barefoot, beaming proudly, hands planted on her towel-clad hips. These girls seem to know, even as they casually enjoy their sleepover party, or their post-swim-practice locker-room hangout, that they're headed for the *New York Times* Bestsellers' List (five million copies sold, at time of writing). Their lashed eyes are inviting and conspiratorial. They have secrets to share with you: about breast development, pimples, hormones, and periods. The book is called *The Care and Keeping of You*. (Its subtitle, then: *The Body Book for Girls*. In later editions, beginning in 2013, it has been divided into two volumes, *The Body Book for Younger Girls* and—seductively, attractively, for those eight- to ten-year-olds who yearn for teenagerdom—*The Body Book for **Older** Girls*).

I've never been particularly skilled at caring for—and, I suppose, *keeping*—myself. My relationship with that self (Should one say *this* self? Here, I am already putting distance between me and her) has ebbed and flowed dramatically for the thirty-six years I've inhabited it. I have not always trusted, nor particularly liked, my body and mind, and I have often questioned the integrity and intelligence of my heart. An inability (or maybe an unwillingness) to extend grace or generosity to my own face, my organs, my skin, my scarred, freckled, and cellulite-mottled limbs—and to the inner thoughts and impulses that steer them through the world—has been a ribbon that runs through every part of my life. It has driven me to self-denial, self-injury, self-destruction. It has informed my aesthetic and dietary choices, my dating habits, my parenting struggles, my creative pursuits. The care and keeping of *others*—my partners, my friends, my pets, eventually my children? Not always easy, maybe, or straightforward, but firmly within my wheelhouse. But the care and keeping of *me*?

And in 1998, on *TCAKOY*'s publication day, when I pulled down my underwear and saw that vivid scarlet bloom, expanding and deepening as if it had a mind of its own, as if it would never stop (I briefly wondered if blood would fill our small downstairs bathroom, our house, the town), that battle to keep and care for myself really kicked off in earnest. I had been taught, in bits and pieces and conversations with a handful of trusted adults—most of whom fumbled—about *menstruation*, a word I loathe as much as the bodily process it describes. I had been told that this moment was special, sacred, a rite of passage into womanhood. I just wanted it to go away, so I could watch *The Disney Channel* or play with my American Girl doll in peace.

The first edition of *TCAKOY* came into my life shortly thereafter, and quickly became a bible of sorts. Its author, a writer for the *American Girl* magazine named Valorie Lee Schaeffer, has spoken of the "cool aunt" voice in which she was determined to speak to the girls experiencing early puberty or prepuberty anxiety and confusion. This aunt, Schaeffer has said, was one of your parents' *younger* sisters. A voice imbued with authority and wisdom but *not*, importantly, that of a parent (or other such form of uncool old grown-up). Schaeffer correctly identified a need, in this pre-texting, pre-social-media landscape, dotted by predecessors like *Our Bodies, Ourselves* and dryly academic sexual health tomes in which an eight- or nine-year-old girl was unlikely to see herself (if she even felt bold enough to *attempt* those dense and annotated texts collecting dust on her mother or grandmother's shelf). Schaeffer gave birth to her own first daughter, in the months before *TCAKOY* was published and hundreds of thousands of girls like me found solace and empowerment in it as we got our first periods, noticed our bodies changing, rode the waves of hormonal mood swings and social-emotional storms endemic of elementary and middle school, and all the dangers and doubts of simply existing in feminized bodies in this world.

Having no cool aunt of my own and no elder sisters, just teenage babysitters and camp counselors (each with their own unique but tenuous grasp on anatomy and reproductive science), the book felt warm, inviting, and—perhaps most important to my terrified, bleeding, self—*safe*. It didn't, like the issues of *Seventeen* magazine I pored over or the MTV music videos I watched in secret when my parents were asleep or occupied in other rooms, leave me with more questions than answers, or an aching (and correct) sense that I would never have access to the belly-chain-adorned flat stomachs and low-rise jeans that would confer the status of (legitimate, worthy, desirable) womanhood. *The Care and Keeping of You* did not (further) frighten or confuse me.

The Table of Contents is divided along the parts of a young body, with sections titled *Heads Up!* (including chapters on acne, hair care, braces, and skincare), *Reach!* (encompassing our underarm hygiene and three separate breast-and-bra-related chapters), *Big Changes* (all pubic-area topics, like periods), and *On the Go* (legs, feet, the ominous "fitness," and issues related to sports and sleep). But the section my thirty-six-year-old-self flips to immediately, including the chapters "Shapes & Sizes," "Food," "Nutrition," and a reprise called "Body Talk: Food," is called, mysteriously, *Belly Zone*.

Because of my decades-long relationship with marijuana, and cold white wine, and possibly some other unnamed illicit substances along the way (not to mention my age, inconsistent sleep and exercise, scrolling on my phone for hours on end in lieu of brain-sharpening crosswords or sudoku puzzles), my childhood memories often feel like riddles, or escape rooms. Can I use context clues to figure out if this memory is taking place in Nantes, France, or in Trenton, New Jersey? Can I envision myself as I *was*, in my lime green jelly sandals and my sparkly butterfly tankini, which shed glitter into the chlorinated depths of backyard pools long forgotten, long confused with one another? Whose house was that, anyway? Reading *The Care and Keeping of You* now, especially in its updated form, feels like an extended bout of deja vu, sprinkled with worry that I might have amnesia. Hadn't there been a step-by-step tampon insertion diagram here, on this page? (There had been, and it was removed from the version meant for younger girls due to concerns from parents that it was "too graphic.")[2] Why isn't sex or pregnancy mentioned at all (aside from a reference to one's period being "practice building a nest") when we know from recent high-profile abortion law cases that nine- and ten-year-olds are becoming pregnant with some horrifying regularity, and struggling to access accurate and affirming information and health care along the way? Why is gender a binary? Why is it assumed so boldly that every one of TCAKOY's millions of readers will identify as a girl, or have crushes on boys?

Quoted in a 2018 feature in *The Atlantic*, written to celebrate TCAKOY's twentieth anniversary, Dr. Cara Natterson (who served as Schaeffer's medical consultant on the book for younger girls, and the author of its sequel) says that while she'd love to publish a book about sex under American Girl's brand name, she feels that there's a place and a time, and that younger girls may need more "safety" from sexual-health-related information as they grow into teenagers. "Tell everyone I would love to write that book with

American Girl, but that's not what these books were meant to do," she says, in her interview with *The Atlantic*. "It's funny how this one book is sort of a safe reminder of what it was like to go through puberty. There's something really comfortable about that."[3] I can't help but wonder, as an adult who remembers those first creeping buds of sexuality and objectification, vines unfurling in *and* around my nine-, ten-, eleven-year-old body, which was commented on and joked about in a sexual way, before I ever reached the age of Dr. Natterson's target *American Girl* readership: Whom does this omission keep safe? I know it would have been safer for me to learn about sex from a "cool aunt"—accurate and affirming—than from the boys on the back of the school bus and the jokes on morning radio shows. I know the very young patients who travel thousands of miles to the abortion clinic where I work could have used a basic primer, and instead have often received only misinformation (or worse, silence) about the things that have been done to and are happening within their bodies. I want to ask Dr. Natterson: "Safe" for whom? But I know that cool aunts can carry their own baggage, their own fears, their own anxiety about the perceptions of the world, of the media, of conservative parents of young readers. Cool aunts can be scared to discuss sex, or feel uncomfortable about sexuality and gender identity, too.

In 2023, a thirty-six-year-old version of myself opens the book again. My life now reads like a list of my eleven-year-old self's wildest dreams, scrawled in gel pen across the pages of a Lisa Frank padlocked diary: *has published a book, has an incredibly kind and funny husband who looks like a movie star, has glamorous and beautiful friends, has an important-feeling career, is a mom.* And yet I am inhabiting a body from her darkest nightmares, weighing more than I know, or care to know. Tattoos. Adult acne. Bisexuality, and casual sex, and outfits she would consider slutty or frumpy or both. *This is actually the body of our dreams*, I tell her now, *because it is the body in which all of our dreams have come true.* My eleven-year-old self rolls her eyes, glares at my thirty-six-year-old body, and silently calls me fat.

That year—the year of *TCAKOY*, the year of my first period—was the year I first noticed the fractures forming, my mother traveling out of state for work and eventually accepting a new position at a prestigious university in another part of the country, and my father staying home to work at our local college and shepherd me through the wilderness of middle school. After that day, when I was given the book which promised to answer all of my bloody questions—my long-suffering American Girl doll went into the

The Care and Keeping of Me: Returning Home to Our Changing Bodies   159

closet. I packed her, and all of her accessories, away that month, a few weeks after my eleventh birthday, removing every trace of her—the bedazzled jean jacket; the plastic, flat-footed Mary Janes (the antithesis, perhaps, of Barbie's terrifyingly spike-heeled pumps); the fluffy white dog on his little leash—from any common or shared spaces of our drafty four-story house. The house I now shared with only my father; my elder brother also having moved out to attend college that summer in my memory of this time.

But wait. Had he? My brother didn't leave for college until I was thirteen or fourteen. So, his absence from the house of my memory is not real; it is a figment of my eleven-year-old self's loneliness, and my thirty-six-year-old self's warped and nebulous timeline, her perception of the empty rooms through which she wandered, bleeding, before she got up the nerve to tell her dad she needed a pad, and could he please go to the drugstore? But the absence of the doll, I know, was real. Her conspicuous absence in the corner of my poster-covered bedroom was commented on immediately, first by my mother and then by a friend one grade below me, who came over to "hang out" (I had stopped saying "play") and wasn't yet ready for nail polish and boy talk to be the sole activities on offer. Exasperated, I finally brought out the doll. I conceded that we could seat her on the bed with us, and include her in our manicure party. I burned with shame, panicked at the thought of this friend telling other girls about what we had done that afternoon at my house. Terrified of anyone finding out that a real-life American Girl With a Period—just like the ones in my new book, smiling as they grew breasts, smiling as they inserted tampons, smiling as they played soccer and rode bikes ("Try to move your body enough so that you are huffing and puffing or sweating for at least 60 minutes every day," *TCAKOY 2* directs its readers in the latest edition)—still played with dolls.[4]

My American Girl doll was not one of the company's historical characters, but instead a contemporary, "look-like-you" doll. Because of their exorbitant cost, I was told by my parents, after years of begging, I could choose ONE (1) doll. And choosing between the most coveted historical Girls—my favorites were Kirsten with her platinum blonde braids and confusing Swedish American lore; Samantha, whom I thought of as "the rich one," with her silky chestnut curls and silver tea set; Felicity, whose cultural context now horrifies me, but who had big hoop-skirted dresses and glamorous green eyes—was simply impossible. If I could only have one, she'd have to be a doll who resembled the popular girls at my school—and thus represented the Ideal Version of Myself that I was sure to become at any moment, if I just bought the right jeans, or was invited to the right pool party. I never named her, because she was not a character in my mind. With her (relative-to-Barbie, and to the girls I saw depicted in movies and magazines) thick, chubby arms and legs, her rounded, blank-but-pleasant face, and her lack of provided backstory or prescriptive character traits, the doll was a projection of all my own girlhood fantasies. Her parents' marriage was *not* slowly unraveling. She was *not* told by a boy at her school that she looked like a dinosaur, or accused on the playground of "giving a hand job" to a different boy, before she knew what that phrase meant. She did *not* bleed into her khaki cargo shorts, caught unprepared and unawares, and with only her dad in the house—nor did anything else gross or embarrassing ever happen to her. She was me, without my flaws and scars. She was me, without my fears. She was me, without my period. And so, she had to go back in the closet, for good.

In September 1998, my knowledge of global politics did yet not extend too far past the impassioned sparkly gel-pen letter I'd written to Bill Clinton that summer, urging him to "help the war-ravaged people of Kosovo" after hearing that phrase on our car radio (always set to NPR) and becoming distraught. When my bimonthly issues of *American Girl* magazine would arrive, glossy and colorful, preteen models beaming up at me from covers full of bright fonts promising me tips for "A Hilarious Halloween Bash" and "How to Solve Your Friendship Problems," I had no thoughts other than: I Must Devour Every Page Immediately. You know that Margaret Atwood poem, the one that goes, *my logic about you is a starved dog's logic about bones*? That was exactly the nature of my primal hunger for all things AG, tearing through jokes from "The Giggle Gang" and binder-decorating tips in the "School Stuff" section of the magazine. Especially now that I was "too old" for the doll, I needed a new portal through which to escape into a world where—even when there were bullies, or pimples, or sick pets, or even fighting parents (I don't recall the magazine tackling divorce, though I'm sure it must have at some point, since much of its readership would have already been intimately acquainted with the concept)—my hair could be straight and shiny, my back-to-school outfit perfectly polished, and my tankini-filled, pineapple-themed summer pool party a smashing success (never mind my own distinct lack of pool, rivaled only by my lack of tankini-clad Cool Girls to swim in it).

The Care and Keeping of Me: Returning Home to Our Changing Bodies   161

"I think I look fat," writes a reader, in the "Body Talk" subsection of *TCAKOY*'s *Belly Zone*. "I know I'm not, but I just can't help feeling this way and hating the way I look. I'm miserable. . . . . I exercise, but I still feel too big. What should I do?"[5]

"If you need to lose some weight," the book answers, "that's one thing. But if your brain is just seeing your body in a way that's not true, you might need help changing that."[6] And then: "Try not to obsess over the mirror until you and your parent figure this out." Which parent, I wonder, would be figuring this out with me? My mother, who had recently become enamored of the Atkins Diet? Or my father, who would warn me about "empty calories" in sports drinks, and speak often with disgust about how our state was named "the fattest in the nation" thanks to all the fast-food drive-throughs. My father who, one night when I was fourteen, out of frustration with my refusal to join him and my mother on a family walk, said to me five words that will remain tattooed on my brain for the rest of my life: "This is why you're overweight!" I wasn't, as it happens, overweight when he said this. I had just recently been informed by my pediatrician that I was in fact *not* on the wrong side of that imaginary, arbitrary red line—whatever number on the scale marked its location—but needed to be mindful, as my weight was "toward the high end of normal." More words I hadn't asked for, more words that I can recite from memory now, as someone who could not tell you the capital of Montana or identify the correct application of Pythagorean Theorem.

"Taking care of your body is a lifelong job," reads the Twentieth Anniversary Edition of *TCAKOY*.[7] "Puberty is a special time of growth and change. Everybody goes through it. It begins for most girls between the ages of 8 and 13," narrates Emily Woo Zeller in the audiobook script of the book, "and it ends **when your body has reached its adult height and size**"—here, thirty-six-year-old me bursts into rueful and angry laughter—"**around ages 15 to 17.**"[8]

To teach eleven-year-old girls, in no uncertain terms, that our high school bodies *are* our adult bodies may promote a certain "keeping" of ourselves, alright—a vigilance, a border and the implied violence of its maintenance, a tight control by any methods those oft-mentioned "trusted adults" may prescribe—but confidence, self-celebration, *care*? My thirty-year-old body, an ocean of cellulite and stretch marks and therapy undertaken to unlearn those very same methods of "keeping" between it and its seventeen-year-old iteration, shakes its head.

In *Body Work*, a shimmering and sharp examination of her own memory and perception, Melissa Febos writes: "Each person who was present for the events of which I have written has a different true story of them."[9] Valorie Lee Schaeffer and Dr. Cara Natterson, I'm sure, have their own true stories to tell, about what has been helpful and harmful to *their* young-girl selves, and to the young girls in their own lives. I know they did not envision the garden that would grow in *my* psyche, for example, from the seeds they planted with their words about fitness and diet and body size. Cool aunts can have internalized misogyny and disordered eating patterns. Cool aunts can be fatphobic, too.

And what am I forgetting, if the granular details of these sentences, written twenty or ten or five years ago by these cool aunts of mine—each syllable and sound—do take up so much of the increasingly limited parking space in the run-down garage that is my memory in adulthood? What am I misremembering, or not seeing clearly, if the calories in one hard-boiled egg are such permanent fixtures, blocking the light from other angles? Maybe I forget the look on my father's face when he apologized, and said that's not what he meant, and all of the ice cream cones he has shared with me, the elaborate meals he has cooked for me and encouraged me to enjoy. Maybe I mischaracterize my mother, who wrestled the very same 1990s and 2000s demons that almost killed me (Weight Watchers, *SELF* magazine, diet yogurt commercials), and so many other demons before those. A woman subjected to nearly four decades more of "friendly" or "healthy" diet and fitness advice than I have been, and who told—and tells—me about how beautiful she finds me, how strong and athletic, how acceptable and worthy and good in all my forms.

In the sequel for readers further along on their puberty journeys, *TCAKOY: The Body Book for **Older** Girls*, food, nutrition, exercise, and weight are a major focus from the very first page. Dr. Natterson, the author of the second volume, is particularly concerned with setting strict and explicit limits around our dietary choices for us. For example: "Even though ice cream is a dairy product, it has so much sugar that it really isn't a healthy source of calcium or protein—it counts as a treat instead."[10] And foods that count as "treats," we learn on the next page, are to be avoided and feared.

The Care and Keeping of Me: Returning Home to Our Changing Bodies   163

"Respecting your body is as much about keeping bad things out of it as it is about putting good things in," Dr. Natterson scolds us, in a sentence that makes perfect sense to my eleven-year-old self, and makes my recovering-orthorexic-and-anorexic-adult-self clutch at my throat and my heart.[11] Keeping bad things out of my body. Bad things. *Bad things.*

The bad things I should try to keep out of my body, I want to scream now—at Dr. Natterson, at the magazine editors, at all of our parents, at my eleven-year-old self, at my *current* self and at any children who have been or may ever be born from this body–might include: cigarettes, excessive alcohol or caffeine, sexual partners who don't respect me or like me, partners who don't treat said body with care and tenderness and the reverence it deserves.

That category does *not* include: ice cream.

But even as my cool aunts forget, or shy away from—or maybe even intentionally ignore, as we all are want to do along the path of unlearning our biases and blind spots—the subjects and concepts that other books for kids have since tackled gracefully and accurately, I don't fault them entirely. American Girl is, in some ways, an inherently conservative and cautious brand. Careful about its history lessons, careful about its depictions of our girlhoods (and of the bodies those girlhoods inhabit, and what we should do with them). That even now, there are *no* fat American Girls; that the scholar Dr. Sami Schalk has written at length about the brand's occlusion of disability and disabled American Girls themselves; that the aforementioned tampon diagram was enough to be considered "controversial" and "too graphic" by a loud minority of parents who bought the book; these should tell us plenty about the America in which we were Girls.[12]

Notes

1. Valorie Lee Schaefer, *The Care and Keeping of You* (Middleton, WI: American Girl, 1998).

2. Allison Pohle, "The Puberty Book Embraced by Preteens, Parents, and Sex Educators Alike," *Atlantic*, August 31, 2018, Accessed January 14, 2024, https://www.theatlantic.com /education/archive/2018/08/the-puberty-book-embraced-by-preteens-and-sex-educators /569044/

3. Pohle, "The Puberty Book Embraced by Preteens, Parents, and Sex Educators Alike," *Atlantic.*

4. Cara Natterson, *The Care and Keeping of You 2: The Body Book for Older Girls* (Middleton, WI: American Girl, 2012), 72.

5. Schaefer, *TCAKOY*, 63.

6. Schaefer, *TCAKOY*, 63.

7. Schaefer, *TCAKOY*, 8.

8. Schaefer, *TCAKOY*, 8.

9. Melissa Febos, *Body Work: The Radical Power of Personal Narrative* (New York: Catapult, 2022), 95.

10. Natterson, *The Care and Keeping of You 2*, 8.

11. Natterson, *The Care and Keeping of You 2*, 9.

12. Sami Schalk, "BeForever? Disability in American Girl Historical Fiction," *Children's Literature* 45 (2017): 164–87.

"Selfish or Annoying"

Etiquette, Gender, and Race in
Oops! The Manners Guide for Girls

Mary Berman

I don't remember who gave me a copy of *Oops! The Manners Guide for Girls*, although I'm pretty sure it was a woman. Maybe it was a gift from my mother, or a well-meaning aunt. I can't have been older than seven or eight. I was one of those children who brought a book everywhere, and since *Oops!* was a very slim book and vaguely educational, it was often the book I was allowed to bring. The minutiae of it have stayed with me all these years; I remember, even now, to put a cherry tomato into my mouth whole instead of biting into it, because they can squirt juice onto unsuspecting fellow diners. Always start from the outside when picking up silverware. Spoon your soup from the closer edge of the bowl. And—believe it or not—you can eat asparagus with your fingers.

The book pitches itself as a book about manners, and it defines manners themselves as "a common-sense guide to getting along with other people."[1] More elaborately: "[Manners] prevent you from being selfish or annoying. They remind you to be kind. They make you better company—and a better person. A girl with nice manners gets respect because she gives it."[2] A better person! Who knew there were morals involved with how you eat your soup?

But the way people—and more specifically women—behave does often impact whether or not they get respect. As children socialized as girls are future women, the message is clear: girls must be taught how to behave. This also impacts what respect looks like. It impacts how girls move through the world, and more pressingly how they are *permitted* to move through the world. Consider my mother's constant directive, when I was eleven years old, to sit with my legs together. Her remark, conveyed with a sigh, that because I'd never learned to twirl my spaghetti, I should be careful when I was older and on a date never to order it. My friend's mother, telling her that she had to learn to ski or else no one "worthwhile" would want to date her. My other friend's mother, telling her not to cut her hair or else all the boys would think she was a lesbian. These lessons are ridiculous and often cruel, built on nonsensical social constructs. But just because something is a construct doesn't mean it doesn't have a consequence. The existence of a book like *Oops!* is predicated on this fact.

How is it that such cosmetic behaviors can mean so much to us? How can a book like *Oops!* cross the wires between manners and morals? Such wire crossing is rooted in the development of etiquette itself; even the term *etiquette* translates as "the little ethics" in French. In his essay "Impolitics: Toward a Resistant Comportment," Trent Hamann references an explicit eighteenth-century shift from courtesy to etiquette, distinguishing between the moralistic quality of the former and the classist quality of the latter:

> In the middle of the eighteenth century, etiquette . . . was unveiled in Lord Chesterfield's letters to his son as a new form of propriety that was clearly different from its historical antecedents, courtesy and civility. Whereas courtesy had been an economy of behaviors radiating from the central figure of the Christian God and civility was focused around the European sovereign, etiquette allowed new and diverse practices of propriety to become multiply defined by various distinct aristocratic groups. In addition . . . etiquette thoroughly disengaged the norms of propriety from their former foundation in religion and morality. The new secular forms of propriety began to exhibit the apparently more trivial characteristics of class convention and fashion.[3]

Today, Merriam Webster defines *manners* not as "a common-sense guide to getting along with other people" but "social conduct or rules of conduct as shown in the prevalent customs."[4] It defines *etiquette* as "the conduct or procedure required by good breeding or prescribed by authority to be observed in social or official life."[5] *Politeness* is the noun form of *polite*, which indicates a quality "showing or characterized by correct social usage."[6] I shan't go down the rabbit hole of defining "correct."

Oops! The Manners Guide for Girls does not distinguish between the three. Apologizing when you've done wrong, letting an old lady take your seat on the bus, and removing your hat in the house are all grouped together. This isn't actually a book about how to be nice to people; it's a book about how to behave—about how *girls* ought to behave. The book does contain some self-awareness about the gendered bent of manners, though without meaningful critique: "Women still get special treatment when it comes to manners: many men will hold a door open for a woman, and women are generally served first in restaurants and at parties. These traditions don't make much sense now that we all know men and women are equal. Lots of people keep them up anyway simply because they like them."[7]

But *Oops!* is also careful to tell its young female readers that above all, they should keep themselves safe: by refusing to give out their information to strangers on the Internet; by politely answering men who ask you a polite question, but refusing to engage beyond that; by, in one example, screaming and hitting someone to get away if they touch you in an inappropriate fashion; by instructing you to "trust your instincts" and get away from people who make you uncomfortable, even if they try to "trick [you] into [a] bad situation" by saying something like, "Don't be rude."[8] In doing so, the book implicitly acknowledges that being a girl or a woman can be dangerous. That the conciliatory behaviors that girls are trained to deploy—that *Oops!*, in fact, is actively teaching—can heighten that danger.

So, to a very limited extent, the book distinguishes between manners, expectations, and realities for people of different genders. But it doesn't, interestingly, distinguish between expectations around manners or behavior for people of different races. All of the illustrative characters in the book are girls of indeterminate early-middle-school age, and the book, in classic American Girl fashion, makes an effort to include racial and cultural diversity in its depictions. There are occasional illustrations of dark-skinned and Asian children, as well as examples of different or unfamiliar customs to expect at, say, a Jewish wedding as opposed to a Christian one, or while traveling abroad.

But one comes away with the impression that as far as *Oops!* is concerned, societal expectations for American girls of every race are the same—which, of course, is not the case. For example, compared to white girls of the same age, Black girls are often perceived as more "adult" than their white peers, requiring less nurturing and support. As a consequence, when they perform behaviors that society considers "bad," Black girls are often thought to be exhibiting malicious intent rather than childlike error, thus receiving harsher punishment for the same behavior.[9] Black children, both boys and girls, are also more readily perceived as loud or angry than white children, and so are expected to be quieter and more controlled.[10]

Separate societal and behavioral standards also apply to other nonwhite children. Asian American children, for example, demonstrate higher levels of academic- and family-related worry than white American children, due at least partially to a different set of parental expectations and personal standards.[11] Latina girls are often expected from a young age to cultivate a caregiving role, more so than their white peers.[12] And so on.

Etiquette has always served the function of excluding members of a nondominant culture, and of training members of those cultures to act in a way that keeps the dominant culture comfortable. As Dinitia Smith wrote in a 2008 *New York Times* review of a biography of quintessential etiquette writer Emily Post, "[Etiquette] books had always been popular in America: the country's exotic mix of immigrants and newly rich were eager to fit in with the establishment. . . . Etiquette books were part of 'the leveling-up process of democracy,' an attempt to resolve the conflict between the democratic ideal and the reality of class."[13] In this tradition, *Oops! The Manners Guide for Girls* walks the razor's edge between societal expectations, gender conformity, and authentic self-expression, meanwhile both reinforcing and undermining the way in which women are expected to behave in a certain manner—including by effacing themselves—in order to garner respect and/or likability. It is also, as you can probably tell, a book that hugely informed my own patterns of behavior.

Oops! The Manners Guide for Girls was published by Pleasant Company Publications in 1997. It was written by Nancy Holyoke, previously a copyeditor for the *New Yorker*, who also cofounded *American Girl* magazine alongside Pleasant Company's founder, Pleasant Rowland. (Holyoke also wrote many of the American Girl *Smart Girl's Guide* books, including not only *A Smart Girl's Guide to Manners*—which is not to be confused with *Oops!*—but *A Smart Girl's Guide to Money* and *A Smart Girl's Guide to Boys*.) To write the book, Holyoke consulted with Dorothea Johnson, founder of a "protocol school" in Washington, DC. By 1997, Pleasant Company had been around for eleven years. It had long since expanded from coaxing little girls into history lessons to teaching them how to navigate the world.

Gendered systems of conduct are probably as old as the patriarchy itself. In *Troping the Body: Gender, Etiquette, and Performance*, Gwendolyn Audrey Foster roots her study of etiquette and conduct literature in writings as old as those of fourteenth-century Italian French poet Christine de Pizan. But in the contemporary era, when we think of American etiquette, most of us think first of Emily Post.

Post was born in 1872, a member of the Baltimore elite, and wrote her first etiquette book, aptly titled *Etiquette*, in 1922. She published ten editions of *Etiquette* over thirty-eight years. Her descendants continue to publish updated editions (as of 2023, we are on edition nineteen) and run The Emily Post Institute, which "[promotes] etiquette based on consideration, respect and honesty."[14]

Post walked (or jogged, or sprinted) so that such etiquette gurus as Amy Vanderbilt, Judith Martin a.k.a. Miss Manners, Martha Stewart, and, yes, Nancy Holyoke could run. Indeed, the regulations laid down in *Oops! The Manners Guide for Girls*, as well as elements of its style, are rooted very explicitly in those put forth by Emily Post. For example, Post's etiquette books used little narratives to illustrate her points, featuring a cast of evocatively named characters, like "Mrs. Newly Rich." In a similar narrative fashion, *Oops!* shows its main character, the second-person "you," reacting to various etiquette boggles, such as your brother's girlfriend dying her hair an ugly color and asking what you think, or you joining a group of your friends and discovering that they're actually having a party they didn't invite you to. (The characters in *Oops!* have much more standard names than "Mrs. Newly Rich," although one of them *is* named Squidge Mealy.) Additionally, the etiquette genre often uses declarative statements, rhetorical questions, and "quizzes" that "foster a model of instruction," all of which are devices that one trips over page after page in *Oops!*: a straightforward directive to "address a woman before a man," a rhetorical question presenting a list of questions and asking which of them would be considered rude (hint: all of them), and—believe it or not, given that this is a book for children—a personality quiz about your hosting skills.[15]

Oops! posits, again, that "a girl with nice manners gets respect because she gives it," and "manners are a kind of code. You use the code to let people know that you're kind and respectful. At the same time, others read the code to decide what they can expect from you."[16] Similarly, Post's *Etiquette* draws a causative line between behaving in a mannerly fashion and being perceived as kind, respectful, or here, "solicitous" and "charming":

> Women reading etiquette texts were encouraged not only to observe gender defined behaviors designed to supposedly protect themselves but also to cultivate an affected air of solicitude. In Post's 1922 etiquette manual, *Emily Post's Etiquette: In Society, in Business, in Politics and at Home*, Post includes an essay entitled "The Bow of a Woman of Charm." Post adopts a friendly conversational tone, encouraging women to "acquire a charming bow. It is such a short and fleeting duty. Not a bit of trouble really; just to incline your head and spontaneously smile as though you thought 'why, there is Mrs. Smith! How glad I am to see her!'"[17]

Similarly, Post and *Oops!* are equally concerned with movement and bearing. From Post: "The practice and cultivation of outward affectation in performance is continually stressed. . . . 'Her body is perfectly balanced[,] . . . she holds herself straight[,] . . . she takes steps of medium length, and . . . [she] walks from the hip, not the knee. On no account does she swing her arms.'"[18] From *Oops!*: "Hold your head up. . . . Hold your head high and don't shuffle your feet. . . . Try not to slump."[19]

However, *Oops!*, being a book for young girls, sets itself apart by tying these rules to positive lessons about self-esteem: "Your body says a lot about what you think about yourself. Take charge of your posture, and you're saying 'I'm a girl who's ready for the world.' Others will see you that way too. . . . Stand straight with your shoulders back. Bodies come in all sizes and shapes. Don't let anybody, but *anybody* [sic], make you feel bad about yours."[20] Pleasant Company and American Girl, after all, self-identify in their branding materials not, like Post's *Etiquette*, as attempting to train their readers in the ways of "Best Society," but as "inspiring," training young girls to be not only well-behaved according to the dominant paradigm but to be resilient, confident, and kind."[21] Which is why it's so interesting that— even with this open-faced dedication to young female empowerment, or in spite of it—the actual lessons in *Oops! do* cleave so neatly to those in early editions of *Etiquette*, the ones concerned not with inner self-esteem but with Society's impression of a person.

Why should this be, in spite of apparent differences in motive? Foster writes, "Power is tied not only to institutions and their purveyors but also to the corporeal body, specifically performativity."[22] In other words, a woman's willingness and ability to behave in a cleanly circumscribed, solicitous fashion with her body correspond, in both midcentury and contemporary American society, to whatever level of power she is able to wield. And *Oops!* and *Etiquette* are both fundamentally concerned with power:

> The fragmentation of the performing body in the utopic, idealized home reveals an ideological concern with maintenance of gender, race, and class order. . . . The body of the reader receives discipline from the author, who continually regulates the desired performance in a manner that obsequiously urges reader identification through textual strategies designed to submit her to a system in which she is consistently urged to deny the "natural" self. One particularly important reason for a critical examination of the popular etiquette book is that the performance of etiquette allows for the signification of gendered roles that are "engendered before being fixed in the world." . . . If contemporary critical theory examines these charged zones of "power and space" in societal discourse, it is the etiquette text that first created them.[23]

Oops! slots cleanly into this tradition of controlling, even imprisoning, the body in order to maintain existing strata of class, gender, and race; even though—or perhaps because!—it's intended not for grown women but for younger girls. Indeed, *Oops!* is representative of the ways in which American women and girls are encouraged to *think* of themselves as powerful, in spite of the glaring evidence of the ways in which they're not, not only in terms of things like a gender pay gap, antiabortion legislation, and disparity in leadership representation, but the more elementary-school realities of the fact that girls are expected to behave a certain way in order to be respected or taken seriously, whereas boys are permitted significantly more flexibility in their behavior. That's why a book like *Oops!* exists in the first place, and the book freely acknowledges this: "[With manners], you'll look more confident, and that can often make you feel more confident, too. . . . A little work on the outside girl lets the girl inside shine through—and that, of course, is the entire point."[24] Not *person*. Girl.

These rules of etiquette, both old and new, are also highly concerned with a woman or girl's utility. Books like Post's *Etiquette* are deeply preoccupied with how a woman manages the domestic sphere: keeping a clean and fashionable home, entertaining guests, exhibiting hospitality, and generally maintaining and prioritizing the comfort of people who are not her. Similarly, girls in *Oops!* are encouraged to show "signs of deference," to ignore "the little imp inside . . . that says 'Me first!,'" and—in one memorable section—to serve a table properly.[25] Such expectations are reflected everywhere, not just in decades-old etiquette books but in life. How many dinners and parties have we all attended where the women offer to help and the men do not, and all the women end up in the kitchen while the men hang around and chat? For this reason, I've actually started biting my tongue when the urge strikes me at a party to offer to help clean up—a behavior that both *Oops!* and *Etiquette* certainly would not condone.

Of course, this question of utility, just as it cannot be divided from gender, also cannot be divided from race. Throughout American history, people of color and—given the horrific legacy of chattel slavery—Black people in particular have been relegated to positions of what Shannon Winnubst, in her essay "Make Yourself Useful!," calls utility: *worker, helper, servant*, even, of course, *slave*; almost never permitted access, and certainly not intrinsic access, to the societal roles with which books like *Etiquette* and, by extension, *Oops!* concern themselves. Winnubst suggests that this very "valuing of that which is useful as the ultimate criterion for all actions" operates so deeply that it becomes "a sensibility . . . written on and in and through our bodies, shaping us to fulfill its needs without even the question of our consent. An imperative aesthetic style. An unwritten code. An etiquette."[26]

It may seem unexpected to frame etiquette in this way. As Foster elucidates in her writings on Emily Post, "Those on the outside of the boundaries of the working class family, including people of color . . . are largely ignored by Emily Post, with the exception of domestics who are bodily troped as extensions of a proper (white) home. Not surprisingly, few etiquette books have been written by and for African Americans."[27] But Winnubst adds: "Reading utility as a primary force in shaping proper comportment, we begin to see how this imperative shapes all bodies—racializing, sexualizing, gendering, classing, even spiritualizing and nationalizing according to how bodies fall on either one or the other side of the command, 'Make yourself useful, boyyy.'"[28]

In other words, if etiquette is synonymous with rules of behavior and comportment, and if the question of utility is ingrained in those rules, and if the very question of utility is tied, as indeed it is, to race and gender—if simply raising the blood-deep specter of utility begs the question of *whose* utility to *whom*—then etiquette *cannot* be divorced from racism and sexism. Etiquette *is* racism and sexism, no matter how much language about girl power you throw in there. Indeed, as previously stated, *Oops!* does not actively acknowledge differences of race at all, the way it at least nominally does with gender.

These race-based rules of comportment are also reflected in societal customs. Hamann points out that Rosa Parks, when refusing to give up her bus seat to a white man in Montgomery, Alabama in 1955, was fined specifically for "disorderly conduct": "In the moment when she refused to move, it wasn't the letter of the law that became an issue for the passengers on the bus. It was the discomfort produced by an impolitic challenge to *custom* (emphasis mine), behavior, and the unwritten rules of proper orderly comportment."[29] *Oops!*, and other etiquette books like it, trained the generation of American girls that read it to *adhere* to custom, even when it might be more beneficial for those girls *not* to do so. *Oops!* does advise girls to prioritize their own safety, as for example when talking to a stranger, but not in a way that ever goes beyond the boundaries of social mores. Above all—unlike Post's *Etiquette*, which is concerned primarily with "Best Society" without meaningfully considering the question of whether acceptance into that Society is actually worth striving for; or questions of racial utility, which don't concern themselves at all with the well-being of their subject   *Oops!* insists that such adherence to custom is *good* for girls! Per *Oops!*, manners make you "a better person"; they give you "the tools to handle all kinds of situations"; a "girl with nice manners" "finds confidence she never knew she had."[30] Here, a girl or woman is better off knowing how to behave within the boundaries of custom, not only externally but internally.

And to some extent, who is to say *Oops!* is wrong? Just because etiquette is inherently racist and sexist, that doesn't mean that learning to operate according to those rules doesn't give a person—say, for example, an American girl—a certain amount of a certain type of power; at least within the framework of American society, which is a framework in which she is probably, especially at the young age of *Oops!*'s target audience, compelled to operate.

Oops! is, again, a book that affected me deeply. For better or worse, it did teach me to eat my food in a particular way, to address older people before younger people, to introduce people to each other in conversation, to give up my seat on the bus, to write thank-you notes, to use my fish fork for my fish. (Although I still never remember if you're supposed to cross your silverware or leave it parallel when you're finished with your meal. And to my mother's horror, I still can't twirl spaghetti.) I'm also white; I strongly suspect I'm personally unable to perceive thousands of ways in which rules of etiquette and societal expectations reflect differently off a Black or otherwise nonwhite body than off mine, the same way that I frankly doubt that even the most enlightened man is able to really grok the expectations, both internal and external, that are placed every millisecond upon the body of a woman. Only later, as an adult, did it occur to me to examine the patterns of behavior that I learned in *Oops!*, to consider both their intended and their actual effects. I work every day to hang on to the behaviors that feel important, and to discard or unlearn the ones that don't. Above all, I try to be careful not to judge other folks for arbitrary patterns of behavior that don't fit into what's commonly regarded as *custom*.

Given this, I must ask myself: Was *Oops!* right? In spite of everything I've written here, did learning "manners" make me more confident, kinder, better? Did it make it easier to live my life?

I would love to say no. But I find, in the end, that it's often impossible to tell.

Notes

1. Nancy Holyoke, *Oops! The Manners Guide for Girls* (Middleton, WI: Pleasant Company, 1997), 3.

2. Holyoke, *Oops!*, 3.

3. Trent H. Hamann, "Impolitics: Toward a Resistant Comportment," in *Etiquette: Reflections on Contemporary Comportment*, ed. Ron Scapp and Brian Seitz (Albany: State University of New York Press, 2007), 59–60.

4. Merriam-Webster.com Dictionary, s.v. "manner," accessed July 3, 2023, https://www.merriam-webster.com/dictionary/manner.

5. Merriam-Webster.com Dictionary, s.v. "etiquette," accessed July 3, 2023, https://www.merriam-webster.com/dictionary/etiquette.

6. Merriam-Webster.com Dictionary, s.v. "politeness," accessed July 3, 2023, https://www.merriam-webster.com/dictionary/politeness.

7. Holyoke, *Oops!*, 17.

8. Holyoke, *Oops!*, 89.

9. Phillip Atiba Goff, et al., "The Essence of Innocence: Consequences of Dehumanizing Black Children," *Journal of Personality and Social Psychology* 106, no. 4 (2014): 526–45, https://doi.org/10.1037/a0035663.

10. "Prospective Teachers Misperceive Black Children as Angry," American Psychological Association, accessed October 16, 2023, https://www.apa.org/news/press/releases/2020/07/racialized-anger-bias.

11. Anne Saw, Howard Berenbaum, and Sumie Okazaki, "Influences of Personal Standards and Perceived Parental Expectations on Worry for Asian American and White American College Students," *Anxiety, Stress, & Coping* 26, no. 2 (March 15, 2012): 187–202, https://doi.org/10.1080/10615806.2012.668536.

12. Denise A. Longoria, Nelda M. Rodriguez, John M. Gonzalez, and Romeo Escobar, "Latina Daughters and Their Caregiving Roles," *Journal of Mental Health and Social Behaviour* 2, no. 2 (June 29, 2020), https://doi.org/10.33790/jmhsb1100120.

13. Dinitia Smith, "She Fine-Tuned the Forks of the Richan Vulgars," *New York Times*, October 16, 2008, https://www.nytimes.com/2008/10/17/books/17book.html.

14. "About," The Emily Post Institute, accessed July 3, 2023, https://emilypost.com/.

15. Holyoke, *Oops!*, 24, 94, 50; Gwendolyn Audrey Foster, *Troping the Body: Gender, Etiquette, and Performance* (Carbondale: Southern Illinois University Press, 2000), 3.

16. Holyoke, *Oops!*, 3, 10.

17. Foster, *Troping the Body*, 7.

18. Foster, *Troping the Body*, 8.

19. Holyoke, *Oops!*, 14–15.

20. Holyoke, *Oops!*, 14.

21. Emily Post, *Etiquette in Society, in Business, in Politics and at Home* (New York: Funk and Wagnalls, 1922), https://www.gutenberg.org/files/14314/14314-h/14314-h.htm; "Our Story," American Girl, accessed July 3, 2023, https://www.americangirl.com/pages/our-story.

22. Foster, *Troping the Body*, 9.

23. Foster, *Troping the Body*, 2.

24. Holyoke, *Oops!*, 14.

25. Holyoke, *Oops!*, 16, 18, 72–3.

26. Shannon Winnubst, "'Make Yourself Useful!'" in *Etiquette: Reflections on Contemporary Comportment*, ed. Ron Scapp and Brian Seitz (Albany: State University of New York Press, 2007), 153.

27. Foster, *Troping the Body*, 14.

28. Winnubst, "Make Yourself Useful!," 153–54.

29. Hamann, "Impolitics," 65.

30. Holyoke, *Oops!*, 3.

PART 4

MAKING AMERICAN GIRL OUR OWN

"Maybe I Could Be Part of the Story Too"

Making Meaning and Understanding American Jewish Identity through American Girl

Rebekkah Rubin

When American Girl released a Hanukkah outfit and gift set in 1996, Jewish kids across the United States coveted the "soft angora sweater sprinkled with sparkling rhinestones" and the "skirt of royal blue velvet," along with the doll-sized menorah, candles, dreidel, Star of David necklace, and gelt (chocolate coins).[1] As one of those Jewish kids in the nineties, Laura remembers how she felt upon seeing the Hanukkah outfit and accessory set: "I BEGGED my parents for it," she said. "I kept all of the pieces and the outfit in the box it came in, carefully putting them back after I played with them every single time."[2] For the first ten years of American Girl's existence, there was no Jewish representation. The original three historical characters, all white and Christian, complete with Christmas books and dresses, set the moral tone for the company.[3] Pleasant Rowland's conceptualization of what it meant to be "American" necessarily excluded any character who was not Christian; the Christmas-centric book formula left no room for a non-Christian character and, consequently, positioned Jewish pasts outside of the American norm.

By selling dolls alongside books, the brand models how consumers of all ages should engage and make meaning with their dolls.[4] Yet, how American

Girl shapes collectors' understandings of Jewish identity has its limits due to the fluid nature of the dolls' identities once they are in the hands of the consumer. For adult collectors, both Jewish and not, American Girl's Jewish dolls, stories, and accessories are a means to learning about and interacting with Judaism, Jewish history, and Jewish culture. And, for Jewish adult collectors, interacting with American Girl's Jewish dolls also involves pushing back against the narratives created by American Girl, using dolls to make sense of their own identities, and sharing their Jewish culture and identities with other adult collectors in online fandom spaces.

My entry into this topic is twofold; I am both a public historian and an adult doll collector who participates in the American Girl fandom online. I also have created an online public history project where I use American Girl dolls to educate about history and Jewish culture.[5] The American Girl fandom is vast, and adult doll collectors flock to various social media sites, including Instagram, Facebook, and YouTube, to share their collections with others and find friends who share their interests. According to Rebecca Joan West, doll collectors, who are often stigmatized for their hobby, seek community among other doll collectors online.[6] These online fan communities have distinct attributes and cultures, and adult doll collectors engage in these fandom spaces for varying reasons, whether to stay apprised of American Girl releases, to share their collections with others, to create and share videos or photographs of their dolls, or to find like-minded friends. My primary focus here is the American Girl fan community on Instagram (called AGIG), where collectors interact with American Girl dolls, characters, and collections by building on American Girl's canonical stories and creating their own original stories and characters, often sharing narratives alongside photos of dolls. While other studies could focus on the ways in which non-Jewish collectors use Jewish dolls and accessories, here I am amplifying the voices of Jewish collectors and how they make meaning using American Girl dolls in the overwhelmingly white and Christian fandom. To include the widest number of voices possible, I circulated a survey to Jewish American Girl adult collectors who participate in AGIG, as well as Jewish adults who may not actively collect dolls, but who interact with some AGIG accounts and grew up with American Girl dolls and books.

In this essay, I briefly discuss American Girl's Jewish characters and collections before turning my attention to the ways Jewish collectors use American Girl dolls to understand and craft Jewish identity.

A Century (Almost) of Jewish American Culture in Four Dolls

Due to American Girl's original emphasis on Christmas morality, Jewish representation has been minimal since the brand's founding. It was not until 1996, when the brand released a Hanukkah outfit and accessory set, that consumers could purchase any specifically Jewish items. Because there were no Jewish dolls available for sale at the time, consumers had to use these Hanukkah accessories with either a doll from the contemporary American Girl of Today line—noncharacter dolls that came in a variety of face mold, hair color, and eye color combinations—or with a canonically Christian historical character.[7] Additionally, the lack of options available for the original American Girl of Today dolls—almost all of which had straight hair—limited how Jewish consumers could relate to the dolls in this line.[8] Although this line, which is currently known as Truly Me, has expanded greatly since its release, it remains the subject of critique by scholars and collectors for its lack of diversity. Scholar Victoria Davion recounted a visit to the American Girl store in New York, where an employee picked out the same doll to represent her, a self-described Middle Eastern Jew, as her young friend who had "Asian features."[9] As of writing, the Truly Me line includes both a blue velvet Hanukkah dress and a Hanukkah sweater that features an image of a smiling latke in a pan.

In 2001, the brand launched the Girl of the Year line with their first Jewish character, Lindsey Bergman. However, Lindsey's Jewish identity was obscured in promotional materials and her limited collection did not include any physical markers of her Jewishness.[10] Additionally, as the brand retired the Hanukkah outfit two years prior, the only specifically Jewish accessory one could purchase for Lindsey was the Hanukkah menorah set in the contemporary line. The Lindsey doll and her accompanying book, *Lindsey* by Chryssa Atkinson, were only available for one year—a characteristic of the Girl of the Year line. In 2009, American Girl released their first Jewish historical character, Rebecca Rubin, whose stories take place on the Lower East Side of New York City in 1914.[11] Unlike Lindsey, Rebecca's Jewish identity is visible in her book series, authored by Jacqueline Dembar Greene, and in her collection, which includes the only Judaica sold by American Girl that is not part of a Hanukkah set—a loaf of challah and Shabbat candlesticks—although much of her collection has been quietly retired in recent years. In February 2023, American Girl released two new historical characters, Isabel and Nicki Hoffman, twins from 1999 living in an interfaith Christian and Jewish family; however, the only references to their Jewish identity in their collections or in their book, *Meet Isabel and Nicki*, by Jennifer Rozines Roy and Julia DeVillers, are mentions of celebrating Hanukkah.

"No Coherent Approach to Using History": Educating in the Fandom

My own entry into the American Girl online fandom coincided with the period between 2009 and 2016, which scholar Emilie Zaslow identifies as an era when American Girl had "no coherent approach to using history as a selling point for dolls."[12] The rebranding of the historical line included eliminating much of the educational aspect of the brand. As a result, in American Girl fan spaces, I encountered many adult collectors who owned Rebecca or Lindsey, yet had very little understanding of Judaism or Jewish culture, including collectors who told me they have only ever encountered Judaism through American Girl, or that the brand was their introduction to Jewish culture.[13] As Jews make up just 2.4 percent of the population of the United States and 0.2 percent of the population worldwide, this is unsurprising.[14] However, without guidance from American Girl, many collectors engaged in behaviors erasing the Jewish identities of American Girl's characters, and, often, imposed Christian identities on Rebecca and Lindsey by sharing photographs of the dolls in specifically Christian contexts, including donning cross necklaces or Christmas, Easter, and First Communion dresses, posing with Christmas trees, and, on occasion, portraying scenes from the New Testament. By sharing photographs online of their canonically Jewish dolls in Christian contexts, non-Jewish collectors are not only shaping their own understanding of Jewish identity but also the understandings of other non-Jewish members of the fandom.

In this environment, I began educating about Jewish history and culture on AGIG to provide non-Jewish collectors more meaningful ways of interacting with their Jewish dolls. Over the years, my educational efforts have expanded from Q&As on holiday traditions to leading other collectors in bake-alongs of Jewish recipes representing Ashkenazi (Central and Eastern European), Sephardi (Iberian), and Mizrahi (Middle Eastern and North African) traditions to hosting discussions of books on Jewish history and culture, as well as antisemitism. To tell a multitude of stories that reflect the vast Jewish experience, I have created my own historical and contemporary Jewish characters, and I often share Instagram posts drawing on the lived experiences of Jewish girls in the past. As my Instagram project has expanded, so too has the number of Jewish collectors on AGIG, many of whom share their own insights and experiences with Judaism and Jewish culture. Although the education about Judaism and Jewish history I share was originally intended for non-Jewish doll collectors, many of my project's followers are now Jewish doll collectors as well as Jewish folks who do not collect dolls, but who want to learn more about Jewish history and culture, particularly women of my generation who grew up without a Jewish American Girl doll to represent them.

"A Roadblock to Full Relatability": American Girl's Canonical Characters and Collections

Before any Jewish characters or accessories were available from American Girl, the absence of Jewish representation distanced Jewish kids from the brand. Both Vera and Aviva remembered writing to American Girl as children and asking the brand to create a Jewish character. For Anneliese, the ever-present Christian stories led to frustration when she was a child. She recalled, "I could relate to the characters so much, but there was always a roadblock to full relatability [because of their Christianity]." In the absence of a Jewish character, Jewish kids had to make do with what limited options were available. Aviva gravitated toward Swedish immigrant Kirsten because her "immigrant narrative and distinct cultural identity was the closest I could come . . . to finding my own family history and version of Americanness in one of the characters." For one collector, in whose family American Girl dolls were the "big Hanukkah gift," deciding which doll to ask for meant determining how "not-Christmas-y" each character was. "I owned some of the Christmas books for the historical characters, but I didn't want to own physical items that were Christmas-y, which is why I felt, even at the time, I had to stay clear of characters like Kirsten, or Josefina, because her necklace looked like a cross," she said.

The awareness that their families' stories were not being told was present for many Jewish collectors who also had American Girl dolls as kids.

According to Angela, "Even as a child, I noticed I wasn't seeing my own family's story in American Girl's original characters. Our experiences as Jews within the timelines of the historical characters would not have been the same as our Christian counterparts." Drew felt similarly: "I think American Girl was one of the first places I really saw how prevalent Christianity is in this country." Another adult collector expressed that playing with non-Jewish dolls was merely another way she felt different from other kids because of her Jewish identity. "We are constantly reminded from birth that we are different in many ways. [My American Girl dolls] were a quiet reminder of [that] difference," she said.

The introduction of the Hanukkah outfit and accessory set in the contemporary line marked the first time Jewish kids saw themselves represented by the brand. "American Girl always made me feel othered, since there weren't any Jewish dolls. The Hanukkah set made me feel like maybe I could be part of the American Girl story too," Laura said. Aviva, who is Orthodox, also remembers her excitement when American Girl released the Hanukkah outfit, particularly as so few outfits in the contemporary line adhered to Orthodox standards of modesty. "I was BLOWN AWAY . . . especially because it was modest by Orthodox standards. I could get a soccer uniform or a hiking outfit for my doll that I liked, but hardly anything that I actually would wear myself," she recalled.

For American Girl adult collectors who grew up with the brand, Lindsey's release in 2001 was a departure from Jewish identity being relegated to a Hanukkah outfit and a menorah set. Adult collectors, including myself, remember feeling ecstatic that we were finally represented with a character doll within the glossy pages of the American Girl catalog. Because Lindsey was released when one adult collector was in the target audience, she "never felt the brand as a whole was alienating despite the overall emphasis on Christmas." However, nothing in Lindsey's collection related to the character's Jewish identity; without reading her accompanying book, *Lindsey* by Chryssa Atkinson, it is possible to completely overlook her Jewishness. And, indeed, among non-Jewish doll collectors—and some Jewish collectors—in the online fandom, there is a lack of awareness that Lindsey is Jewish.

While the plot of *Lindsey* involves, among other things, preparations for her older brother Ethan's forthcoming bar mitzvah, collectors who read the book as children tended to have more positive responses to it than those who read the book as adults. "At around age eight . . . I read Lindsey's book with my dad and I loved it," Nell, who runs a Jewish meme account on AGIG, recalled. "My brother was becoming a bar mitzvah . . . and I thought it was so cool that my life was mirrored in a medium I care so much about." Anneliese disagreed: "Lindsey deserves more than just an off-handed mention of a bar mitzvah," she said. Despite the emphasis on a Jewish life cycle event, there is little in *Lindsey* about the eponymous character's own relationship with Judaism and Jewish culture.

The few references to Lindsey's Jewish identity in her book privilege assimilation to American culture. This is primarily expressed by disparaging traditional Ashkenazi Jewish foods—one of the many ways non-Jews historically marked and continue to mark Jews as Other. Examples include describing a matzo ball as a "slippery, dumpling-like blob of mush" and complaining about chopped liver and pickled herring, wishing instead for "normal stuff, like cookies or potato chips."[15] Lindsey's internalization of the disdain for traditional Ashkenazi Jewish foods and her preference for foods coded as "American" emphasizes the Otherness of Jewish foods, and, consequently, the Otherness of Jewish culture as a whole. One adult collector recalled that the ways she played with her Lindsey doll emulated the privileging of assimilation, as modeled by American Girl: "I definitely took out my own angst about my 'Jewish hair' on my Lindsey doll. I spent about as much time trying to make her hair 'nice' like my friend's [straight-haired, blonde] Kit doll as I did on my own, very curly, frizzy hair. It did not work." Although Lindsey was retired a year later, the privileging of assimilation would continue to model how kids and adults interacted with American Girl's Jewish characters.

American Girl's introduction of Rebecca, eight years later, drew many Jewish folks back to the brand as adult collectors. I also became reinterested in American Girl at this time, as I could not resist the lure of a Jewish historical character, particularly one who happened to share my name. Vera, who is a cantor, said: "I feel less diffident about playing with a doll as an adult knowing that Rebecca's Jewish identity is helping me think of fresh and engaging methods (doll-related or otherwise) to open Judaism up to inquiring and fun-loving Jews of all ages."[16] She has incorporated her Jewish practice into her doll collecting, including hand-sewing a *tallit* (prayer shawl) for her Rebecca doll. Similarly, Nell attributes her scholarly interests in the American Jewish diaspora to Rebecca's books.

However, in Rebecca's book series, American Girl again emphasizes the Otherness of Jewish culture. Scholar Emilie Zaslow contends that Rebecca's books "often [portray] those who are willing to hide their differences more favorably than those who struggle to maintain their ethnic identity."[17] This is also evident through the brand's attempts to fit a Jewish character into a mold created for Christian characters. Instead of a Christmas book, Rebecca has a Hanukkah book, *Candlelight for Rebecca*, yet Hanukkah is neither a very important holiday in the Jewish calendar, nor one that would have been a major celebration for Rebecca, as the daughter of immigrants living in the United States in 1914.[18] Despite this, Rebecca receives a special Hanukkah dress, just as the Christian historical characters who preceded her received Christmas dresses. "I always found it odd the very fancy dress Rebecca owned was for Hanukkah and not for Rosh Hashanah, Yom Kippur, or Passover," Anneliese shared. "I realize now that . . . Hanukkah is [better known] than other [Jewish] holidays due to its proximity to Christmas."

Because the Jewish calendar does not follow the predetermined format of American Girl's historical books, more significant Jewish holidays receive either a brief mention or none at all.[19] Indeed, the editor of Rebecca's books, Jennifer Hirsch, has emphasized that Rebecca is "a Jewish girl but she's American first and foremost," suggesting that there is an incompatibility with being both Jewish and American.[20] Forcing Rebecca—and, consequently, her Jewish identity—into a Christian framework echoes the many ways in which Jewish Americans have historically been pushed to assimilate into Christian American culture, and how Jewish identities were historically categorized in ways that reflected Christian understandings, or the lack thereof, of Judaism.[21]

Jewish collectors are also cognizant of the ways in which American Girl has diluted the intrinsic Jewishness of the Judaica in Rebecca's collection. For example, American Girl has sold the challah included in Rebecca's "Sabbath Set" in other, non-Jewish contexts over the years, including in an accessory set in the contemporary Truly Me line, and as part of the bakery in Claudie's 1920s Harlem Renaissance–themed collection, gradually eroding the significance of challah as a Jewish ritual food.[22] Rebecca's plastic challah also remains the only part of her "Sabbath Set" that is used for Shabbat ritual; when American Girl rebranded the historical line, they removed the Shabbat candlesticks from the set and packaged them with her "Parlor Table" instead.[23] One collector expressed dismay by the brand's lack of attention to Rebecca's accessories: "I've been disappointed by how [Rebecca's collection has progressed], from the 'Sabbath set' that doesn't include candlesticks to the generally uninspired outfits, it feels like [American Girl has] stopped caring." However, other collectors find great meaning in Rebecca's Judaica. "In my house, I have a table where I have my Shabbat candles [and] more Judaica, and I have my Rebecca standing behind her parlor table with the Shabbat candles and challah from her collection," Alyson said.

While Rebecca's collection is distinguished by the presence of specifically Jewish accessories, Isabel and Nicki's collection notably lacks any physical markers of their interfaith family or Jewish identities at all. Much like Lindsey, Isabel and Nicki's Jewish identities are restricted to their book and the marketing copy for accessories in their collections.[24] Consumers reading the marketing copy on the American Girl website need to draw their own conclusions about why the characters celebrate both Hanukkah and Christmas.[25] According to writer A. R. Vishny, "The problem here is that American Girl has completely abandoned the pretense that these are educational toys and have buried the Jewish identities of these dolls deep enough that it can be ignored."[26] Indeed, within the online fandom, Isabel and Nicki's Jewish identity is often and easily ignored by non-Jewish collectors, while Jewish collectors largely hoped for a deeper and more thoughtful representation from the brand.

"When Isabel and Nicki were debuted, I felt almost like a little girl again," Sasha said. "They're Jewish, and from Seattle just like me! I think they are a wonderful representation of what modern Judaism can look like, especially for young women and girls." Holly, who has experienced antisemitism due to her blonde hair and green eyes, particularly appreciates that Isabel's physical appearance is much like her own, and that it goes against stereotypes of Ashkenazi Jews. "I do find it frustrating that . . . Rebecca [with light brown hair and hazel eyes] is portrayed almost as 'more Jewish,' because she is from a more strongly practicing household and has a more stereotypical [physical appearance]," Holly said. However, she wished Isabel and Nicki's book had a deeper exploration of their Jewish and interfaith identities. Another collector concurred: "It is such a good opportunity to showcase a somewhat modern view of Jewish girlhood—in an interfaith family, which is so important!—and I hope that comes into play as the twins are developed further. Even if they are written with a more secular Jewish identity (also important!) I don't want their Jewishness downplayed." For Kirsten, who converted to Judaism as an adult, Isabel and Nicki's release prompted conflicting feelings: "I was . . . a little let down by how little Jewishness actually made it into their stories (so far), but I remain pumped that there are canonically Jewish dolls that are being sold right now and might serve as an educational tool for people who grew up like I did—without any concept of what Jewishness looks like. Hopefully it might spark some interest in kids to go to libraries and look things up." Still, for Kirsten, American Girl's decision to have Hanukkah as Isabel and Nicki's sole connection to Judaism is "a very Christian way of approaching Jewishness." Yet, due to the fluid nature of Isabel and Nicki's identities, Jewish collectors are able to engage with these characters, as well as Lindsey and Rebecca, in ways that are particularly meaningful to them, often by expanding and amending the characters' canonical stories.

"All My Dolls Are Jewish": Making Meaning as Jewish Consumers and Collectors

Despite the ways in which American Girl prescribes play and models behavior by selling dolls alongside books about the characters, many Jewish collectors have found meaning in straying from those canonical stories by making canonically Christian characters Jewish, creating Jewish identities for noncharacter dolls in the Truly Me line, and imagining richer storylines for canonically Jewish characters. "Growing up all my dolls were Jewish by default because I am, I don't see why that should change as an adult," Nell said. Creating additional Jewish characters, including Sephardi and Mizrahi characters, as well as characters with other intersectional identities, including LGBTQ+ characters, is one method collectors use to address the lack of diversity in American Girl's canonically Jewish dolls. "As an Ashkenazi Jew, I feel represented by American Girl, but I wouldn't . . . if I weren't Ashkenazi," Alyson said. Nell also brought up the prevalence of Ashkenazi representation in the brand. "As a Jewish community we should strive for more than just white Ashkenazi representation," she said. "I've decided that all my dolls are Jewish," one collector shared. "It means that despite a wide variety of ethnic and cultural backgrounds, they all share Judaism—much like Jews in real life." For Malkah, having a diverse doll collection beyond Jewish dolls is also connected to their Jewish identity: "I think [the] desire for diversity in my collecting is tied to Jewish values of building solidarity."

"Maybe I Could Be Part of the Story Too": American Jewish Identity

Holly, who feels similarly, said, "I try to express *tikkun olam* [the Jewish value of repairing the world] in my doll collecting and [elsewhere]."

However, when expressing Jewish identity through the medium of photos, as on AGIG, Jewish collectors are hindered by the lack of doll-sized Judaica sold by American Girl. For some, American Girl's Jewish dolls and Judaica take on the meaning and significance of human-sized Judaica. [27] As such, collectors are conflicted about the best way for American Girl to represent Jewish material culture while also recognizing that non-Jewish consumers purchase the brand's doll-sized Judaica as well. Ellie hopes for more doll-sized Judaica from American Girl: "I want to see . . . a modern Jewish girl (or any gender child!) and . . . her stories of celebrating Shabbat and [the High Holidays]. I want to see more doll play sets for customers to purchase to tell those stories with their dolls." While Kirsten hopes for more Jewish representation in outfits and accessories, including a costume for the carnivalesque holiday of Purim, or a Rosh Hashanah outfit, when it is traditional to dress in white, she feels torn about American Girl selling ritual items, due to the ways in which non-Jewish collectors often misuse and misunderstand them. "I don't really want [American Girl] to release [ritual objects] like *kippah* or *tallit* . . . I don't want people putting a *tallit* on their doll and calling it a cute spring shawl," she said. Instead, Kirsten suggests a Shabbat set that would include an educational pamphlet on Shabbat traditions and practices. Although American Girl has released countless Christmas and Easter dresses and accessory sets over the years, the brand largely has not offered Christian ritual objects for sale that fall outside of these two holidays. While doll-scale Christian ritual items are readily available from crafters who sell their wares online, doll-scale Judaica offerings from independent creators are sparse, and the majority of those who profit off of doll-sized Judaica are not Jewish.

Despite the lack of doll-sized Judaica, some collectors who were not born Jewish reported that their explorations of Judaism through American Girl dolls, often within fandom communities, led them to feel more connected with Jewish family or to pursue Jewish conversion. One adult collector shared that although they had been raised Catholic, Rebecca's books allowed them to feel closer to their grandmother, who had been Jewish before converting to Catholicism. As a kid, Sasha was gifted a Samantha doll by a Jewish family friend who had grown out of dolls, which Sasha now sees as a defining moment in her decision to pursue conversion as an adult: "When

I was handed Samantha, she had a small Magen David [Star of David] around her neck. . . . Having a doll who I deemed Jewish made me feel more connected to Judaism. . . . Perhaps she is who I owe my entire Jewish identity to." Kirsten, whose conversion process began around the same time she became reinterested in American Girl as an adult, similarly traces her interest in Judaism back to her childhood play with American Girl dolls, particularly her desire for the American Girl of Today Hanukkah outfit. "I would secretly pretend [my doll] was Jewish, even though as a child I had no idea what that actually meant or entailed. [I didn't know anyone who was Jewish], but I would check books out from the library about Jewish celebrations and have my childhood doll try to enact them," she shared. When Kirsten completed her conversion, her partner gifted her a Rebecca doll. For Malkah, who also converted to Judaism, collecting American Girl dolls as an adult is a way to reconnect with their childhood, so much of which is a reminder of their Catholic and Mormon upbringing: "By purposefully collecting the Jewish American Girl dolls, I feel like I can finally connect with a piece of my childhood in a way that's authentic to who I am now." Ellie, who is in the process of conversion, expressed that their decision to make their Marisol doll (a Latina character from the Girl of the Year Line) Jewish inspired their own exploration of Judaism. "The more I learned, the more I connected with Jewish spirituality and my own fractured beliefs," Ellie said.

"Jewishness without Apology": Jewish Collectors and the Online Fandom

In addition to finding and making meaning through American Girl, Jewish collectors also face the challenges of being Jewish in an overwhelmingly white and Christian fandom. Jewish collectors reported a lack of inclusivity regarding Jewish representation from both ends of the political spectrum and in various American Girl fandom communities and platforms. In more progressive parts of the community, collectors expressed frustration that Jewish dolls were not viewed as diverse. "It makes me sad when people dismiss [Isabel and Nicki] as just more white dolls when, in fact, they do represent a minority group—one that I'm part of. But Jews often get left out of the diversity conversation," Angela said. Toby agreed, saying, "I feel like a minority most of the time [on AGIG] and non-Jewish collectors just don't get it." Kirsten also pointed to the absence of intersectionality when non-Jewish doll collectors thought about Jewish dolls, particularly among fans calling for new dolls of color at the time of Isabel and Nicki's release. "People were forgetting that [Isabel and Nicki] were Jewish, not the usual Christian or Christian-coded characters that American Girl puts out. But very few people were arguing that they could have been Jewish dolls of color—it was like they couldn't reconcile how the two identities could be present in one character," she said. Another collector expressed concerns that American Girl's Jewish characters do not reflect the diversity of the Jewish experience: "I worry that the sliver of representation that American Girl has produced in Jewish characters reaffirms common stereotypes and misconceptions about American Jews and Judaism—that we're all white, that Hanukkah is just 'Jewish Christmas,' and that all Jewish practices look the same."

More politically conservative fan spaces, including collector groups on Facebook, many of which tend to have Christian undertones if not explicit Christian messaging, have led to similar feelings of disconnect with the fan community. "I find that those who are not Jewish are often interested in our culture and love to hear our stories, but sometimes fall short from actually understanding," Angela said. She shared that when Jewish collectors have spoken out against non-Jewish adult collectors who make canonically Jewish dolls Christian, for example, by having a Jewish doll wear a cross necklace or a First Communion dress, the Jewish collectors are often accused of bullying. Kirsten has had similar experiences: "[The fandom] has a really large, loud Christian segment who are very particular in how they wield their Christianity."

Additionally, the brand's emphasis on Christmas leads to an outpouring of doll Christmas photos in online fan spaces. Angela finds it particularly difficult to be a Jewish member of the fandom when most of AGIG is sharing Christmas photos. "There's something about Christmas that makes me uncomfortable, but it's hard to express that in a country in which it is such a beloved holiday," she said. Angela pushes back against this discomfort by sharing Jewish holiday-themed photos, particularly during the month of December.

Regardless of the platform, Jewish collectors are cognizant of the challenges of being Jewish online, even among others who share their hobby. "I don't often actively show my Jewishness online. I tend to hide behind my appearance and name. . . . I worry that being more open will lead to more unkindness," Holly said. For Ellie, avoiding antisemitism on AGIG means "curating my circle of friends very closely." Other collectors feel more comfortable being outwardly Jewish due to the other Jewish members of the community. "I'm inspired to broadcast my (and my dolls'!) Jewishness without apology," one collector shared. Still, she is cautious about antisemitism: "I've been on social media long enough to anticipate the [inevitability] of antisemitism. . . . Sometimes it feels like the vitriol is unescapable, even when it's not wearing swastikas—people don't realize how much venom we can taste behind casual Christian supersessionism, or soft Holocaust denial, or unthinking erasure."

Look to the Past, Learn for the Future

In early 2023, when I learned Isabel and Nicki's stories would not foreground their Jewish identities, I created my own 1990s historical character, Rivkah, based on my experiences as a Jewish girl growing up in Ohio in the 1990s. When I introduced her on Instagram, I drew upon my longing for a Jewish American Girl doll as a kid: "It's 1999 and Rivkah is dreaming about visiting the American Girl Place in Chicago and picking out her own American Girl of Today doll. When she was younger, her parents gave her Samantha for Hanukkah. Although she loves Samantha, Rivkah doesn't have a doll like her. Because Samantha, like all the other character dolls sold by American Girl in 1999, celebrates Christmas, and Rivkah is Jewish."[28] I was overwhelmed by the public response to this post. "I see so much of myself in this," one commenter wrote. "Now I wish I could buy a Rivkah doll," someone else shared.

By studying the voices of Jewish collectors of American Girl, we can see that much of the meaning Jewish collectors take from American Girl's dolls, stories, and accessories, are of the collectors' own making. When Jewish collectors circulate their own narratives about Jewish characters (both canonical and not) in fandom spaces, those narratives can and do wield just as much power as the canonical narratives from American Girl. In this way, Jewish collectors will continue to push the fandom forward in terms of representing the diversity of the Jewish experience. Even as the future of Jewish representation from the brand is unknown, Jewish collectors will certainly continue to make their own meaning with American Girl dolls, and, in doing so, continue to shape and transform the ways members of the fandom, both Jewish and not, interact with and understand Jewish identity.

Notes

1. American Girl catalog, Holiday 1996, Chagnon Family Museum of Toys and Collectibles, accessed August 15, 2023, https://toysandcollectiblesmuseum.org/aghd1996.

2. Uncited quotes come from an online survey circulated by the author to members of the AGIG community.

3. See Emilie Zaslow, *Playing with America's Doll: A Cultural Analysis of the American Girl Collection* (New York: Palgrave Macmillan, 2017), 8–9.

4. See Molly Rosner, *Playing with History: American Identities and Children's Consumer Culture* (New Brunswick, NJ: Rutgers University Press, 2021), 4.

5. See Rebekkah Rubin, @iamexcessivelydollverted, accessed August 20, 2023, https://www.instagram.com/iamexcessivelydollverted.

6. See Rebecca Joan West, "Some of My Best Dolls Are Black: Colorblind Rhetoric in Online Collecting Communities," (PhD diss., Loyola University Chicago, 2014).

7. See American Girl catalog, Holiday 1996.

8. See American Girl catalog, Holiday 1996. Hair is one of several physical traits frequently involved in the racialization and othering of Jewish people. Ashkenazi Jews in particular are frequently stereotyped as having frizzy, dense, curly, and dark hair. For more information about Jewish hair stereotypes, including in American Girl, see *What Is Jewish Hair?* by the Jewish Women's Archive, https://jwa.org/blog/jewish-hair.

9. See Victoria Davion, "The American Girl," *Metaphilosophy* 47, no. 4/5 (October 2016).

10. See American Girl catalog, Fall 2001, Chagnon Family Museum of Toys and Collectibles website, accessed August 15, 2023, https://toysandcollectiblesmuseum.org/kkhcfa01.

11. No relation, unsurprisingly, to this author.

12. Emilie Zaslow, "Which Vitamins are in the Chocolate Cake? How American Girl Marketing Has Responded to Shifting Discourses About Gender and Race," *Public Historian* 43, no. 1 (February 2021): 20.

13. In addition to my own conversations with members of the AGIG community, some major figures in the community have mentioned that Rebecca's stories were their introduction to Judaism. See "All About Rebecca," interview of Jacqueline Dembar Greene by Sydney Paulsen and Kristen Washington, *American Girl Fan Club*, August 17, 2022, https://www.everand.com/podcast/591855774/All-About-Rebecca-In-this-episode-Sydney-Paulsen-and-Kristen-Washington-are-joined-by-special-guests-Jacqueline-Dembar-Greene-author-of-the-Rebecca.

14. See "Jewish Americans in 2020," Pew Research Center, May 11, 2021, https://www.pewresearch.org/religion/2021/05/11/the-size-of-the-u-s-jewish-population.

15. Chryssa Atkinson, *Lindsey* (Middleton, WI: Pleasant Company, 2001), 1, 106.

16. Cantors are Jewish members of the clergy responsible for the musical part of the service.

17. Zaslow, *Playing with America's Doll*, 157.

18. See Melissa R. Klapper, *Jewish Girls Coming of Age in America, 1860–1920* (New York: New York University Press, 2005).

19. See Jacqueline Dembar Greene, *Rebecca and the Movies* (Middleton, WI: American Girl, 2009); Jacqueline Dembar Greene, *Rebecca and Ana* (Middleton, WI: American Girl, 2009).

20. See "All About Rebecca," interview of Greene by Paulsen and Washington.

21. See Eric L. Goldstein, *The Price of Whiteness: Jews, Race, and American Identity* (Princeton, NJ: Princeton University Press, 2006).

22. See "City Market Goodies," American Girl Wiki, accessed August 22, 2023, https://americangirl.fandom.com/wiki/City_Market_Goodies; "Angelo's Bakery," American Girl, accessed August 22, 2023, https://www.americangirl.com/products/angelos-bakery-hjr00; "Rebecca's Sabbath Set," American Girl, accessed August 14, 2023, https://www.americangirl.com/products/rebecca-sabbath-set-gjh73.

23. See "Rebecca's Parlor Table," American Girl, accessed August 25, 2023, https://www.americangirl.com/products/rebecca-parlor-table-gjh72.

24. See Julia DeVillers and Jennifer Roy, *Meet Isabel and Nicki* (Middleton, WI: American Girl, 2023).

25. See "Isabel & Nicki's Pet Set," American Girl, accessed August 15, 2023, https://www.americangirl.com/products/isabel-and-nickis-pet-set-hnr76; "Isabel & Nicki's Computer & Desk Set for 18-inch Dolls," American Girl, accessed August 15, 2023, https://www.americangirl.com/products/isabel-and-nickis-computer-and-desk-set-for-18-inch-dolls-hnr85; "Isabel's Bedroom Accessories for 18-inch Dolls," American Girl, accessed August 15, 2023, https://www.americangirl.com/products/isabels-bedroom-accessories-for-18-inch-dolls-hnr83.

26. A. R. Vishny, "Are the New '90s American Girl Dolls Really Jewish?," Hey Alma, February 24, 2023, https://www.heyalma.com/are-the-new-90s-american-girl-dolls-jewish/.

27. See Rachel B. Gross, *Beyond the Synagogue: Jewish Nostalgia as Religious Practice* (New York: New York University Press, 2021).

28. Rebekkah Rubin (@iamexcessivelydollverted), "It's 1999 and Rivkah . . . ," February 21, 2023, https://www.instagram.com/p/Co78z_OOzzW.

Interpreting, Imagining, and Inventing Queer Pasts and Futures through American Girl

Laura Traister

> If you don't know you have a past,
> how can you believe you have a future?
> —The Pop-Up Museum of Queer History[1]

We don't know for sure who first publicly suggested that Molly Jean McIntire is gay. We do know that her name cropped up on articles titled "The 100 Most Lesbianish First Names"[2] and "American Girl Dolls Ranked in Order of Gayness" in 2016 and 2017, and that many tweets over the years have said she is gay.[3] But although a modest number of people gleefully responded to each of these claims, no post created more conversation than the one shared on American Girl's official Instagram account on June 1, 2022 (June is the start of Pride month).

The post showed a Molly doll in her summer-camp outfit, and the caption read, "To all the Molly girls in the world: We see you. And we celebrate you. A classic is back!"[4] Although the brand was referring to their decision to bring the doll out of retirement, some adult American Girl fans interpreted the announcement as evidence that Molly is canonically gay. After *The Cut* requested comments from American Girl, the brand responded with a statement that read, "The new Molly collection releasing today is simply aligned with when all of our new summer product is debuting. Nothing more."[5] But many adult fans' imaginations had already been sparked. Some even jokingly interpreted the brand's response in an affirming way: "Hey, whose parents *didn't* try to push them back into the closet after a flashy coming out online?"[6]

Much of this discussion was playful, but the need for LGBTQ+ representation—including adult fans' desire for retrospective representation in a brand from their childhood—is serious. When the historical and current lives of people in a marginalized group are erased, people in that group (especially kids) are left to their own imaginings. As Dr. Rudine Sims Bishop wrote in her historic 1990 article "Mirrors, Windows, and Sliding Glass Doors," calling for more children's books about people of color,

> Literature transforms human experience and reflects it back to us, and in that reflection we can see our own lives and experiences as part of the larger human experience. Reading, then, becomes a means of self-affirmation, and readers often seek their mirrors in books. . . . When children cannot find themselves reflected in the books they read, or when the images they see are distorted, negative, or laughable, they learn a powerful lesson about how they are devalued in the society of which they are a part.[7]

Adults look for these reflections too. One study of American Girl nostalgia found that adult fans also looked to "their childhood memories in order to give their constructed identities credibility in the present."[8] For example, a woman's "assertion that the brand facilitated her love of history may be interpreted as an attempt to ground her identity in the historical past: through her nostalgia, she can claim she has always loved history and that this love is an essential part of her identity that has existed since childhood."[9] Because many LGBTQ+ adults, including me, lacked representation as kids, it's not hard to see why some of us derive validation and joy from interpreting a doll and book character from our childhoods as being queer.[10]

Although "the American Girl doll and book collection represents perhaps the most serious and successful attempt in twentieth-century American culture to use dolls and books to teach children about their history," the brand does not acknowledge queer history or contemporary queer life.[11] (As of 2023, the one exception is the story of Kira, Girl of the Year 2021. Her first book mentions how the law in Australia changed so that her queer great-aunts could marry. The story does not discuss US law.)

Some adult AG fans might say that discussing gender identity and sexuality is inappropriate since the American Girl books and dolls were originally made for "girls ages 8 and up."[12] Indeed, the brand has defined itself against more sexualized dolls like Barbie and Bratz.[13] The dolls "appear innocent" compared with Barbie's adult figure; "they are unambiguously childlike, and romantic relationships do not factor into their stories. Instead, the American Girl goes to school and makes friends."[14] But the brand has never shied away from content (however minor) about gender nonconformity (think Felicity's breeches and Kit's preference for baseball over frills). And there's a long record among fans of heteronormative "shipping," or excitedly expressing potential romantic pairings, between AG girls and boys from their books—e.g., Felicity/Ben and Kit/Stirling. So while it's probably not realistic to think that the brand will ever explore a main character's crushes (straight or queer), neither is it fair to expect LGBTQ+ fans to not dream about queer AG ships.

The brand's lack of an openly queer main character means that some fans have long been interpreting canon content as queer, imagining queer futures for canon characters, and even inventing their own queer characters—and probably will as long as the fandom exists. This essay provides a glimpse into these fan activities and focuses on fan content that is "openly available for public view"[15] on the internet, which is usually the hub of many fandoms' activities. Since some of the sites I examined have a minimum age of thirteen for users,[16] I'm acting on faith that the content examined in this essay is from "teen and adult fan communities."[17] I focused on three sites of queer AG interpreting, imagining, and inventing: playful listicles, slash fanfiction, and fan accounts on "American Girl Instagram" (AGIG).

A few notes for readers before I expand on these three sites: Some of these content creators use multiple pronouns, which I alternate between when writing about their work. My choice of sources is, of course, informed and limited by what parts of the fandom I have been organically exposed to. I write from my position as an adult AG fan and as a cisgender gay woman, but I cannot and do not speak for all AG fans or all LGBTQ+ people. Although this essay has limits, the creativity of the AG fandom does not; countless wells spring forth online for anyone interested in learning more.

Interpreting Canon Content as Queer

The most visible and popular listicle about American Girls and queerness I know of is "American Girl Dolls Ranked in Order of Gayness," written by Peyton Thomas in 2017 for *The Niche* blog. Thomas argues that the brand's stories are "inherently gay. Or, at the very least, relatable and safe for young, questioning lesbian and bi girls in a way that the vast majority of media isn't."[18] The list ranges from Caroline Abbott at #15 to Kit Kittredge at #1, with justifications for each historical doll's ranking. Because Thomas closely reads and interprets the canonical narrative around each character, he focuses mainly on their identities as nine- or ten-year-olds. This list isn't so much about who the girls may crush on or date in a few years, but about who they already *are*. Most of his justifications fall into one of two categories: (1) gender-nonconforming identities and (2) female homosociality, by which I mean not only "social bonds between persons of the same sex" but also specifically "relations that are based on emotional closeness, intimacy, and a nonprofitable form of friendship."[19]

Looking at nonconforming identities, Thomas starts with the obvious: the doll clothes. He deems Josefina's summer riding outfit—a little feminine (the dress's puffed sleeves and ruffled hem), a little masculine (the straw hat and leather vest)—"one of the gayest things American Girl has ever produced."[20] Nanea's high-waisted shorts, which mark "the first time ever that a doll's intro outfit has included pants rather than a dress or a skirt" is "cause for gay celebration."[21] Molly's "butchest looks" include her aviator outfit, cowgirl costume, summer-camp uniform, and roller-skates. Although Thomas does not mention Felicity's nighttime adventures wearing stolen breeches, several commenters point to it as sartorial evidence of queerness. For Rebecca, he simply points out that she "wears purple all the time." This is one of the listicle's satisfying "if you know, you know" moments; Thomas assumes that readers will recognize the longstanding association between the color lavender and LGBTQ+ people, from the Cold War–era Lavender Scare and the Lavender Menace collective to lavender marriages and lavender graduations.[22]

Thomas also mines the historical books for behavior and interests that don't conform to the gendered expectations of each character's era and culture. Kaya'aton'my spends time "training to become a warrior or declaring confidently that she's going to lead her people one day."[23] Felicity is a horse-obsessed tomboy who finds domestic work a drag. Samantha aspires to be the first female president or a painter "like Mary Cassatt," who was a feminist and never married. In a slightly earlier article about tomboy heroines, Thomas named Kit as "the gayest and butchest" American Girl doll, pointing to her "iconic transmasc stunt" of "dressing as a boy to ride the rails," as well as to her resistance to "the frilly pink decor her mother's chosen for her bedroom."[24] Despite Maryellen's setting during "the halcyon, repressed days of the Eisenhower administration," she, too, is a tomboy who likes TV shows like *Davy Crockett* and *The Lone Ranger* and wants to be a rocket scientist. Of Julie's campaigns to play on the boys' basketball team and to save the Bay area's endangered golden eagles, Thomas cheekily writes, "Short of writing a book called, 'Julie Joins the Milk Campaign,' [American Girl] couldn't possibly have been more direct." These examples show how, even in a canon that's not clearly queer, a character's resistance to the gendered norms of her day "represent these categories as cultural constructions, opening a space for nonconforming fans to see themselves reflected and normalized."[25]

It's worth nothing here that Thomas also interprets even mainstream interests as justification for a character's gayness. He writes that Rebecca is "obsessed with Yiddish theatre and vaudeville shows" (an obsession many people around her would have shared).[26] Thomas also argues that Melody's interests in Motown and civil rights are "inherently gay," because "rock and roll was invented by a black bisexual woman" and gay people made "invaluable contributions . . . to the push for civil rights."

The other main category of justifications for the characters' gayness is female homosociality.[27] Thomas writes, "It is a rare thing for an American Girl to even speak to a boy to whom she's not related. And when this does happen, it's probably because the boy was antagonizing [her], and she had to put him in his place." Examples include Rebecca clapping back at schoolmate Leo when he calls her a "street sweeper," Kit pushing schoolmate Roger for insulting her family, and Melody staging a "swift and decisive verbal takedown" of a white schoolmate and bully named Donald.

Fierce love between female friends is more evidence of queerness. Thomas calls the simultaneous release of best-friend dolls Marie-Grace and Cécile "a blatant marketing ploy to sell two $115 dolls at once" but concedes that "it was undeniably gay." When Kirsten loses her BFF Marta to cholera, she "gains major lesbian cred for the fact that she fell victim to Bury Your Gays in her very first boo."[28] Addy gets "sucked into what's essentially a love triangle" between classmates Sarah and Harriet, "so really, Addy has two girlfriends." Thomas's allusions to these fierce female friendships naturally expand into shipping. Relationships named in the listicle are Cécile/Marie-Grace, Kirsten/Marta, Addy/Sarah/Harriet, Samantha/Nellie, Kit/Ruthie, and Maryellen/"forbidden Italian girlfriend." But grounded as this article is in the time of the books (i.e., in the characters' childhoods), these pairings are not the focus.

We need look no farther than the comment section to see why queer interpretation of the historical dolls and books matters. The listicle boasts ninety-eight comments as of August 2023, some of them posted five or six years after the article was published. The comment section is joyous, funny, and deeply creative. Commenters add their own theories and call for more representation. They say Felicity is bi and enjoys relationships with both her BFF Elizabeth (a Loyalist!) and her father's apprentice Ben (a Patriot!). They point out that Julie's friend Ivy owns cats *and* a rainbow romper. They discuss Kaya's crush on her role model, Swan Circling, and Molly's crush on her teacher, Miss Campbell. They ship Kirsten/Singing Bird and interpret even the most mundane moments as queer, like Molly sitting in a patch of poison ivy at summer camp. The fans want to see Molly/Emily content and a ranking of the gayness of Girl of the Year dolls (with calls for Lindsey, Chrissa, Gwen, and Sonali). Though most of these comments are gleeful, fans also express frustration—e.g., about the "bury your gays" media trope in the early deaths of Marta and Swan Circling. One commenter points out that Caroline could be queer despite her heteronormative appearance. Thomas, the listicle's author, replies to her comment to change his interpretation: "you are so right. caroline is femme4femme."[29]

As you read the comments, you can witness AG fans' delight in recognizing their younger selves in the characters, and in connecting with other strangers who are doing the same. Together, these fans are engaged in "the work of making historic queerness visible in the present," which allows them to "make for themselves another version of history."[30] In doing so, they "not only create a community in the present but also, through this collective reconstruction, connect with lesbian [and wider LGBTQ+] history."[31] The commenters share funny memories from their childhoods, such as making their dolls share beds and scandalizing their family members. But underneath all the humor is a feeling of validation and relief. Something like "Now I finally understand why I was so drawn to this doll as a kid."

Imagining Queer Futures Postcanon

What happens when fans decide to step beyond the confines of canon? This is what Yashwina Canter does in her 2022 *Autostraddle* listicle "Which Historical Lesbian Bars Would American Girl Dolls Have Visited?" They imagine queer futures for nine twentieth-century characters (this was pre-Claudie, sadly), listing each with her birth year and the year she would've turned eighteen—from 1913 for Samantha to 1994 for Courtney. "Imagining them older, in subsequent decades," she writes, "lets these vibrant characters expand beyond their original narrative confines." In this listicle, the girls are officially young women, which opens space for adult fans to more freely imagine their sexual identities.

As Thomas does in his article, Canter employs a playful tone while serving up deeply researched knowledge of queer history and of American Girl lore, including the characters' styles and personalities. They call Samantha a "badass femme queen," Kit a "rough-n-tumble butch queen," Melody a "pop culture icon," and Julie a "sweet little long-hair-butch San Francisco sports gay." But the listicle's strongest and most unique offering is its focus not just on each woman's identity, or on a partnership with her canonical "best friend," but rather on her connection to the larger queer community of her specific time and place. In fact, the listicle reads almost like a (very gay) "Peek into the Past."[32] By mapping lesbian bars across the country and throughout the twentieth century, Canter makes visible a history of queer resistance and community that many of us did not grow up learning.

It's particularly valuable that she sheds light on the queer history of places outside well-known LGBTQ+ havens like San Francisco or New York City. We visit those cities—and, in them, historical places like Eve's Hangout, Amelia's, and Maud's—but only because Samantha, Rebecca, and Julie live there. Canter also invites readers to visit dive bars with Kit in Cincinnati, meet "lesbian former-WACs [Women's Army Corps members]" with Nanea in Honolulu, attend "mixed-race drag balls" with Molly in Chicago, watch Maryellen bartend and jam to jukeboxes in Central Florida, go disco dancing with Melody in Detroit, and hit up The Palms in West Hollywood with Courtney.

Canter expertly blends each place's history with each character's interests and personality. Since Nanea is "a creative, headstrong, often-impulsive girl," she "wouldn't be having any trouble shaking up gay adventures" as a teen.

"I'm betting that Julie would've been fielding Maud's softball and basketball teams," Canter writes, "and driving the girls to the bar after practice in her beat-up van." Though they acknowledge each era and place's oppressions, such as "police surveillance or harassment," it's still gratifying to imagine the joy each character could find in her local area—no transplant to San Francisco or NYC needed. Crucially, Canter also imagines some characters past age eighteen. "By the time of Cincinnati's first pride parade in 1973," she writes, "Kit would have been 50 years old—a beloved butch elder."

Though there are fewer comments on this listicle than on Thomas's piece, the reader response is much the same. This comment section is another example of a space where people who "may have perceived themselves and their histories as invisible" are "using historic invisibility as a means of connection in the present."[33] Readers suggest books and archives that are useful for more queer history, and they call for historically informed fan fiction about the characters.

Shipping Queer Love Through Slash Fanfic

Fan fiction, or "fanfic," refers to "stories involving popular fictional characters that are written by fans and often posted on the Internet."[34] Historically informed AG fanfic does in fact exist. A *lot* of it. Writing fanfic is a popular way for people from all sorts of fan communities to imagine storylines beyond canon, and shipping characters is an especially common type of storyline. One scholar's observation about fanart surrounding Monster High dolls (another line owned by Mattel, which bought American Girl in 1998) also applies to the AG fandom: "Shipping is a way for artists [or writers] to add sexuality to characters to include same-sex desire as well as heteronormative desire. The images [or stories] ascribe an overt sexuality to the characters that Mattel avoids."[35]

AG fans have been shipping characters online through fanfic since at least 2005, when the oldest AG fic was posted on the fan platform I was most familiar with growing up: FanFiction.net. Incidentally, some have suggested a connection between this early content and the first American girl movie, *Felicity: An American Girl Adventure*, which also came out in 2005.[36] As it happens, most fanfic on that site ships Ben/Felicity, a.k.a. Benicity.[37] When I scanned the descriptions of the 276 stories in the American Girl category in June 2023, I could not find any clearly queer content. Felicity/Ben, Samantha/Eddie, and Kit/Stirling stories, however, abounded.

I then turned to Archive of Our Own (AO3), a "noncommercial and nonprofit central hosting place for fanworks" that is associated with the Organization for Transformative Works, a nonprofit created in 2007 by fans.[38] Surveys have found that the majority of users on AO3 are queer,[39] and it's a popular site for "queering narratives."[40] AO3 hosts a lot of "slash fanfic," which "refers to fan-written texts that recast cis/heteronormative[41] content with queer characters, relationships, and themes."[42] On fanfic sites, creators often use the slash symbol to express a romantic and/or sexual pairing (as opposed to the ampersand, which denotes platonic pairings). Female/female (F/F) slash is often called "femslash." Such content is "unique in that it expresses queer possibilities that transform past, present, and future cis/heteronormative trends."[43] Although such writing can be "positive and subversive," we must keep in mind that fan communities often reproduce "wider structural inequities" such as "normative whiteness and heteronormativity" and "demand a great deal of time and labor from their participants."[44]

These limitations likely exist in the AG fanfic community and content on AO3. Even so, slash fanfic is worth examining, because it is another way adult (and likely some teen) AG fans connect AG and queerness. These creators reach forward, past the books' end dates, to give historical characters a queer future. But they also reach backward, before their own lifetimes, to give themselves and other queer fans today what many of us need: queer elders, a queer archive, and a sense of queer history that is seldom taught.

When I searched AO3 in August 2023, there were over two hundred fics under the fandom tag American Girl.[45] The oldest F/F one was from 2010—eleven years before AG debuted Kira's queer great-aunts. Some fics are from Femslash February, a month dedicated to celebrating F/F content. Inspired by scholar Diana Floegel's ethical approach to analyzing fanfic, I chose to analyze filters and tags rather than specific works, since these works are created with more expectation of privacy than, say, a blog post or a public social media account. I searched for LGBTQ+ content by focusing on tags. There are six category tags:

- General (no romantic and/or sexual relationships)
- F/M (female/male)
- F/F (female/female)

- M/M (male/male)
- multi (multiple types of relationships, or a relationship with multiple partners), and
- Other (relationships outside of these categories).[46]

I chose to focus on F/F fics because that is the largest category of queer slash fiction. It's worth noting, however, that even on AO3, the majority of romantic pairings are still F/M.

- General 94
- F/M 58
- F/F 48
- M/M 3
- Other 1
- Multi 1

Historical characters who have been around for a long time and have established best-friend characters seem to make the most popular F/F pairings. In the Relationship tag, this is what we see:

- Nellie O'Malley/Samantha Parkington 21
- Ben Davidson/Felicity Merriman 18
- Kit Kittredge/Ruthie Smithens. 13
- Molly McIntire/Steve Rogers [Captain America] . . . 9
- Cornelia Edwards/Gardner Edwards 8
- Elizabeth Cole/Felicity Merriman 7
- Stirling Howard/Kit Kittredge 6
- Samantha Parkington/Eddie Ryland 6
- Marie-Grace Gardner/Cécile Rey 4
- Emily Bennett/Molly McIntire. . . . .

I also noticed a few ships of Girls of the Year characters that were not represented in these tags. These include Chrissa Maxwell (2009)/Gwen Thompson (Chrissa's companion doll), Chrissa/Gwen/Sonali Matthews (also Chrissa's companion doll), and Chrissa/Tara (a bully in Chrissa's books), as well as Luciana Vega (2018)/Blaire Wilson (2019).

Additional Tags (also called "freeform tags") provide more detail about a given fic.[47] Many are simple descriptors to set readers' expectations.

Tags about romance include "First Love," "Growing Old Together," and "Soulmates." More queer-specific tags include "WLW character" (women loving women) and "Lesbian Character," as well as AG-specific tags like "nonbinary!Kit"[48] and "Kit grows up to be a trans guy."

Many stories explicitly age up the characters, as Yashwina Canter did in her lesbian-bars article. We see this trend in the general tag "Aged-Up Characters," as well as in more specific tags like "It's 1883—Felicity and Elizabeth Are 18," "Sam and Nellie are 17ish," "Samantha and Nellie Are 21 (1916)" and, for Kit/Ruthie, "It's 1938 So They're Like 13–14ish." Though mostly set in the characters' exciting teen or young-adult years, some fics stretch farther into the future, imagining couples like Nellie/Samantha and Kit/Ruthie in old age, having spent a lifetime together.

Many fics acknowledge the grim realities of the historical characters' eras through tags like "Period-Typical Sexism," "mentions of conversion therapy," "Internalized Homophobia," and "Disapproving Family." Other tags show how queer people in those eras navigated such danger. Many of the tags are well-established euphemisms for queer love (and many of them are very funny): "becomes a spinster," "Gals bein' pals," "Boston marriage," "Samantha and Nellie are Officially Spinsters (shh they aren't but don't tell anybody)," "Women Wearing Pants," and, simply, "Pants." One fandom researcher explains why some fans might enjoy poking fun at the "hidden in plain sight" nature of "close friendships" between women throughout history: "Pleasure is found in the act of making lesbians visible across time, the pleasure arising from a feeling of intuitive and intimate knowledge of what queerness might look like. By highlighting unacknowledged examples of historic queerness, contemporary queers share in this knowledge and their ability to reshape stories of what this queerness looks like, moving from 'lifelong companions' to lovers."[49] Fans are making visible what Adrienne Rich once called "a history of female resistance which has never fully understood itself because it has been so fragmented, miscalled, erased."[50]

Inventing Queer Characters on American Girl Instagram

In the American Girl fandom, AGIG refers not to the brand's official Instagram account, but to the community of fans who post doll content on their Instagram accounts. While the listicles and fanfic focus on interpreting canon content as queer and imagining queer futures for canon characters, a lot of queer creators on AGIG tend to take their creativity a step further and invent their own characters and storylines.

AGIG gained media attention in June 2022, shortly after all the buzz about Molly. A few AGIG creators coordinated anti-Pride posts, backing their opinions with Bible verses. In response, many creators spoke out on Instagram against the homophobia in some areas of the AG fan community. Three of those creators were quoted in an NBC News article.[51] I have chosen to analyze their public Instagram content and, like NBC, quote the creators by only their first names. Unlike the fanfic on AO3, the queer representation in these accounts' content is not limited primarily to F/F shipping. The characters in these posts are also more ethnically diverse than what we see on AO3, with all three creators participating in Dolls of Color month each September.

The account @honeyag_ is run by Reese, who is queer and has thirty-nine dolls. Reese creates their own names and stories around the dolls, whether they are from the historical collection, World By Us, or Truly Me. She posts her LGBTQ+ dolls with Pride flags in June. A 2020 post showed six of his dolls and this educational caption: "Here we have all of their sexualities in case you do not recognize the flags! Left to right we have Marlow, Pansexual. Daphne, Asexual. Summer, Bisexual. Last three, Maisie, Phoenix, and Asia my little lesbeans! Summer and Maisie are a couple." Hashtags included #agigpride and #loveislove.[52] Another couple is Ainhoa and Nova,[53] and another even appears to have their own couple name, Aphorjune, and appears in posts with hashtags like #gaydolls and #couplegoals.[54]

Another account, @sapphic.ag, is run by Kyra, who is also queer. Her account features a highlight called "gfs" with photos of dolls next to each other at AG stores and captions like "do y'all think they're dating" and "they're so gfs."[55] On every post of their custom dolls, Kyra includes their names and pronouns. Some of her Pride posts include flags and more details about the dolls' identities; followers can meet Fin (he/they), who is nonbinary and transmasc;[56] Juliet (she/they), who is an asexual lesbian;[57] Paisley (she/her), who is pansexual;[58] and many more characters. At times, Kyra uses their platform to critique the American Girl brand and antitrans legislation, and to ask followers to "please support the trans community this month, and the next month, and forever."[59]

Finally, the account @prettylittleelizabeth is run by Kelsey, who calls herself an ally to the LGBTQ+ community. The characters she invents aren't

Interpreting, Imagining, and Inventing Queer Pasts and Futures   207

necessarily queer, but they do celebrate queerness. Responding to the homo-phobic posts in June 2022, she posted a photo of a Truly Me #63 doll named Peyton wearing a "Let love win" pin. The caption read, in part, "Peyton is happily wearing her Pride pin, because she has two moms. . . . and twice the love 🏳️‍🌈 🩷."[60] A later post showed a Truly Me #86 doll named Kali stand-ing in front of an easel and a canvas with a rainbow and the words "Love is greater than hate." In the caption, Kelsey wrote that being an ally "means being a friend, listening, and educating yourself when necessary, not just in June but all year long."[61] A Pride 2023 post shows how creative fans can be in using official AG products to write their own stories. We see Peyton again, in a scene that uses two AG products: the rainbow Pastel Party Dress and the rainbow layer cake from the Take the Cake Party Set.[62]

Insisting on More Queer Characters and Stories

As LGBTQ+ people, including youth, become more visible in American history and the present day (while also increasingly under attack, especially trans youth[63]), what characters and stories might yet populate the official AG universe, as well as AG fan works?

One fan has already deemed the newest historical dolls—twins Nicki and Isabel from 1999—as possibly "the gayest yet."[64] In an *Autostraddle* article, Analyssa Lopez writes, "*The L Word* would have come out when they were 15! Callie and Arizona get together when they're in college! At least one of them is coming out, and you can't convince me that both of them aren't queer."[65]

It can take a lot of imagination to understand yourself as queer, especially if you grow up in an environment that erases or demonizes people like you. It's a heavy task for a child to imagine a future they've never seen and relationships that don't follow their culture's dominant scripts. American Girl seems to be addressing these gaps in some of their nonfiction guides for today's kids.[66] But what about the stories? Will young fans in the future have to imagine queer storylines on their own? Or will queerness someday be normalized in the AG books they read, freeing fans to imagine more queer characters and stories because they want to, not because they have to?

American Girl books have told story after story of young people who become agents of change throughout history. What stories will they tell about kids of the 2000s, 2010s, 2020s, and beyond? As Peyton Thomas points out in his article for *LGBTQ Nation* questioning American Girl's partnership with J. K. Rowling, "Today, trans girls are fighting for the same right to equality in sports that Julie won so long ago."[67] Will American Girl ever create nonbinary characters or trans girls who fight for their right to play their favorite sports? What about a story that centers a trans girl whose transness is normal—just one of many aspects of who she is?

What gaps will those stories leave, and how will the fandom fill them? As any American Girl knows, history is continually being shaped by all of us. The stories we tell in the coming years will depend on the history we write today.

Notes

1. Pop-Up Museum of Queer History, https://queermuseum.tumblr.com/.

2. Riese Bernard, "The 100 Most Lesbianish First Names, Ranked By Lesbianism," *Autostraddle*, December 15, 2016, https://www.autostraddle.com/top-100-most-lesbianish-first-names-346521/.

3. Jamie Kenney, "Twitter Thinks American Girl Just Confirmed Molly's 'Queer Icon Status' & Here's Why," *Romper*, June 2, 2022, https://www.romper.com/life/american-girl-molly-gay-tweets.

4. American Girl (@americangirlbrand), Instagram photo, June 1, 2022, https://www.instagram.com/p/CeQ-YrlLZ6p/?utm_source=ig_web_copy_link.

5. Katie Heaney, "Did American Girl Just Out Molly?," *The Cut*, June 1, 2022, https://www.thecut.com/2022/06/american-girl-molly-pride-month.html.

6. Carmen Phillips, "Also. Also. Also: American Girl Denies Molly Came Out for Pride Month, but We Know the Truth," *Autostraddle*, June 2, 2022, https://www.autostraddle.com/molly-american-girl-doll-gay-pride-2022/.

7. Rudine Sims-Bishop, "Mirrors, Windows, and Sliding Glass Doors," *Perspectives* 6, no. 3 (Summer 1990), https://www.readingrockets.org/sites/default/files/migrated/Mirrors-Windows-and-Sliding-Glass-Doors.pdf.

8. Molly Brookfield, "From American Girls into American Women: A Discussion of American Girl Doll Nostalgia," *Girlhood Studies* 5, no. 1 (2012): 59.

9. Brookfield, "From American Girls into American Women," 59.

10. I am using *queer* and *queerness* to refer to "non-normative gender identities and sexual orientations," as in Diana Floegel, "'Write the Story You Want to Read': World-Queering through Slash Fanfiction Creation." *Journal of Documentation* 76, no. 4 (2020): 785.

11. Molly Rosner, *Playing with History: American Identities and Children's Consumer Culture* (Lewisburg, PA: Bucknell University Press, 2021), 119.

12. "Our Story," American Girl, https://www.americangirl.com/pages/our-story.

13. Emilie Zaslow, *Playing with America's Dolls: A Cultural Analysis of the American Girl Collection* (London: Palgrave Macmillan, 2017), 30.

14. Rosner, *Playing with History*, 126.

15. Sarah Mariel Austin, "Valuing Queer Identity in Monster High Doll Fandom," *Transformative Works and Cultures* 22 (2016): para. 2.1, https://doi.org/10.3983/twc.2016.0693.

16. "Terms of Service: II. Archive Age Policy," Archive of Our Own, Organization for Transformative Works, accessed October 15, 2023, https://archiveofourown.org/tos#age.

17. Austin, "Valuing Queer Identity," para 2.1.

18. Peyton Thomas, "American Girl Dolls Ranked in Order of Gayness," *The Niche* (blog), July 9, 2017, https://the-niche.blog/2017/07/09/american-girl-dolls-ranked-in-order-of-gayness/.

19. Nils Hammarén and Thomas Johansson, "Homosociality: In Between Power and Intimacy," *SAGE Open* 4, no. 1 (2014), https://doi.org/10.1177/2158244013518057.

20. Thomas, "American Girl Dolls Ranked."

21. Thomas, "American Girl Dolls Ranked."

22. The *Global Encyclopedia of Lesbian, Gay, Bisexual, Transgender, and Queer (LGBTQ) History* defines the Lavender Scare as "a Cold War campaign targeting gay people in the US government for reasons of national security that paralleled the anti-Communist campaign known as the Second Red Scare" and the Lavender Menace as "an informal lesbian feminist collective formed in New York City in 1969 to advocate for lesbians within the women's liberation movement." A "lavender marriage" refers to a marriage of convenience between a man and a woman meant to conceal the sexual orientation of one or both people. Today, many LGBTQ+ student centers celebrate "lavender graduation" ceremonies.

23. Thomas, "American Girl Dolls Ranked." American Girl books often follow a simplistic and formulaic narrative of a girl straining against the sexist limitations of her time. It's important to consider whether Thomas or the brand are mapping this narrative onto Kaya's story and Nimíipuu culture in 1764, especially since the books were written by a white woman. The Kaya doll and books were developed with the permission and input of the Nez Perce Tribe, including an eight-person advisory board. In the *Kaya* books, women do not typically become warriors as men do. We see this in *Kaya's Hero*, when Kaya asks Kautsa, her maternal grandmother, what makes a woman warrior named Swan Circling so "different." For this reason, I believe Thomas's suggestion—that Kaya's goals of becoming a warrior don't conform to her society's expectations—is accurate.

24. Peyton Thomas, "Nine Plucky Tomboy Heroines Who Made You the Butch Lesbian or Transmasc Icon You Are Today," *The Niche* (blog), June 28, 2017, https://the-niche.blog/2017/06/28/nine-plucky-tomboy-heroines-who-made-you-the-butch-lesbian-or-transmasc-icon-you-are-today/.

25. Austin, "Valuing Queer Identity," para. 5.9.

26. Thomas, "American Girl Dolls Ranked."

27. Although, according to Nils Hammarén and Thomas Johansson, the term homosociality is "frequently used in studies on men and masculinities . . . to refer to how men, through their relations to other men, uphold and maintain patriarchy," it is also possible to use the word without focusing on hierarchy. Here I am using "female homosociality" to refer to what Hammarén and Johansson call "horizontal homosociality"—i.e., "more inclusive relations . . . that are based on emotional closeness, intimacy, and a nonprofitable form of friendship."

28. "Bury Your Gays" refers to a media trope that "pertains to a systematic pattern in which SGM [sexual and gender minority] characters, typically lesbians and bisexual women, die in violent ways and often in service of another character's development." Ansley Birchmore and Heather Hensman Kettrey, "Exploring the Boundaries of the Parasocial

Contact Hypothesis: An Experimental Analysis of the Effects of the 'Bury Your Gays' Media Trope on Homophobic and Sexist Attitudes," *Feminist Media Studies* 22, 6 (2022): 1312.

29. A femme is "a person who is feminine of center in dress, attitude, and/or presentation. It is often, but not exclusively, used in a lesbian context." ("Femme," LGBTQ+ Glossary, PFLAG, accessed October 15, 2017, https://pflag.org/glossary/). The term *femme4femme* "derives from a romantic shorthand used in lesbian personal ads, and indicated one femme-identified person seeking another for a sexual or romantic liaison. The erotic impulse of femme4femme has since been politicized and is used in social media and other public intellectual work to index a [sometimes reductive] femme centrism." Savannah Shange, "Play Aunties and Dyke Bitches: Gender, Generation, and the Ethics of Black Queer Kinship," *Black Scholar* 49, no. 1 (January 2019): 52. doi:10.1080/00064246.2019.1548058.

30. Ellie Turner-Kilburn, "Reimagining Queer Female Histories through Fandom" *Transformative Works and Cultures* 37 (2022): para. 5.11, 5.3.

31. Turner-Kilburn, "Reimagining Queer Female Histories," para. 0.1.

32. "Peek into the Past" is the nonfiction section in the back of some American Girl books that provided more historical context for the stories.

33. Turner-Kilburn, "Reimagining Queer Female Histories," para 6.1.

34. *Merriam-Webster*, s.v. "fan fiction (n.)," accessed October 16, 2023, https://www.merriam-webster.com/dictionary/fan%20fiction.

35. Austin, "Valuing Queer Identity," para. 5.4.

36. "American Girl," Fanlore, last modified July 2, 2023, https://fanlore.org/wiki/American_Girl.

37. Benicity is an example of a couple nickname—a combination of the names of people who are in a romantic relationship. Well-known examples of celebrity couple nicknames include Brangelina (Brad Pitt and Angelina Jolie) and Kimye (Kim Kardashian and Kanye West). Benicity is also an example of a ship name, which fans use to express their desired pairings. Examples include Rizzles (Jane Rizzoli and Maura Isles from *Rizzoli & Isles*) and Stony (Steve Rogers and Tony Stark from Marvel).

38. "About the OTW," Archive of Our Own, Organization for Transformative Works, https://archiveofourown.org/about.

39. Casey Fiesler, "Why Archive of Our Own's Surprise Hugo Nomination Is Such a Big Deal," *Slate*, April 9, 2019, https://slate.com/technology/2019/04/archive-of-our-own-fan-fiction-2019-hugo-nomination.html.

40. Floegel, "'Write the Story You Want to Read,'" 787.

41. PFLAG's LGBTQ+ Glossary defines cisnormativity as "the assumption that everyone is cisgender and that being cisgender is superior to all other genders." Heteronormativity is "the assumption that everyone is heterosexual and that heterosexuality is superior to all other sexualities."

42. Floegel, "'Write the Story You Want to Read,'" 785.

43. Floegel, 787.

44. Floegel, 787.

45. "Fandoms > Books & Literature," Archive of Our Own, Organization for Transformative Works, accessed August 1, 2023, https://archiveofourown.org/media/Books%20*a*%20Literature/fandoms.

46. "Archive FAQ > Tags," Archive of Our Own, Organization for Transformative Works, accessed August 1, 2023, https://archiveofourown.org/faq/tags?language_id=en#tagtypes.

47. "Archive FAQ > Tags."

48. According to PFLAG's LGBTQ+ Glossary, nonbinary "refers to people who do not subscribe to the gender binary." Gender binary refers to "the disproven concept that there are only two genders, male and female, and that everyone must be one or the other."

49. Turner-Kilburn, "Reimagining Queer Female Histories," para 5.9.

50. Adrienne Cecile Rich, "Compulsory Heterosexuality and Lesbian Existence," *Journal of Women's History* 15, no. 3 (Autumn 2003): 37.

51. Morgan Sung, "American Girl Doll Collectors Are Fighting Homophobia within Their Online Community," NBC News, June 6, 2022, https://www.nbcnews.com/pop-culture/viral /american-girl-doll-collectors-are-fighting-homophobia-instagram-agig-rcna32219.

52. Reese (@honeyag_), Instagram photo, June 3, 2020, https://www.instagram.com/p /CA-jeUZsbzt/?utm_source=ig_web_copy_link.

53. Reese (@honeyag_), Instagram photo, January 13, 2022, https://www.instagram.com /p/CYrnPQ3L3Om/?utm_source=ig_web_copy_link.

54. Reese (@honeyag_), Instagram photo, June 10, 2023, https://www.instagram.com/p /CtTqfDpuUxD/?utm_source=ig_web_copy_link.

55. Kyra (@sapphic.ag), Instagram story highlight, 2021, https://www.instagram.com /stories/highlights/17871936386748861/.

56. Kyra (@sapphic.ag), Instagram post, June 5, 2023, https://www.instagram.com/p /CtHdHQXrUs5/?utm_source=ig_web_copy_link.

57. Kyra (@sapphic.ag), Instagram post, June 11, 2023, https://www.instagram.com/p /CtWyMRTLltP/?utm_source=ig_web_copy_link.

58. Kyra (@sapphic.ag), Instagram post, June 23, 2023, https://www.instagram.com/p /Ct1kLQAsJXE/?utm_source=ig_web_copy_link.

59. Kyra (@sapphic.ag), Instagram post, June 5, 2023, https://www.instagram.com/p /CtHdHQXrUs5/?utm_source=ig_web_copy_link.

60. Kelsey (@prettylittleelizabeth), Instagram post, June 6, 2022, https://www.instagram .com/p/CeeAbkdrZHr/?utm_source=ig_web_copy_link.

61. Kelsey (@prettylittleelizabeth), Instagram post, June 23, 2022, https://www.instagram .com/p/CfJ4kTur_gu/?utm_source=ig_web_copy_link.

62. Kelsey (@prettylittleelizabeth), Instagram post, June 11, 2023, https://www.instagram .com/p/CtXGDCZO3kN/?utm_source=ig_web_copy_link.

63. Williams Institute, "Prohibiting Gender-Affirming Medical Care for Youth," March 2023, https://williamsinstitute.law.ucla.edu/publications/bans-trans-youth-health-care/.

64. Analyssa Lopez, "These New 90s American Girl Dolls Might Be the Gayest Yet," *Autostraddle*, February 24, 2023, https://www.autostraddle.com/these-new-90s-american -girl-dolls-might-be-the-gayest-yet/.

65. Lopez, "New 90s American Girl Dolls."

66. WRAL News, "American Girl Doll Kira Is the Brand's First with An LGBTQ Storyline," February 16, 2021, https://www.wral.com/newest-american-girl-doll-kira-is-the-brand-s -first-with-an-lgbt-storyline/19530243/. 2/; Camille Fine, "American Girl Stands behind Body Positivity Book amid Unprecedented Spike in Anti-LGBT Reviews," *USA Today*, December 9, 2022, https://www.usatoday.com/story/news/nation/2022/12/09/american-girl-body-book -anti-lgbtq-backlash/1085842900; Peyton Thomas, "American Girl Is All about Equality. So Why Did It Partner with JK Rowling?," LGTBQ Nation, October 25, 2022, https://www .lgbtqnation.com/2022/10/american-girl-equality-partner-jk-rowling/.

67. Thomas, "American Girl Is All about Equality." Rowling, the author of the Harry Potter series, has publicly and repeatedly made transphobic comments. American Girl

partnered with The Wizarding World of Harry Potter to release the American Girl® Harry Potter™ Ultimate Collection in September 2022. Some AG fans, including Thomas, question or criticize this partnership. Thomas writes that the collection "contribute[s] to . . . the substantial wealth" of Rowling.

An Interview with the Creators of the "Hellicity Merriman" Meme Account

Justine Orlovsky-Schnitzler

On October 2, 2021, I was surrounded by dear friends who had traveled from both near and far to celebrate my impending nuptials. After two days of overproof cocktails, too much sun exposure, and limited sleep, my head was swimming as nine of us jockeyed for seats at the dinner table in my parents' home, close by to the beach house we had rented for the weekend. I smiled drowsily (and a little drunkenly) as I watched my friends from different parts of my life become friends with each other. *I knew Tirthna and Irene would hit it off,* I thought as I watched the two of them in animated conversation, feeling less like a bride and more like a proud parent. *I bet they're sharing how much they have in common—starting with me!* I felt satisfied that I had masterminded the most seamless integration of friend groups of all time. "Oh my *god*," I heard Tirthna say, incredulous. "I wish you hadn't told me that. I have to look at you all weekend," Irene apologized immediately. "I'm so sorry." I felt panic rising in my chest as Irene caught my gaze. "I was just telling Tirthna that I have American Girl Teeth,"[1] she explained, and then grinned with her lips pulled up to display said Teeth to the table. Everyone screeched with delight. "I said I wish she hadn't told me that," Tirthna repeated, "because now I can't unsee them."

Moments later, I was bounding upstairs to dig my Molly doll out of the closet in my childhood bedroom (a closet that was also temporarily

Photograph of the author's friend Irene Newman and the author's American Girl doll, Molly.

storing my wedding dress—surely, there is poetry yet to be written about having to dig around such a heavy symbol of adulthood to find a beloved pre-adolescent toy). I asked Irene to pose with Molly, to preserve the absurdity of the moment and direction the evening had taken. I had started the weekend with zero intention of including my American Girl doll in my bachelorette party, and yet, there she was—now propping up a champagne bottle as we toasted to everyone and everything from the man I was marrying to *The Care and Keeping of You*'s infamous diagram on how to insert a tampon.

That all of this came about because Irene thought to describe her teeth as "American Girl Teeth"—and that everyone at the table knew exactly what she meant—is a testament to the American Girl online renaissance, propelled along in no small way by meme creators. In late July 2021, a TikTok trend of identifying celebrities with American Girl Doll Teeth picked up steam, a few months after a user first coined the term in reference to themselves.[2] By 2022, the trend had led us to a place both bizarre and oddly predictable: a NYC-based tattoo artist named Michaela began offering a close-up of an American Girl doll's chompers as part of an American Girl–themed flash (preprepared tattoo designs) sheet (other options include Molly's glasses, a keychain featuring Coconut the dog, and Samantha's legs, surrounded by a heart).[3] The official American Girl TikTok account commented, "The girls who get it, get it." We know at least one person in the world is sporting American Girl Doll Teeth pride for the rest of their natural life.

The internet provides easy access to the American Girl universe for those who didn't have the dolls as a child. Anyone can make a meme, comment on a post, or take a What Doll Are You? quiz; there is virtually no barrier to entry, in contrast to the high price tags of the physical dolls and accessories. On a deeper level, these memes, essays, and posts offer their creators and the users who share them a way to reconcile their childhood with who they have actually become.

There is also the potential for people to transcend matters of privilege and the missteps of the company behind a beloved cultural touchstone by imagining the characters to be as enlightened as we feel we are today. American Girl memes, especially those involving the dolls directly, give us a chance to interact with a childhood staple as *older* and therefore *wiser* versions of ourselves. One of the earliest sites to imagine American Girl characters in the era of the internet, Betches.com, ranks the original lineup of dolls by "betchiness"—that is, their social capital by way of real or imagined attitude. "The betchiest thing about Felicity is that she owns a horse," the article asserts. "Felicity is not higher on the list because [she] . . . would probably say things like 'I just get along with guys better than girls.'"[4] The original article went viral, and subsequent publications have imagined the American Girls in quarantine ("Molly spends all her free time . . . calling Governor Cuomo's office just to cry"), with Hinge profiles ("It's pretty obvious Josefina will be courted by numerous suitors attempting to take her for Tex-Mex"), and attempting to navigate turning thirty-five.[5] Ultimately, this is mythmaking. Psychologist Dan McAdams posits: "We do not discover ourselves through myth, we make ourselves through myth."[6]

American Girl memes, by and large, have sorted themselves into two categories: hyper-specific and innocuous ("we need an American Girl doll who eats cheese out of a bag with her hand") and struggling-adjacent ("we need an American Girl who tried to do her own bikini wax and failed"). Users recognize themselves in the meme and feel relief that they can construct their own narratives about their lives, in the same way doll play as a child encouraged them to worldbuild and self-mythologize. Taking Prozac, loving Phoebe Bridgers, and smoking a lot of weed can all become character traits of fictionalized dolls; features, not bugs. And we can find new ways to challenge what otherwise could be seen as flaws. I don't, I have learned, have rather short, childlike legs with undefined, soft knees. I have *American Girl Doll Legs*. And how.

On January 30, 2023, I spoke via Zoom to the creators behind "Hellicity Merriman," an American Girl meme account with close to two hundred thousand followers on Instagram.[7] We talked about the lifecycle of memes, the lure of nostalgia, and adult friendships mediated by the dolls (and brand) of our youth.

Justine Orlovsky-Schnitzler: If you don't mind, would each of you share your name?

Barrett: My name is Barrett.

Carter: And my name is Carter.

Justine: How do y'all know each other? And how did you get this account going?

Barrett: So we met at work about five and a half years ago. And the lore of the account is that it was Carter's idea. She sometimes likes to share credit with me, but it was her idea—she's the brilliant one. And it came from a long history of, like, bonding over the shared experience of having had these dolls growing up, and reading their books, and laughing about how oddly dark the books can be, while also being silly with it. We'd make each other—and other coworkers—take personality quizzes like "What American Girl Doll Are You?"

. . . I think it was on Twitter first that I saw American Girl memes start to really pop up, and we'd send them back and forth to each other. I thought they were hilarious. And almost a year ago, at this point, Carter let me know she had the account and shared the password with me.

Justine: Carter, did you have anything you wanted to add?

Carter: I think what Barrett shared is a great summary of how we met . . . and the inspiration behind our account was definitely swapping memes that we were seeing primarily on Twitter, and then on Instagram. And I think it happened very organically. We were both coming up with ideas . . . I think it was after, probably, one extra glass of wine that I actually made the account. And it was pretty slow-going in the beginning. Like, I have ADHD. I literally never finish anything. I'm the kind of person that has twelve journals that I've started and only made it four pages into before abandoning it. This is the only thing I feel like I've ever done that I have stuck with. And I think Barrett is a huge reason for this, because I have some accountability. We're doing it together, which is *way* more fun. But yeah, it totally started as a joke. I didn't think it was going to last more than a week.

Barrett: I tell people all the time, privately, that I would never in a million fucking years do this on my own. And people are surprised by that! But I feel like we're very similar in a lot of ways, but also able to foil each other. It keeps us level, and helps us not take it too seriously, while also being like, how can this be fun and maybe even educational?

Carter: I really would not want to do that dance by myself.

Justine: When did it seem like things were taking off into a new direction, with a larger audience? You know, when suddenly there's like one hundred thousand people following you, and people are engaging with you in a different way. Was that scary? Or just exciting?

Barrett: In June 2022, things really took off. The "We need a ___ who" meme format just exploded. We started seeing some of our memes get reshared to other platforms. We went from 10K followers to 15K or 20K. And then I remember seeing, organically, a TikTok that had billions of likes and views on it, that was just screen-grabbing from our Instagram. It was a person, using the green screen feature, to look through our account. It was like ten seconds long. But after that, things happened very quickly. We got to like 75K or 85K followers. Then finally, the big day that sticks out: we realized we were probably going to hit 100,000 followers on the day that *Roe v. Wade* was overturned. And I think by the end of that day, we'd hit 135K or 145K. We posted a one-off meme about the decision and it just got shared *everywhere*.

Justine: I work for an abortion fund currently, and I can tell you within my own sphere . . . I was really grateful for accounts that were offering a release valve, so you feel like you can get up and keep doing this work. Your post made it into our orbit pretty early. But it's been great because y'all have continued to lift up abortion funds and other organizations keeping people safe and keeping care accessible. From my perspective, it seems like y'all are not worried about trying to appeal to everyone with your memes. . . .

This is more niche, but it's great that Felicity is the face of the account in some ways. I've tried to explain to my husband how the jokes about Felicity being the "conservative" American Girl doll came about. Was there a particular reason you chose Felicity? Or did it just really work with the pun you wanted to accomplish with her name?

Carter: I had Felicity! I actually had two dolls as a child. Felicity was my first and I was gifted her because I grew up in Virginia and I have red hair. . . . Felicity, of course, is from Colonial Virginia, and has red hair. That was really the whole thought process for my parents. Even though I eventually got another doll—Lindsay, which was the very first Girl of the Year in like 2001—I've always been loyal to Felicity. So I wanted to make the name of the account something like a pun, and *Hellicity* just worked. I threw some devil horns on her and it all came together.

Barrett: I would ask for dolls like, every year for Christmas. I couldn't get enough of these things. Samantha was my first, and main one, though. I had a Bitty Baby when I was little. I also had Samantha's friend Nellie. I had Josefina. And I had two of the Girls of the Year—Kailey, which was 2003, and then Marisol, who was 2005.

Justine: I had Molly. But it's funny . . . what Carter just said, about getting Felicity because she had red hair and lived in Virginia . . . you're kinda like, yep! That's enough! That's enough for this doll to *be me*. That was the thought process for my parents. I have a grandfather who fought in WWII, and they thought—great, she'll love Molly! Hilariously, I ended up with the same glasses that Molly wears, as an adult. But as a kid, my peers were like, *that's the ugly doll*. Which felt *great*.

Barrett: I identify so strongly as a Samantha girl, but I know I was definitely too young to have chosen that for myself. I looked like her when I was like a little kid. I had, like, thick brown wavy hair and blunt bangs. I'm sure my parents thought—this one looks like her! This is going to be her person! Our parents were assigning us an identity in these dolls, and they had no idea [*laughs*].

Justine: Yeah—no one thought we would, as adults, be calling ourselves "Molly girls" or "Samantha girls." I don't know how old you are, but I'm twenty-seven. And right around twelve and thirteen is when my peer group and friends stopped playing with dolls. I missed my chance to have a Jewish doll, because Rebecca came out right after I got my first period and everyone was casting aside their childhood toys. And so Molly became an artifact

An Interview with the Creators of the "Hellicity Merriman" Meme Account   219

in the corner of my room. But I remember thinking that American Girl was only going to continue to produce more and more diverse dolls, and simultaneously that the historical dolls would creep closer and closer to my mom's childhood. Or, God forbid, *mine.* They just recently released a doll living in the nineties. You can get a tiny Pizza Hut cup for your doll. She can have a Macintosh 128k. And that was really the point of no return—where I looked at the company and I thought, all right, I'm officially an adult now. . . . And I don't know what the longevity of the company is. I mean, no one does. They've obviously done great. They had a resurgence in the last few years, though they were on a sharp decline right before. Bringing back the historical lineup, the original six dolls, was a huge hit. Clearly they're aware there's an appetite for revisiting this company and these dolls. I don't know if y'all have contributed to this nostalgia-frenzy in some capacity, but I'd like to think that you have.

Barrett: We've gotten a few DMs from people who are American Girl employees.

Carter: The company itself has never reached out. But I think one of the first interviews Barrett did on behalf of the account also had some quote in there from American Girl corporate that was generically like, not *loving* it, but not *hating* it. Just something like, "we love to see how girls who play with our dolls turn into adults; American Girls turn into American women." That was the gist of it. I can say I don't think they hate us, which is good [*laughs*].

Justine: I wouldn't see how they could. That's the thing, right? There's this enormous resurgence of people engaging with the company through your account, and through accounts like yours. No matter how you slice it, it translates into engagement with the company, and one of those methods of engagement is through purchasing. There was an article in the *New York Times*, which I'm sure you are familiar with, profiling Harry Hill and Serena Kerrigan going to the American Girl Café in NYC to day drink. And the company can't officially comment on people getting drunk at a children's cafe, but they are *probably* benefiting financially from it in some way. So, it's a tricky line, I'm sure, that they have to walk.

Carter: One anecdote that springs to mind—and this is slightly off—topic, but I think about it all the time because it's funny . . . we have a highlight reel where I occasionally let Felicity try new things because she did spend about fifteen years of her life in a box in a basement. Somebody online suggested that she get her ears pierced. And so I took a drill and I pierced her ears with the drill. And someone wrote to us and said, "I used to work at American Girl, and I did doll-ear piercing. And that's *literally* how we did it. We would use a drill." And they said that there was like a back room with just doll heads that you could practice on. I don't know for sure if this is true. But I think about that all the time . . . imagining a back room at the American Girl doll store full of . . . brave doll heads.

Justine: Have y'all dealt with harassment in any form?

Barett: Carter, I feel like you've probably got more stories than I do. It hasn't happened in a while.

Carter: Yeah, usually things are very positive. Whenever we've posted anything nostalgia-related, we see a lot of activity in the comments. Folks tag each other in, and we absolutely love that. That's my favorite thing that happens. But the only flip side of that is on the post we made the day *Roe v. Wade* was overturned, comments just got way out of hand. That post got *thousands* of hate comments. This was in part because the post reached so far beyond our typical audience. Celebrities were sharing it. Right. And I *was* scared, because I had never been in a situation online where I "blew up" like that.

Justine: *Totally.*

Carter: And so I was reading the comments, which was not a good thing to do. I was coming back from a trip and my boyfriend was driving, so I just sat in the front seat and deleted comments for like two hours on the way home. Just the most heinous, horrible, god-awful shit I have ever read. But since then . . . it really hasn't ever been as intense as that. Although a couple of days ago someone called us satanic, which I am obsessed with. I was like, thank you, yes.

Justine: I'm curious generally about how you conceptualize longevity, or if you're really thinking that far forward. Do you want to just do this as long as it's fun? Or do you feel pressure to keep up, like you'll have to run this account longer than you intended? Or do you try to not think about it at all?

Barrett: I do feel some pressure. I think—and I might be speaking for both of us here, but Carter, cut me off if I'm not—both of us thought it would have petered out by now. I work in digital marketing full time. You expect a peak, and then valleys. . . . And that still hasn't *really* happened. We don't have days or weeks where there's exponential growth on the account. But we're also not losing our audience en masse. And so as long as it's fun, and it feels useful, we'll do it.

Justine: That makes total sense—and there's no correct or wrong answer here.

Carter: Yeah, I agree. Right now, it still feels fun. And there definitely are moments where it *doesn't* feel fun . . . but the good outweighs the bad. We don't post on a schedule and I think that helps.

Barrett: There's probably been two or three weeks where we were posting every day, multiple times a day. And then two or three days of quiet passed, and people were in the comment section, in our direct messages, asking if we were okay and what was going on. But now—we can just let things happen organically. I can post when I have inspiration, and not sit and try to force it.

Justine: I'm curious if there's anything you feel very strongly about, with the brand. I'm not an ambassador for American Girl, and neither are y'all— but is there anything that's stuck with you or come up for you, internally, once you started running this account?

Barrett: There's definitely a massive gap between when I stopped playing with these dolls, or when the catalog stopped coming to my home—and then us making this account. Like, a good fifteen-year gap. In the interim, American Girl as a brand wasn't on my radar. . . . I remember when we started the account, I was getting up to speed on what American Girl has been doing in that fifteen-year gap between my childhood and now. I noticed right off the bat how much more *diverse* the dolls and characters are, and what efforts have been made toward that. And of course, there are still shortcomings. We talked about this recently for an outlet, but: I know over the last few years the brand has wanted to update some of its books to have gender inclusive language, and to talk more about exploring gender identity. And there was this immediate conservative backlash. And what we said was: this brand may still fall short on things, but has *never* been a really conservative brand. Like the foundation was: these are little girls who are imperfect, but they all are solving problems by themselves and becoming better people. And they wanted to educate little girls about history, try to build empathy for folks who are different from you, and provide good accurate information about puberty and feelings while they're at it. This was *always* a fairly decent brand. So, it's crazy to me that there has been so much conservative backlash against this brand at every possible fucking turn. American Girl has never tried to cater to outright regressive people.

Justine: I guess there's a sliver of possibility that for some folks, these dolls were just expensive toys. A status symbol. And maybe those folks didn't look around and dig deeply into the lessons of the books, or pay any attention to the entire suite of materials American Girl produces. And so now these folks can come back around and claim American Girl is suddenly "sneaking in" progressive ideas. Like you said—to me, those ideas always seemed obviously present. And sure, they're a corporation, and sure, they're owned by Mattel now—and they want to make money. But I'd rather give my money to a brand trying to be more inclusive in helping kids learn about puberty and gender and independence and creativity.

Carter, I don't know if you had anything you wanted to add to that? No pressure.

Carter: Like you mentioned earlier . . . for me, it's not just about the dolls. It was never just about growing up. I think seeing and hearing the shared experiences of people has been so helpful for me personally. Like . . . at a time where I felt super lonely, it was really nice to have this outlet where I could share what I was feeling and see what other people were feeling too. We made a meme about needing an American Girl guide to navigating your mental health in your midtwenties; that was only *kind* of a joke.

Everyone engaging with our page has had this experience of knowing about American Girl dolls as kids, or having one; we know their stories, some of which are God awful and dark. And we realize that we should be grateful we don't have to deal with cholera now, but also sometimes getting out of bed is really hard. And I think that is the tone of a lot of our humor. And we can read the comments or look at our messages and see how many people are sharing what we make to their stories and into the world. To me—it's about *that*. It's about our community, where we're still growing up in some ways. Being a person in this world can be difficult. Maybe it's not cholera-killed-my-sister tough, but it doesn't mean it's not tough.

Justine: Absolutely.

Barrett: I think doll culture has emerged in the past, like one and a half years as a way for us to relive our childhoods a little bit and also synthesize our adulthood. It's not unrelated to other waves of nostalgia, especially with the internet. But we've had the Barbie movie come out. *M3gan* came out. I don't know what the obsession is exactly . . . which is funny to say, as someone who has kind of capitalized on this nostalgia and obsession, but . . . there's a kind of humor in twisting a symbol of girlhood into our relationship with womanhood.

An Interview with the Creators of the "Hellicity Merriman" Meme Account   223

Justine: I think that makes sense. I had Barbies as a kid, but it was always evident to me that Barbie is a *woman*. She's very small, but she's a woman. Whereas when you're engaging with an American Girl doll as a kid, they're meant to be a kid your age. My parents weren't ever really worried about the broader questions of Barbie being oversexualized. And Barbie's had, like, three hundred jobs, and she seems to have been good at all of them. But with an American Girl doll, you're playing with a representation that's meant to be close to your likeness and age. More representational, less aspirational.

It definitely makes that meme about having "American Girl Doll Teeth" or "American Girl Doll Legs" as an adult even funnier. I have the latter. One of my best friends proudly claims the former.

Barrett: People find a lot of joy in it. Like Carter mentioned, in some of our earliest posts, we tried to make slightly more specific connections to American Girl characters as the brand created them. And now, it's more general life observations. And for now, it seems like people are still with us, and they like it. I definitely don't think the doll resurgence is going anywhere as quickly as some other bits of nostalgia have. American Girl is still very much of the moment.

Barret and Carter jointly created and run the American Girl meme account "Hellicity Merriman" (@hellicitymerriman on Twitter/X and Instagram)

Notes

1. Most American Girl doll facial molds feature an open mouth with two prominent front teeth. In common usage, having "American Girl Teeth" means your two front teeth are especially visible when you speak, and also visible whenever your jaw is relaxed.

2. Emerald Pellot, "What Are 'American Girl Doll Teeth' And Why Do People Want Them?" *In the Know by Yahoo!*, July 30, 2021, https://www.intheknow.com/post/american-girl-doll-teeth/?guccounter=1&guce_referrer=aHR0cHM6Ly93d3cuZ29vZ2xlLmNvbS88&guce_referrer_sig=AQAAAK7OtPaGs5rk3noEol9Ja1vDRv754-EOUvmssZnVq8OsolWUb5uubAB6kUBPdkCGbE7jvQhGA2nU4lmvj_slUeBxXm5JKdjcZfWNRKKDGmKWPTpncPDw3NRF6FiqLfb7R7SYvMLoehYfwoZa8NPOfwfdIwKoaXSbX77-tImjUgfy.

3. @kale.tat, "all my julie girlies rise UP," TikTok, January 6, 2023, https://www.tiktok.com/@kale.tat/video/7185594546825317674.

4. Alise Morales, "American Girl Dolls Ranked by Betchiness," *Betches*, December 14, 2016, https://betches.com/american-girl-dolls-ranked-by-betchiness/.

5. Alise Morales, "How the American Girl Dolls Would Spend Quarantine," *Betches*, April 1, 2020, https://betches.com/how-the-american-girl-dolls-would-spend-quarantine/.

6. Angela Chen, "How We Create Personal Myths, and Why They Matter," *Catapult Magazine*, July 18, 2018, https://catapult.co/stories/column-data-stories-we-tell-about-our selves-and-why-they-matter.

7. Barret and Carter, @hellicity_merriman, Instagram, https://www.instagram.com /hellicity_merriman/.

CONCLUSION

American Girls Forever

Justine Orlovsky-Schnitzler and KC Hysmith

On November 30, 2023, at 6:00 a.m. (EST), preorders went live for a collaborative event that in the first year of Pleasant Company's existence would have likely seemed impossible: *Barbie x American Girl*. For the price of $300, American Girl (and Barbie) rewards members could order a doll expected to arrive by mail a full year later, sometime in November 2024. The doll itself was curiously adult in its execution: she dons permanent makeup and sports a version of Barbie's iconic black-and-white bathing suit studded with Swarovski crystals. It is unsettling, in more ways than one, to see Barbie's visage and aesthetic grafted onto the body of a doll always intended to represent a girl roughly nine years of age. Though the limited run of five thousand dolls sold out within twenty-four hours of the preorder release, reactions within the American Girl doll community and wider online forums were mixed. One Reddit user lamented, "It feels a little weird to me to have a doll who was designed to look like a child done up like a sex symbol. I think I just have a very limited idea in my head of what an American Girl doll is . . . and this isn't it."[1]

A *Fast Company* profile of American Girl from 2019 noted that the company's sales had been in free-fall, declining 28 percent in 2018 alone. "American Girl is tasked with a tricky business challenge: It must win over today's children by creating dolls, content, and experiences that resonate with them, while also winning over their parents, who like me, are yearning

American Girl x Barbie collector doll marketing image. Credit: Mattel Creations

for the brand that shaped their own childhood," profiler Elizabeth Segran writes. "And based on American Girl's financial woes, it may be struggling to cater to the needs of two very different generations of consumers."[2]

Who is the Barbie-fied American Girl doll for? She cannot stand under her own power (she is the first American Girl doll to come with a necessary display stand, much like the original Barbie who was unable to support herself on her perpetually tip-toed feet). She will depreciate in value the moment she is sprung from the box she arrives in (that is, if she's even let out of the box). She is, by all indications, not meant to be a plaything at all. This, in and of itself, is not entirely outside the realm of reasonable: American Girl dolls have always been expensive, and many, many passionate fans of the company—adult and child alike—are dedicated and thoughtful collectors, preferring to keep their dolls in particular condition. American Girl encourages you to make your dolls your own, however you see fit to engage with them. Still, there is something oddly finite in this doll, and this release. Perhaps it is because it feels like a cash grab at the tail end of an exhaustive promotional cycle tied to the summer 2023 Barbie movie directed by Greta Gerwig (and the doll will only arrive in mailboxes a full year after a preorder is placed). Perhaps it is for the reasons articulated by so many online—that Barbie's look is simply too adult to be transposed onto a child. Or perhaps it's simply because Pleasant Rowland created American Girls not to argue with nor belittle Barbie, but to be something *different* from her. An American Girl character might have played *with* Barbies within her universe, but she was—at the center of it all—herself.

In seemingly unrelated news, barely twelve hours before the Barbie collaboration launched, Henry Kissinger, former Secretary of State, died at his home in Connecticut. As soon as the news broke widely, AG parody account Hellicity Merriman sprang into action. "If this is how u found out Henry Kissinger is dead," the post on Instagram read, "be honest."

On X/Twitter, user Tyler McCall (@eiffeltyler) confessed to being one such individual. "I found out Henry Kissinger died from an American Girl doll meme account on Instagram," she wrote. "Exactly what Pleasant Rowland intended when she invented them in 1986."[3] Others agreed. "Hellicity is exactly how I found out," user Bre (@brewrites) replied. "And I printed out the screenshot so I would always remember," attaching a photo showing she had, in fact, done exactly that.[4]

Obviously, the introduction of an official brand collaboration between Mattel subsidiaries and the death of one of the most reviled war makers of the twentieth century are not, strictly speaking, linked. But they are two points in a broader constellation of American capitalism that keeps American Girl in the (frequently absurd) zeitgeist of the twenty first century. The internet excels at collapsing seemingly disparate worlds together, to the point that at least a few hundred people learned of a major world event from a doll meme account.

Moreover, this overlap speaks to American Girl's continued relevancy as a nostalgic entity operating under its own power—outside of and *away from* the company itself. This creates somewhat of a dilemma for American Girl: many of the people talking about the company most excitedly and keeping it public discourse are doing so in a way that the company cannot publicly endorse or engage with. American Girl is spreading itself thin: it wants to speak for and to girls of the present moment, shaping emerging generations, while simultaneously courting nostalgia that may or may not pay off in financial engagement.

On May 4, 2021, American Girl announced the return of the six dolls that comprised the original lineup.[5] Samantha, Kirsten, and Molly had been discontinued between 2008 and 2013, while Josefina, Felicity, and Addy had been retired between 2013 and 2016. A Smithsonian article about the launch summarized the excitement on the internet: "When American Girl announced the news [to bring back the 'original 6' doll lineup] on May 4 [2021], nostalgic social media users reacted with glee, sharing anecdotes about their favorite characters and making plans to purchase replacements for well-worn childhood dolls."[6] As part of the promotion, they also released a short book explicitly aimed at adults, entitled *Everything I Need to Know I Learned from American Girl*, which was, according to the brand, "sort of tongue-in-cheek" and "explicitly nostalgic."[7]

Nostalgia is at once a comfort and an attempt to freeze time, to return to so-called simplicity or process new experience through a supposedly simpler lens. That processing can sometimes look downright heretical: take, for example, the stunning upswing in adults visiting the American Girl Café in NYC to "get sloshed." A February 18, 2022 *New York Times* article entitled "Dolls and Drinks for Likes and Clicks" documents the phenomenon of social media influencers reveling at their new destination:

> On this occasion, the two influencers posed for selfies, recorded content and mugged for their phones as servers brought several courses that included cinnamon buns, crudités, buttered noodles and chicken fingers. The vast cafe was mostly empty apart from five other parties, each made up of children and their chaperones. Mr. Hill and Ms. Kerrigan took their seats, got their dolls situated and toasted rose martinis served in glasses rimmed with pink sugar. For some, 11:30 is early for a drink, but Mr. Hill had already spent the morning mixing water with cranberry juice to simulate cocktails for a sponsored Instagram post. This time, the vodka was real.[8]

Whether or not American Girl can officially underwrite millennials treating the AG Café like a neighborhood bar is beside the point; AG is, directly and indirectly, benefiting from the arrangement.

In 2023, American Girl participated in no less than seven other partnerships with outside brands and companies: a second release with Disney and Swarovski, a second Harry Potter release, the National Football League, Something Navy (a fast fashion brand popular amongst users of the video app TikTok), *Wicked* (the musical), and Jeni's Splendid Ice Cream.[9] Of all these joint efforts, Jeni's feels the most obtuse.[10] American Girl debuted new Jeni's tee-shirts for dolls, tiny plastic pints, and an ice cream truck sporting the Jeni's logo retailing for $325. It is hard to imagine any preteen was yearning for officially licensed merchandise of an ice cream company known for pints often retailing for north of $10.

Recall Juliette Holder's essay about consumerism: "Courtney doesn't just buy things—she buys real brands, including American Girl. In a meta-moment, you can buy your American Girl doll an American Girl doll of her own (Courtney is, I guess, a Molly fan)."

This is not to lament official releases in every form; there are undoubtedly many consumers who have derived a lot of joy from these efforts, as evidenced by (some) strong sales numbers. But there is something to be said for collapsing into monoculture. Brand-name collaborations stray from what made American Girl truly unique at its outset. A separate, but related issue is the quality of items making their way to consumers. Since 2010 (considered to be an important year of transition in manufacturing, after which dolls were no longer stamped with "Pleasant Company" on the back of their necks), collectors and ordinary consumers have identified a noticeable shift in the sturdiness and material composition of dolls. Arms and legs come out of their sockets at a much more frequent clip; dolls arrive with mussed hair and irregularly painted faces, their torsos floppy. The vinyl composition of the doll's skin has a tendency to turn gray or green over time; some specific dolls, like Nellie and Kailey (both discontinued) have a tendency to turn orange.[11] Similarly, furniture and accessories no longer designed hold the promise of becoming heirloom pieces; real wood for doll beds has been replaced by particle board and most clothing is made of plastic fibers. For some reason, you can buy segment of the Hogwarts Express (made entirely of plastic) in collaboration with Warner Bros./the Harry Potter franchise for $550, while historical dolls continue to see their collections shrunk or outright retired (Mattel retired Samantha in 2008, her fellow historical doll Kirsten went in 2009, and Molly in 2010.)

A few years later, in 2014, the original book series, one of the last vestiges of several historical characters, was rereleased as the BeForever series in two-volume bundles each packed with several of the historical stories and, notably, none of the original illustrations.[12] In 2019, the books underwent further revisions including the abridgement of events, side stories, descriptions, and other important contextual information that arguably attracted young historically inclined readers in the first place. It does not feel like a projection to point to these decisions as a real loss for the brand, and for future generations of would-be historians (as argued by Tara Strauch in this collection). On a more existential level, there is the lingering worry that gutting the historical line in particular means American Girl has firmly moved away from what many would consider to be the *soul* of the company (if a company could, in fact, have such a thing).

There is much we did not cover in this anthology: the annually changing Girl of the Year dolls, the Bitty Baby and Wellie Wishers product lines, the complexities of the BeForever rebrand, the varying television or direct-to-DVD historical character movies produced since 2004 (as of December 2023, Mattel has announced intent to pursue a *Barbie*-sized blockbuster adaptation of the American Girl line, with scant details at time of writing).[13] And though we were fortunate to hear from many doll collectors, it would take an entirely separate volume to speak to the richness and diversity of collectors and creators, who have been making American Girl their own since its debut.

We hope, then, that you take from this anthology a sense of appreciation for the kinds of conversations American Girl has inspired since 1986. Maria Santa Poggi, writing for *InStyle*, summed it up beautifully:

> Lately, I've been thinking about the girl I used to be. She was awkward, funny, and had a mouth of braces. She had synchronized handshakes with her friends and lived off of inside jokes. She was embarrassed over her body and mortified to talk to her first crush. She spent her free time reading next to her Molly McIntire American Girl Doll, and she dreamed of a world full of choices. She wanted to dye her hair, get tattoos and piercings, have her first kiss, and go to college. A lot of my girlhood was waiting and preparing to choose who I could be. That feeling never goes away—and maybe that's why American Girl Dolls haven't either. They remain, as always, a way to process who we are, what we want, and who we want to become.[14]

To that end, when we think about where American Girl is heading—as an idea, as a company, as a part of ourselves—we're thinking (ever optimistically) about generations to come. We're imagining what it will be like to share our dog-eared copies of *The Care and Keeping of You* with a niece, with an air of conspiratorial *cool aunt* energy. We're hoping that children continue to feel empowered to use American Girl as a springboard—to create their dolls and their backgrounds in their own image. We're purchasing the menorah set for our doll that we would have loved to have as a child, just because we can. And we're comfortable with diverging from Pleasant Company (and Mattel) as much as we feel we need to. We know corporations are not people. We know we have the power to critique, to fill in the gaps, to rip it all up and start from scratch. Our creativity is endless; our nostalgia is *ours*, in all of its complexities and contradictions.

Notes

1. "Are you purchasing the AG Barbie collector doll?" r/americangirl, Reddit, November 30, 2023, https://www.reddit.com/r/americangirl/comments/187obvq/are_you_purchasing _the_ag_barbie_collector_doll/.

2. Elizabeth Segran, "American Girl Sales Are Plummeting. Can the Iconic '90s Brand Be Saved?" *Fast Company*, December 17, 2019, https://www.fastcompany.com/90439667 /american-girl-is-in-free-fall.

3. Tyler McCall (@eiffeltyler), "I found out Henry Kissinger died from an American Girl doll meme . . ." X, November 29, 2023, https://twitter.com/eiffeltyler/status/1730045783901077801.

4. McCall, X, 2023.

5. Megan Reynolds, "American Girl Is Getting the Old Band Back Together," *Jezebel*, May 4, 2021, https://jezebel.com/american-girl-is-getting-the-old-band-back-together-1846820142.

6. Meilan Solly, "The Enduring Nostalgia of American Girl Dolls," *Smithsonian Magazine*, June 3, 2021, https://www.smithsonianmag.com/history/evolution-american-girl-dolls -180977822/.

7. American Girl Editors, *Everything I Need to Know I Learned From American Girl: Timeless Advice for Girls of All Ages* (El Segundo, CA: American Girl, 2021).

8. Shane O'Neill, "Dolls and Drinks for Likes and Clicks," *New York Times*, February 18, 2022, https://www.nytimes.com/2022/02/18/style/american-girl-cafe-harry-hill-serena -kerrigan.html.

9. This is especially stark given the rich individual creator's market—Etsy artists have been making and selling unofficial Harry Potter attire for American Girl dolls for years.

10. "Jeni's Splendid Ice Creams," American Girl, accessed January 14, 2014, https://www .americangirl.com/collections/jenis-splendid-ice-creams.

11. The Doll Ranch (@desertdollranch), "I know a few other people have mentioned this in the notes, but Kailey is very often afflicted by Cheeto Disease," Tumblr, May 3, 2023, https://desertdollranch.tumblr.com/post/716341998041366528/i-know-a-few-other-people -have-mentioned-this-in.

12. "Central Series," American Girl Wiki, accessed January 14, 2024, https://americangirl .fandom.com/wiki/Central_Series#:~:text=There%20have%20been%20many%20changes, publication%20run%20by%20its%20traits.

13. Meredith Woerner, "American Girl Dolls Movie in the Works from Mattel, 'Pet Sematary: Bloodlines' Screenwriter," *Variety*, December 13, 2023, https://variety.com/2023/film/entertainment-industry/american-girl-dolls-movie-mattel-1235837140/.

14. Maria Santa Poggi, "We Need an American Girl Doll Who Will Save Us," *InStyle*, July 19, 2022, https://www.instyle.com/reviews-coverage/american-girl-doll-memes.

Acknowledgments

This book project began in October 2022, at the 134th annual meeting of the American Folklore Society in Tulsa, Oklahoma. Justine traveled from North Carolina to present her talk, "American Girl, the Business of Self-Expression, and the Future of Nostalgia," conceived as a love letter to the burst of internet-driven creativity around American Girl during the pandemic. By the end of the weekend, she'd met with the University Press of Mississippi—and left KC a very excited voicemail with a proposition you only get to make a few times in your life: *Do you want to edit a book with me?*

Thankfully, KC said yes.

Over the last two years, we've had an incredible time ... mostly dreaming about how to fit a research trip to the American Girl Store into our project budget and whether an American Girl themed party (complete with matching doll costumes and hors d'ocuvrcs from thc historical cookbooks) was an appropriate way to celebrate a book launch.

To that end: we would like to thank a number of people who made this book a reality.

From Justine

My husband Max, my first and best editor (always). My Grandma Sally, for giving me my Molly doll in 2002. My parents, Steve and Lisa Schnitzler, who raised me 1) wonderfully 2) with the stubborn confidence that I could publish a book. To their incredible coterie of friends who raised me alongside them (and never complained when I came to dinner parties). My sister,

Olivia, the true doll expert in my life. My *machatunim*, Gerri, Jeff, and Ethan. My Grandma Barbara, of blessed memory, who passed away during this publication process. To Irene Newman and Tirthna Badhiwala: thank you for letting me romanticize 1) your conversations 2) your beautiful teeth. And thank you to John Chavez and Ken Oots, for photography and cover design wizardry.

In no particular order whatsoever: Baz Armstrong, Kyla Dehart, Mackenzie Kwok, Robert Lazo and Amanda Moffett, Jordan, Greyson, and Charlotte Feurer, Robert Wallace and Elisa Pelgrift (and Elinor), Ethan Tyler, Jessie Taylor, Charles Lumsden and Tara McKinnon, Sabrina Golling, Ana Elezovic, Mia Lehrer, Sloan Godbey, Grace Morrison, Sierra Lawson, Zachary Faircloth, Pat and George Lee, Seth Kotch, Annie Crowther, Grace Esposito, and Samantha Sugerik.

Last but *never* least: our cats, Fritz and Miró, who mostly knocked papers off my desk (but were an integral part of the process nonetheless), and Katie Crutchfield/Waxahatchee, who provided the soundtrack to almost every page I wrote.

From KC

My dad for instilling a love of historical trinkets (also known as *material culture*). My husband for not complaining about said affinity for historical trinkets, which eventually served as the impetus for getting a PhD (and the acquisition of more trinkets for *research purposes*) and how I eventually met Justine! To Esther, who shares this love of history and is a fount of AG knowledge and the absolute best coauthor. To my children for letting me check out AG books with their library cards. And lastly, thank you to name-not-remembered from elementary school for inviting me to my first American Girl themed costume birthday party sleepover even though I didn't own a single item from the highly coveted brand; you welcomed me as I arrived in my mom's old frilly nightgown with my creepy knock-off vintage porcelain doll in tow nonetheless. Little did you know the historic moment we were about to make together.

From Both of Us

To our brilliant contributors who put both their clever minds and compassionate hearts into every line of their essays. For many, these words were personal, deeply nostalgic, and at times painful and embarrassing. We cannot thank you enough for your candor and the skill with which you melded it into thoughtful, critical, and constructive analysis of everything American Girl was and is. Thank you all for enduring our emails, our memes, and our edits. We are so proud to be part of this anthology with you.

To the American Girl fans, devotees, and estranged besties who still check in from time to time, but make sure to keep those boundaries up: This is for you. We hope you find yourself amongst these pages and hope to hear your AG story someday. A special thanks goes out to the AGIG community and others in the AG world who kindly allowed our contributors to interview them.

To Mary Heath and the entire University Press of Mississippi team. Thank you for helping us share this idea with the world.

To the Orange County Social Club (the best bar in the world), where many a sentence was written and email responded to with perfectly made negronis in hand. We'll hide no fewer than three copies of the book somewhere on the premises for everyone to enjoy.

To Bill and Marcie Cohen Ferris. We are so lucky to be in y'all's orbit.

And to American Girl: you've been there from the beginning and we've whispered so many secrets to our dolls over the years, there isn't much you don't already know. Thanks for being there and for letting us pick you apart. You'll always be our BF*Beforever.*

About the Contributors

Mary Berman is a Philadelphia, PA, USA-based writer of mostly speculative fiction, plus the occasional poem or essay. She earned her MFA in fiction from the University of Mississippi, and her work has been published in *PseudoPod*, *Cicada*, *British Fantasy Society Journal*, and elsewhere. Find her online at www.mtgberman.com, or read her monthly creative writing newsletter at mtgberman.substack.com.

Mary M. Burke, UConn professor of English, is author of *Race, Politics, and Irish America: A Gothic History* (2023) and a cultural history of Irish Travellers (both from Oxford UP). She collaborated with Tramp Press on the 2022 *Juanita Casey Horse of Selene* reissue. A former University of Notre Dame NEH Irish Fellow, she was a 2022 LRH Fellow at alma mater Trinity College Dublin. Her work has placed with *NPR*, the *Irish Times*, and *RTÉ*.

Abigail C. Fine holds a PhD in comparative literature from Queen Mary University of London. Her dissertation examines Cinderella's fairy godmother in adaptations of the tale using a dress-based, sociohistorical lens. Her research interests include fairy tale studies, children's literature, adaptation theory, and fashion studies. She holds an MA in history from the College of William and Mary, and an MA in English literature from Georgetown University. She grew up with a Felicity doll.

Juliette Holder is pursuing a PhD in rhetoric from Texas Woman's University. She previously earned an MA in rhetoric from San Diego State University. She is an instructor of technical writing and first-year composition courses. Her research interests include feminist rhetorics, popular culture, and the writing process. Occasionally, she combines all three by studying what Taylor Swift's rerecording project reveals about the revision process. Her work has appeared in *Ms.* magazine and *USA Today*.

KC Hysmith is a writer, food scholar, historical recipe developer, and the director of communications at the Museum of Food and Drink (MOFAD) in New York City. She holds an MLA in gastronomy from Boston University and PhD in American Studies from the University of North Carolina. With a combination of food scholarship and digital media, KC demonstrates how the past impacts the way we eat and think about food today. Find more of her work on TikTok (@foodherstory) and on Instagram (@kchysmith).

Mackenzie Kwok is a folklorist, writer, and musician based in New York City. She studied folklore at the University of North Carolina at Chapel Hill and social anthropology at the University of Cambridge. Her research interests range from Chinese diasporic foodways to protest chants. She grew up reading all the American Girl historical collection books, subscribed to *American Girl* magazine, and still has her copy of *The Care and Keeping of You.*

Esther Martin is a food scholar, folklorist, and storyteller completing an MLA in gastronomy at Boston University. She has expertise in foodways, material culture, and public history. In her day-to-day life she works as an instructional designer at University of Pennsylvania where she is committed to creating equitable and inclusive classrooms. She is passionate about public-facing food studies and has spent time butchering sheep and cooking over a hearth as an historic interpreter. Her other interests include dressing like Miss Frizzle, gardening, and napping.

Hannah Matthews is the author of *You or Someone You Love: Reflections from an Abortion Doula* (Atria Books, 2023). Her writing has appeared in *TIME, Vogue, ELLE, Esquire, Teen Vogue, Glamour, McSweeney's,* the *Washington Post, Jezebel, Salon,* and other publications. Matthews lives with her family in Maine, where she works as an abortion doula and community care worker.

About the Contributors

Janine B. Napierkowski is a Lifetime Girl Scout, American Girl collector, and board member of Yes She Can, Inc. She has an MA in leadership in museum education from Bank Street College and has worked on projects at museums all over the country for Rube Goldberg, Inc., her favorite being the Children's Museum of Pittsburgh. Janine enjoys reading, theater, and historic houses, all of which she can trace back to the influence of American Girl.

Justine Orlovsky-Schnitzler is a folklorist, writer, and editor. She's a long-term and frequent contributor to *Lilith* magazine, and her work has also appeared in the *New York Times*, *Southern Cultures*, the *Bitter Southerner*, the *Jewish Women's Archive*, the *Jewish Book Council*, and *In geveb*. An excerpt from her master's thesis, *Mir Zaynen Do!*, was published in the 2023 inaugural issue of the *Journal of Jewish Folklore and Ethnology*. She lives with her husband and two cats in Los Angeles.

Samantha Pickette is assistant director of Brandeis University Hillel and a research associate at the Hadassah-Brandeis Institute. She has a PhD in American Studies from Boston University. Her research focuses on Jewish American culture, with a particular emphasis on representations of Jewish women in American literature, film, television, and comedy. Her first monograph, *Peak TV's Unapologetic Jewish Woman: Exploring Jewish Female Representation in Contemporary Television Comedy*, was released by Lexington Books in 2022.

Sheena Roetman-Wynn, Lakota and Muscogee Creek, is the education manager for the Indigenous Journalists Association, as well as a freelance journalist for more than fifteen years. Her work can be found at *Indian Country Today*, the *New York Times*, the *Washington Post*, *Native Peoples Magazine*, *Vice Sports*, and more. Roetman-Wynn holds a degree in journalism with a research specialty in American Indian Media from Georgia State University. She is currently based in Atlanta, GA.

Rebekkah Rubin is a public historian and historical consultant who works with museums, historic sites, and community organizations to communicate historical scholarship to the public and evaluate how we remember and commemorate the past. She also uses American Girl dolls to teach about historical memory, women's history, and Jewish history and culture on Instagram (@iamexcessivelydollverted).

Marissa J. Spear is a disabled writer and historian based in Northwest Arkansas. She received a BA in health equity studies from Goucher College and a graduate certificate in narrative medicine from Columbia University. Her YA fiction work was longlisted for *Voyage Journal's* 2021 Book-Pitch Contest. Her historical research focuses on the Baltimore branch of the Black Panther Party and has appeared or is forthcoming from the *Journal of Women's History, Nursing Clio*, and *All of Us*.

Tara Strauch is an associate professor of history at Centre College located in Danville, Kentucky. Her work has appeared in the journal *Church History* as well as in several edited collections. In addition to her scholarly interest in American Girl, she studies religion and politics during the American Revolution and early American republic. Her current book project examines the history of American holidays.

Cary Tide is a writer.

Laura Traister (she/her) received Kit for Christmas in 2001, when she, too, had freckles and blonde hair. Like Kit, she grew up writing stories on an old typewriter. She's still rocking a bob and writing today but will never dare to walk on a train trestle bridge. She holds an MFA in creative nonfiction and works as a copyeditor in her home state of North Carolina. You can reach her at lauratraister.com.

Index

Page numbers in **bold** refer to illustrations.

accessories and sets, xiii, xiv, xv, xx, 12, 20, 21, 27n2, 30, 31, 32–33, 35, 36, 42, 45, 68, 77, 91, 104–5, 118, 126n31, 148, 149, 179, 180, 181, 184, 186–87, 189, 192, 229, 231

Addy Walker, ix, xv, xvii, 4, 7–9, **8**, 11, 15, 20, 23, 32, 41, 45, 115–29, 200, 228; books, 7–8, **8**, 9, 15

advisors to American Girl: Ann McCormack, 77; Cheryl Chisholm, 127n44; Diane Mallickan, 78; Dorothea Johnson, 168–69; Janet Sims-Wood, 119; Tad Stoermer, 18; use of, xvii, 18, 45, 48, 77, 78, 115, 116, 119, 127, 133, 209; Violet J. Harri, 116–17

AGIG (American Girl Instagram), 180, 182, 183, 185, 189, 190, 191–92, 197, 205–6

American Girl (American Girl magazine), xvi, 23, 142, 146, 147, 148, 151, 156, 160, 168

American Girl (brand), xx, 3, 4, 19, 20, 42, 46; business model, 4, 5, 36, 138; business partnerships, 20, 228–29; ethos, xiii, xiv, xv, xix, 12, 13, 15, 16, 49, 122, 144, 163, 170, 197, 222; mission, xviii, 23, 26, 104, 107, 143; purchase by Mattel, xix, 13, 24. *See also* Pleasant Company

American Girl, The (Girl Scout magazine), 142, 145–46, 147, 151, **152**

American Girl authors/illustrators/editors, 45, 117, 118; Cara Natterson, 157–58,

162, 163; Chryssa Atkinson, 95, 181, 184; Connie Rose Porter, 7, 8, 116, 117, 118, 119; Dahl Taylor, 8; Dan Andreason, 6; Jacqueline Dembar Greene, 3, 96, 97, 99, 100, 102, 103, 104, 107, 108, 110n11, 181; Janet Shaw, 74, 76, 77; Jennifer Hirsch, 186; Megan McDonald, 89, 90; Melodye Rosales, **8**, 117, 123; Nancy Holyoke, 168, 169; Valerie Tripp, 5–6, 18, 42, 48, 137, 142, 143, 144–45, 146, 151; Valorie Lee Schaeffer, 156, 157, 162

American Girl books, xiii, xvi, 30, 34, 60, 68, 116, 129, 131, 132, 133, 134, 135–36, 138, 142, 143, 144, 149, 150, 154, 196, 198, 207; *American Girls Club*, 146; BeForever, 54, 106, 229–30; *The Body Book for Older Girls*, 155, 162; *The Body Book for Younger Girls*, 155; *The Care and Keeping of You*, xvi, 24, 146, 147, 154–64, 214, 231; *Everything I Need to Know I Learned from American Girl*, 228; Family and Friends section, 75, 106; Looking Back/Peek into the Past chapters, 13, 42, 54–55, 67, 90, 106, 144, 145, 201; as marketing tools, 32, 33; *Oops! The Manners Guide for Girls*, xvi, 165–75; Pastimes series, 21, 22; *Smart Girl's Guide to Boys*, 168; *Smart Girl's Guide to Manners*, 168; *Smart Girl's Guide to Money*, 168. *See also* cookbooks; *specific dolls*

American Girl Café, 20, 33, 219, 228

Index

American Girl Library, xvi. *See also* American Girl books; magazine (*American Girl*)
American Girl parties, 19, 20, 24, 29, 34, 35
American Girl Place, xvi, xxi, 20, 29–30, 33, 34, 35, 181, 192
American Girl website, xx, 20, 24, 187
American Girl Wiki, 8, 10, 149, 150
American Girl Women, 146, 151
American history. *See* history: teaching of
American Revolutionary War, 5, 6, 12, 34, 107
Americanization. *See* assimilation
Ana Rubin, 101, 102, 103, 107–8
Andreason, Dan, 6
Angela (Maryellen Larkin's Italian friend), 48, 71n49, 86
Asian American identity, xviii, 83–94, 168
Asian American stereotypes, 89–92
assimilation, xvii, 60, 65, 67, 68, 91, 98, 99, 108, 110n11, 185, 186
Atkinson, Chryssa, 95, 181, 184

Barbie, xiii–xiv, xix, 13, 23, 126, 148, 159, 197, 222, 223, 225–27, **226**
BeForever: books, 45, 54, 58n58, 106, 229; dolls and clothing, 105, 106; historical doll lineup rebranding to, x, 42, 45, 104, 106, 230
Black Hawk's War, 137
Blaire Wilson, 25, 204
body image, 161, 163, 170
Boswell, Megan, 104

Care and Keeping of You, The (TCAKOY), xvi, 24, 146, 147, 154–64, 214, 231
Caroline Abbott, x, 198, 200
Cécile Rey, x, 45, 57n17, 199, 200, 204
Cherokee Trail of Tears, 137
children's literature, 4, 5, 6, 15, 41, 43–44, 48, 55, 109, 129, 131, 132, 196. *See also* middle grade (MG) literature; young adult (YA) literature
Chisholm, Cheryl, 127n44
Chrissa Maxwell, 200, 204
Civil War, 119, 123, 133
Claudie Wells, x, 45, 186

clothing, xv, 3–17, 31, 33, 118, 138, 149, 179, 181, 184, 229; Addy Walker, 7–9, **8**, 11, 15, 118; Felicity Merriman, 5–7, 11, 198; Indigenous, 80; Ivy Ling, 92; Josefina Montoya, 69n25, 198; labor to make, 6–7, 9, 11, 13–14; as marker, 3–5, 7–9, 61, 135, 198; Molly McIntire, 195, 198; Nanea Mitchell, 198; and play, 11–12, 13, 15; Rebecca Rubin, 9–11, **10**, 105–6, 198; Samantha Parkington, 35. *See also specific dolls*
Cold War, 198, 199, 209n22
collectors, xiv, 20, 149, 151, 180, 181, 182–92, 226, 229, 230
Colonial Williamsburg, ix, xv, 5, 128, 135
commodification, 5, 106
consumerism, xiv, xix, xx, 4, 12, 14, 15–16, 30, 32, 33–36, 97, 106, 130, 148, 149, 150, 229. *See also* material culture
contextualization, 3–4, 19, 22, 23, 25, 42, 54, 55, 63, 66, 84, 85, 88, 90, 109n6, 135, 136, 230
cookbooks, xx, 18, 19–26, 27, 35; *The American Girls Cookbook*, 22; *American Girl Felicity's Cook Book*, 18, 21; *Cookies*, 24; *Cooking Studio*, 21, 24; *Samantha's Cookbook*, 35; *Sweet & Savory Treats Cookbook*, 25, 26; *Tea Parties*, 24
cooking, 19, 21, 22–23, 24, 27
Corinne Tan, xviii, 83–84, 86, 92, 93
costume, 11, 12, 21
Courtney Moore, x, xx, 33, **42**, 46, 201, 229
COVID-19, xviii, 18, 83, 84, 86, 92
crafts, 19, 22, 24, 34, 35, 146

disability: in children's literature, 43–44, 50–53; history of in American Girl, 44–46; representation of, xviii, 46–50, 54, 55, 163
dolls and characters: BeForever, x, 42, 45, 54, 58n58, 105, 106, 229, 230; best friend/ companion, x, xvii, 74, 75, 84–85, 86, 199, 204; Bitty Baby, 218, 230; boy, xiv; Girl of the Year, 44, 45, 84, 91, 92, 93, 95, 96, 109n2, 181, 190, 196, 200, 218, 230; Girl of Today, xxi, 147, 181, 190, 192; historical characters, ix, x, 103, 104, 106, 107, 109n4,

204; Just Like You, xvi, 68, 91; Truly Me, 91, 181, 186, 188, 206, 207; WellieWisher, 230. *See also specific names*
dress. *See* clothing

Emily Bennett, 200, 204
etiquette, 34, 165–75; utility, 172–73. *See also* gender norms

facial molds, xviii, 59, 66, 77, 91, 104, 181, 186, 223n1. *See also* physical traits
"Felicity Generation," xvi, 128–30, 138
Felicity Merriman, ix, xv, xx, 4, 5–7, **6**, 11, 12, 15, 18–19, 23, 27, 32, 33, 34, 107, 135–36, 159, 197, 198–99, 200, 202–3, 204, 205, 215, 218, 219–20, 228; books, 5–7, 15, 18, 21, 50, 116, 135; movie, 202
female homosociality, 198, 199–200, 209n27
femininity, 4, 6, 7, 12, 23, 210n29; Jewish, 95–96, 97, 102, 103
feminism, xix, 12–13, 97, 107, 109, 116, 144; Black, 116–17, 118, 119, 120, 122, 124, 125n17
food and drink, 18–28, 135; characters' accessories, xx, 20, 32, 33; Felicity Merriman, 18–19, 21, 27; fictionalization of, 25–27; history, 19, 20–21, 22, 26, 27; Indigenous, 26, 27n2, 28n17; Ivy Ling, 90; Kaya'aton'my (Kaya), 26, 27n2, 28n17; Kirsten Larson, 19–20, 25; Kit Kittredge, 25; Lindsey Bergman, 96, 185; Rebecca Rubin, 25, 186; Samantha Parkington, 21; in *The Care and Keeping of You*, 157, 162. *See also* cookbooks
furniture. *See* accessories

Gabriela McBride, 45
gender: identity, 3, 4, 5–6, 158, 197, 198, 221; norms, 4, 6, 11, 19, 22–23, 27, 98, 150, 157, 167, 168, 169, 170, 171, 172–73, 197, 198–99
Girl Scouts USA, 142–54, **152**; *The American Girl* (magazine), 142, 145–46, 147, 151, **152**; books, 146, 147; branded dolls, 148; differences with American Girl, 149, 150; gear available for American Girl, 148; gear available from American Girl, 147–48; similarities to American Girl, 143–44, 145, 146, 150, 151

girlhood, xiv, 12, 13, 19, 49, 50, 116, 120, 122, 150, 151, 163, 187, 222, 230
Greene, Jacqueline Dembar, 3, 96, 97, 99, 100, 102, 103, 104, 107, 108, 110n11, 181
Gwen Thompson, 200, 204

Harris, Violet J., 116–17
"Hellicity Merriman," xxi, 45, 128, 216–24, 227
Hirsch, Jennifer, 186
historians, 19, 25, 117, 180; Black, xvii, 117; disabled, 42, 46, 55, 65–66; inspired by American Girl, xvi, xviii, 21, 22, 42, 128, 129–31, 138–39, 230; social, 129, 136; women, 117, 129–30, 138
historical accuracy, 19, 54, 55, 60, 67, 77, 78, 102–3, 122, 132, 138
historical inaccuracy, 47–48, 67, 69n25, 70n28
history: curricular development, 134–35; fictionalization of, 25–27, 41; food, xx, 18–28; teaching of, xix, 16n8, 131–35
Holyoke, Nancy, 168, 169

identity: Asian American, xviii, 83–94, 168; Black, 64; gender, 3, 4, 5–6, 158, 197, 198, 221; Jewish, xviii, 10, 70n36, 95–96, 97, 98, 101, 102, 106, 108, 179–94. *See also* representation
immigrant experience, xvii, 59–60, 61, 62, 66–67, 71n47, 89, 91, 96–102, 104, 105, 108, 109, 109n6, 183
Indigeneity, xix, 26, 27n2, 28n17, 47, 72–82, **73**, 137, 150
influencers, 20, 228
Instagram, xxi, 45–46, 130, 180, 183, 192; AGIG (American Girl Instagram), 180, 182, 183, 185, 189, 190, 191–92, 197, 205–6; *American Girl Women*, 146, 151; "Hellicity Merriman," xxi, 45, 128, 216–24, 227; official American Girl account, 195–96
intersectionality, xx, 81, 181, 191
Isabel Hoffman, x, 182, 187–88, 190, 191, 192, 207; books, 182
Ivy Ling, x, xviii, 84–93; book, 84–85, 89, 90–92

Johnson, Dorothea, 168–69
Josefina Montoya, ix, xv, xviii, 23–24, 32, 64, 66, 68, 69n25, 104, 137, 183, 198, 215, 228; books, 45, 137, 142
Josie Myers, 45
Joss Kendrick, 45
Joy Jenner, 45, 46, 48
Julie Albright, x, xiii, 29, 45, 84, 85, 86, 87, 88, 89, 90, 145, 199, 201, 202, 208; books, 89, 92, 145

Kailey Hopkins, 218, 229
Kanani Akina, 89
Kavi Sharma, 93
Kaya'aton'my (Kaya), x, xix, 9, 26, 45, 46–47, 73, 77–79, 86, 137, 198, 200, 209n23; books, 45, 47–48, 54, 77, 209n23
Kira Bailey, 196, 203
Kirsten Larson, ix, xv, 22, 25, 32, 35, 64, 68, 73, 76–77, 135, 159, 183, 199–200, 228, 229; books, xvi, 19–20, 74–75, 76–77
Kit Kittredge, x, xiii, xx, 24, 25, 29, 30–33, 34, 185, 197, 198, 199, 201, 202, 204, 205; books, 20, 145

lesbian. *See* LGBTQ+; queerness
LGBTQ+, xiv, 14, 188, 196, 197, 198, 200, 201, 203–4, 206, 207; representation, 196, 200, 207. *See also* queerness
Lindsey Bergman, 95–96, 181, 182, 184, 185, 187, 188, 200; books, 96, 104, 181, 184–85

magazine (*American Girl*), xvi, 23, 142, 146, 147, 148, 151, 156, 160, 168
Mallickan, Diane, 78
manners. *See* etiquette
Marcie-Grace Gardner, x
Marisol Luna, 190, 218
Maryellen Larkin, x, 42, 45, 46, 48–50, 54, 68, 71n49, 86, 199, 200, 201; books, 45, 48, 49, 54
material culture, xx, 130, 131, 135, 136, 138, 151, 189
Mattel, x, xix, xx, 4, 13, 14, 16, 23, 24, 77, 78, 126n31, 146, 148, 150, 202, 222, 227, 230
McCormack, Ann, 77

McDonald, Megan, 89, 90
McKenna Brooks, 45
Melody Ellison, x, **43**, 46, 199, 201; books, 45
memes, xxi, **42**, **43**, 45, 46, 128, 214, 215–16, 217, 223, 227. *See also* "Hellicity Merriman"; @PinkSaltCollective
middle grade (MG) literature, 41, 42, 43, 50–52, 54, 58n58, 97, 132
molds. *See* facial molds
Molly McIntire, ix, xiii, xv, 22, 23, 25, 29, 32, **43**, 46, 64, 73, 86, 107, 136, 144, 151, **152**, 195, 198, 200, 201, 204, **214**, 215, 218–19, 228, 229, 230; books, xvi, 23, 136, 142, 144–45

Nanea Mitchell, x, xx, 33, 46, 201, 229; books, 45, 145, 198, 201
National History Standards Project, 134–37
Natterson, Cara, 157–58, 162, 163
Nellie O'Malley, x, xvii, xviii, 59–62, 63, 64, 66, 67, 68, 84, 86, 133, 200, 204, 205, 229; books, 67, 68. *See also* Samantha Parkington: books
Nez Perce (Nimíipuu), xix, 26, 45, 46, 47, 54, 77, 78, 137, 209n23
Nicki Hoffman, x, 182, 187–88, 190, 191, 192, 207; books, 182

online community. *See* social media
Oops! The Manners Guide for Girls, xvi, 165–75
othering, 46–50, 62, 63–64, 66–67, 69n19, 74–75, 76, 95–96, 101, 108–9, 168, 184, 185–86, 193n8, 209n23

physical traits, xviii, 44, 59, 66, 77, 91, 104, 181, 186; eyes, xvi, 64, 65, 91, 104, 159, 187; hair, xvi, 59, 64–65, 66, 80, 83, 104, 106, 181, 184, 185, 193n8, 218, 226; legs, 48, 160, 215, 216, 223, 229; mouth and teeth, xviii, 66, 77, 91, 214, 215, 223n1; nose, xviii, 66, 91; skin tone, xvi, 59, 66, 80, 91, 104, 115, 117, 229
Pleasant Company, xiii, xiv, xv, xvii, xviii, xix, 22, 30, 78, 115, 116, 117, 118, 133, 134, 137, 148, 169, 225; advisors, 19, 129 (*see also* advisors to American Girl); books and magazine, 21, 22, 23–24, 135, 136,

146, 168; ethos, xiv, xv, 30, 31–32, 144, 170; goods sold, 19, 121, 148, 149, 229 (*see also* accessories; American Girl books; *specific dolls*); mission, 132, 143; Portfolio of Pastimes, 22, 24; Publications, 23, 168; revenue, ix, xv–xvi, 116, 121; sale to Mattel, x, xix, 13, 24, 148

Porter, Connie Rose, 7, 8, 116, 117, 118, 119

postfeminism, 106

queerness, xx, 195–211; character identities, invented, 205–7; dolls' clothing, 198; fan fiction, 202–5; history, 196, 201–2, 203; representation, 205, 207; shipping, 197, 200, 202, 204, 206

race issues, xix, 3, 4, 5, 9, 11, 22, 25, 44, 46, 116, 120, 167, 171, 173

racialization and racism, xvii–xviii, 74, 89, 117–18, 121, 123, 126n41, 134, 173; in American Girl products, 75, 91, 120, 193n8; anti-Asian, 83–86, 88, 92, 93; "refuge of whiteness," 121, 122; in society, 9, 59, 62–63, 66–67, 70n28, 117, 121, 122, 167–68, 172, 173

Rebecca Rubin, x, xviii, xxiin6, 3, 4, 9–11, **10**, 15, 20, 25, 66, 68, 70n36, 96, 98–109, 110n11, 181, 185–87, 188, 193n13, 198, 199; books, 3, 9–11, 12, 13, 14, 15, 96–97, 98–99, 101, 102, 103, 104, 105, 106, 108, 186, 189

representation, 196; Asian American, xviii, 83–94, 168; Black, xvii, 45, 116, 117, 119, 120, 122, 123, 126n41, 133–34, 168, 172; disability, xviii, 46–50, 163; Indigenous, xix, 26, 27n2, 28n17, 47, 72–82, **73**, 137, 150; Irish, xviii, 59–68, 70n32, 70n36, 71n49; Jewish, 3, 10, 41, 66, 95–109, 179, 181, 183, 184, 187, 188, 189, 190–91, 192; LGBTQ+ and queer, 196, 200, 205, 207

Rosales, Melodye, **8**, 117, 123

Rowland, Pleasant, ix, x, xv, xix, 16n8, 64, 69n21, 116, 117, 121, 131–33, 143, 168, 179, 227

Samantha Parkington, ix, xv, xx, 20, 21, 22, 23, 32, 33, 35, 59, 62, 63, 64, 80, 81–82, 84,

86, 104, 107, 133, 135, 142, 159, 192, 199, 200, 201, 203, 204, 205, 215, 228, 229; books, xvii, 35, 59, 60, 61, 63, 67, 133, 134

Schaeffer, Valorie Lee, 156, 157, 162

sets. *See* accessories

Shaw, Janet, 74, 76, 77

Sims-Wood, Janet, 119

Singing Bird, 73–75, 76–77, 78, 80, 200

social media, xiii, xiv, 128, 150, 180, 182, 184, 187, 190–92, 202, 214, 215, 225, 228; AGIG (American Girl Instagram), 180, 182, 183, 185, 189, 190, 191–92, 197, 205–6; Instagram, xxi, 45–46, 128, 130, 146, 151, 180, 183, 192, 195–96, 197, 205–6, 216–24, 227; @PinkSaltCollective, 42, 43, 46; TikTok, 18, 27, 214, 215, 217, 228–29; X/Twitter, 128, 131, 216, 223, 227

socialization of girls, 5, 11, 23, 132, 143, 150, 165–66, 167, 170

Sonali Matthews, 200, 204

Spanos, Stephanie, 106

Speaking Rain, 45, 46–48, 49, 51, 54

stereotyping: by American Girl, xvii, 12, 44, 59–72, 73, 89, 92–93, 104, 150, 193n8; in society, 23, 27, 59–60, 62, 63, 64–67, 92, 102, 106, 150, 187, 191. *See also* representation

Stoermer, Tad, 18

Swan Circling, 200, 209n23

Taylor, Dahl, 8

TikTok, 18, 27, 214, 215, 217, 228–29

toys and play, xiii, xiv, xix, xx, xxi, 4, 11–13, 36, 68, 75–76, 78, 81, 109, 121–22, 132–33, 138, 150, 184, 185, 187, 188, 190, 216, 218, 221, 226

tradition, 5, 15, 90, 92, 93, 97, 99, 104, 106, 108, 110, 116, 118, 120, 122, 123, 143, 150, 167, 171, 182, 189

trans. *See* LGBTQ+

Tripp, Valerie, 5–6, 18, 42, 48, 137, 142, 143, 144–45, 146, 151

whiteness, xvii, xviii, 60, 62–64, 66, 67, 68, 86, 91, 92, 96, 203; "refuge of whiteness," 121, 122

World War II, xv, 41, 68, 69n19, 86, 107, 136, 144, 145

X/Twitter, 128, 131, 216, 223, 227

Yellow Power, xviii, 86. *See also* Asian American identity
young adult (YA) literature, 41, 42, 43, 50, 52–53, 54

Zeller, Emily Woo, 161

www.ingramcontent.com/pod-product-compliance
Lightning Source LLC
Chambersburg PA
CBHW030501290325
24211CB00006B/23